THE HANGING OF AFZAL GURU

THE HANGING OF AFZAL GURU

AND THE STRANGE CASE OF THE ATTACK ON THE INDIAN PARLIAMENT

WITH AN INTRODUCTION BY ARUNDHATI ROY

PENGUIN BOOKS

An imprint of Penguin Random House

PENGUIN BOOKS

USA | Canada | UK | Ireland | Australia
New Zealand | India | South Africa | China | Singapore

Penguin Books is part of the Penguin Random House group of companies
whose addresses can be found at global.penguinrandomhouse.com

Published by Penguin Random House India Pvt. Ltd
4th Floor, Capital Tower 1, MG Road,
Gurugram 122 002, Haryana, India

First published as *13 December* by Penguin Books India 2006
Revised and updated edition published 2007, 2013

ISBN 9780143420750

Typeset in Sabon Roman by SÜRYA, New Delhi
Printed at Thomson Press India Private Limited

www.penguin.co.in

Pedro Algorta, a lawyer, showed me the fat dossier about the murder of two women. The double crime had been committed with a knife at the end of 1982, in a Montevideo suburb.

The accused, Alma Di Agosto, had confessed. She had been in jail more than a year, and she was apparently condemned to rot there for the rest of her life.

As is the custom, the police had raped and tortured her. After a month of continuous beatings they had extracted several confessions. Alma Di Agosto's confessions did not much resemble each other, as if she had committed the same murder in many different ways. Different people appeared in each confession, picturesque phantoms without names or addresses, because the electric cattle prod turns anyone into a prolific storyteller. Furthermore, the author demonstrated the agility of an Olympic athlete, the strength of a fairground Amazon, and the dexterity of a professional matador. But most surprising was the wealth of detail: in each confession, the accused described with millimetric precision clothing, gestures, surroundings, positions, objects . . .

Alma Di Agosto was blind.

Her neighbours, who knew and loved her, were convinced she was guilty:

'*Why?*' asked the lawyer.

'*Because the papers say so.*'

'*But the papers lie,*' said the lawyer.

'*But the radio says so too,*' explained the neighbours. '*And the TV!*'

—Eduardo Galeano,
The Book of Embraces

CONTENTS

PART TWO: THE HANGING

PREFACE TO THIS EDITION: LYNCHING BY DUE PROCESS

After spending eleven years in prison in New Delhi, most of them in solitary confinement, and on death row, on a clear February morning, Mohammad Afzal Guru was hanged. It was an execution performed in stealth and, as a former Solicitor General of India (and Senior Advocate in the Supreme Court) says later in this book, an act whose legality was gravely questionable.

How could there be legal doubts about an elected government hanging a man who had been given three life sentences and a double death sentence by the highest court in the land? Because only ten months before, in April 2012, the Supreme Court had concluded a series of hearings over the question of executing prisoners who had already served inordinately long prison sentences. One of the cases in that cluster was the case of Afzal Guru. The Bench had reserved its judgement; but Afzal Guru was executed before the Court delivered its verdict.

The government turned down his family's request for his body. He was buried without ceremony next to Maqbool Bhat, the founder of the Jammu Kashmir Liberation Front and the pre-eminent icon of Kashmir's movement for Azadi, freedom.

And so, in the compound of Tihar Jail, a second Kashmiri body awaits a funeral. While in Kashmir's Mazar-e-Shohadda, Martyrs' Graveyard, another empty grave awaits a body. Those who know Kashmir know how those imagined, subterranean, human-shaped hollows have, in the past, unleashed militant insurrections.

In India, once the initial bout of noisy celebrations trumpeting the triumph of the 'Rule of Law' had subsided, once the goons on the streets had run out of sweets to distribute (how long can you keep burning posters of a dead man without snack breaks?), a few people were permitted to express their unease with capital punishment, and to air their doubts about whether or not Afzal Guru had a fair trial. That was nice. And well timed too. Once again we came across as a Democracy with a Conscience.

Except *that* debate too has already taken place, six years ago, and even then it was four years overdue. First published in December 2006, the essays in Part I of this book deal at length with the trial, the miscarriage of justice, the fact that Afzal Guru went unrepresented in the trial court, the ways in which real leads were never followed, and the insidious role of the media at the time. Part II of this new edition is a compilation of essays and analyses written after the execution. The introduction to the first edition ends by saying 'Therefore, this book, offered in hope.' This time, it is offered in anger.

In these very vengeful times, the impatient may well say: Chuck the details and the legal minutiae. Was he guilty or was he not? Did the Indian government hang an innocent man?

Anyone who takes the trouble to read this book would have to come to the conclusion that Afzal Guru had not been proven guilty of the crime he was accused of committing—of being one of the conspirators in the Attack on the Indian Parliament or, more fashionably, the 'Attack on Indian Democracy'. (Contrary to the elaborate misinformation put out in the media, even the prosecution never accused him of being one of the attackers, or of killing anybody. He was only tried for being an accomplice, a mere foot soldier.) Even as the Supreme Court convicted him of this crime and sentenced him to death, in its controversial judgement that invoked satisfying 'the collective conscience of the society' as one of its reasons for putting a man to death, it also went out of its way to say that the evidence before it was not direct, but only circumstantial.

Terrorism experts and other analysts have loftily glossed over this by saying that in cases like these the 'full truth' would always be elusive. In the case of the Attack on Parliament, this certainly seems to be what has happened. The 'truth' seems to have eluded us entirely. Logically, that should have raised the juridical principle of 'reasonable doubt'. It did not. A man whose guilt was by no means established beyond reasonable doubt was hanged.

Let's concede that an Attack on the Indian Parliament *does* amount to an Attack on Democracy. Was the 1983 Nellie massacre of three thousand 'illegal Bangladeshis' not an attack on Indian Democracy? Or the massacre of more than three thousand Sikhs on the streets of Delhi in 1984? Was the demolition of the Babri Masjid in 1992 not an attack on Indian Democracy? Was the Shiv Sena-led slaughter of thousands of Muslims in Mumbai in 1993 not an Attack on Indian Democracy? What about the 2002 pogrom against thousands of Muslims in Gujarat? There is plenty of evidence, direct as well as circumstantial, to connect leaders of our major political parties to these mass murders. But could we ever imagine any of them being arrested, imprisoned for eleven years, let alone executed? Oh no. On the contrary, one of them—who had never held public office—was recently given a state funeral that brought the city of Mumbai to a standstill. Another will most likely be running for the post of Prime Minister of the World's Largest Democracy in the next election.

In this cold, cowardly way, making empty, exaggerated gestures that mimic Due Process, India's own brand of fascism has laid itself upon us.

In the Mazar-e-Shohadda in Srinagar, the epitaph on Afzal's tombstone (which the police removed, and then was forced to replace because of public outrage) reads, in translation:

> The martyr of the nation, Shaheed Mohammad Afzal Guru, Date of Martyrdom: 9th February 2013 Saturday, whose mortal remains are lying in the custody of the Government of India. The nation is awaiting its return.

Knowing what we do, it would be hard to describe Afzal Guru as a warrior in any conventional sense of the word. His shahadat, his martyrdom, comes from having experienced and borne witness to the hell that tens of thousands of ordinary young Kashmiris have lived through. Like them, he has been burned, beaten, electrocuted, blackmailed and now killed. (You can read a description of what was done to him on one occasion, in the picturesque words of his torturer, in Appendix III.) But while Afzal Guru was executed in the greatest secrecy, the events that led to his execution were performed on stage to a full house. When the curtains went down and the lights came up, the audience applauded. The reviews were mixed, but what the hell, the deed had been done.

The 'full-truth' is that Afzal Guru is dead and that we will probably never know who attacked the Indian Parliament. The Bharatiya Janata Party has been robbed of its grisly election ditty: *'Desh abhi sharminda hai, Afzal abhi bhi zinda hai'* (The Nation is Still in Shame, Afzal is Still Alive). It will have to come up with a new one.

Long before he was arrested and jailed, Afzal Guru was a broken man. Now that he is dead, those who prey on carrion are circling over his body, trying to gain political traction, and to contain, co-opt and manage people's fury. For some time to come we will be presented with letters he never wrote, books he never authored and things he never said. These ugly games will not change anything. Because of the way he lived and the way he died, he will live on in popular Kashmiri memory, as a hero, lying side by side with Maqbool Bhat, and sharing his aura.

As for the rest of us, his story makes it clear that the real Attack on Indian Democracy is the continued military occupation of Kashmir.

Mohammad Afzal Guru, Rest in Peace.

1 March 2013   ARUNDHATI ROY

INTRODUCTION: BREAKING THE NEWS

This Reader goes to press almost five years to the day since 13 December 2001, when five men (some say six) drove through the gates of the Indian Parliament in a white Ambassador car and attempted what looked like an astonishingly incompetent terrorist strike.

Consummate competence appeared to be the hallmark of everything that followed: the gathering of evidence, the speed of the investigation by the Special Cell of the Delhi Police, the arrest and charge-sheeting of the accused, and the forty-month-long judicial process that began with the fast-track trial court.

The operative phrase in all of this is *'appeared to be'*. If you follow the story carefully, you'll encounter two sets of masks. First the mask of consummate competence (accused arrested, 'case cracked' in two days flat), and then, when things began to come undone, the benign mask of shambling incompetence (shoddy evidence, procedural flaws, material contradictions). But underneath all of this, as each of the essays in this collection shows, is something more sinister, more worrying. Over the last few years the worries have grown into a mountain of misgivings, impossible to ignore.

The doubts set in early on, when on 14 December 2001, the day after the Parliament Attack, the police arrested S.A.R. Geelani, a young lecturer in Delhi University. He was one of four people who were arrested. His outraged colleagues and friends, certain he had been framed, contacted the well-known lawyer Nandita Haksar and asked her to take on his case. This marked the beginning of a campaign for the fair trial of Geelani. It flew in the face of mass hysteria and corrosive propaganda enthusiastically disseminated by the mass media. The campaign was successful, and Geelani was eventually acquitted, along with Afsan (aka Navjot) Guru, co-accused in the same case.

Geelani's acquittal blew a gaping hole in the prosecution's version of the Parliament Attack. But in some odd way, in the public mind, the acquittal of two of the accused only confirmed the guilt of the other two. When the government announced that Mohammad Afzal Guru, Accused Number One in the case, would be hanged on 20 October 2006, it seemed as though most people welcomed the news not just with approval, but morbid excitement. But then, once again, the questions resurfaced.

To see through the prosecution's case against Geelani was relatively easy. He was plucked out of thin air and transplanted into the centre of the 'conspiracy' as its kingpin. Afzal was different. He had been extruded through the sewage system of the hell that Kashmir has become. He surfaced through a manhole, covered in shit (and when he emerged, policemen in the Special Cell pissed on him.[1]) The first thing they made him do was a 'media confession' in which he implicated himself completely in the attack.[2] The speed with which this happened made many of us believe that he was indeed guilty as charged. It was only much later that the circumstances under which this 'confession' was made were revealed, and even the Supreme Court was to set it aside saying that the police had violated legal safeguards.[3]

From the very beginning there was nothing pristine or simple about Afzal's case. Even today Afzal does not claim complete innocence. It is the *nature* of his involvement that is being contested. For instance, was he coerced, tortured, blackmailed into playing even the peripheral part that he did? He didn't have a lawyer to put out his version of the story, or help anyone to sift through the tangle of official lies and fabrications. Various individuals worked it out for themselves. These essays by a group of lawyers, academics, journalists and writers represent that body of work. It has fractured what—until only recently—appeared to be a national consensus interwoven with mass hysteria. We're late at the barricades, but we're here.

Most people, or let's say many people, when they encounter real facts and a logical argument, *do* begin to ask the right questions. This is exactly what has begun to happen on the Parliament Attack Case. The questions have created public pressure. The pressure has created fissures, and through these fissures those who have come under the scanner—shadowy individuals, counter-intelligence and security agencies, political parties—are beginning to surface. They wave flags, hurl abuse, issue hot denials and cover their tracks with more and more untruths. Thus they reveal themselves.

Public unease continues to grow. A group of citizens have come together as a committee (chaired by Nirmala

Deshpande) to publicly demand a Parliamentary inquiry into the episode. There is an on-line petition demanding the same thing.[4] Thousands of people have signed on. Every day new articles appear in the papers, on the net. At least half a dozen web sites are following the developments closely. They raise questions about how Mohammad Afzal, who never had proper legal representation, can be sentenced to death, without having had an opportunity to be heard, without a fair trial. They raise questions about fabricated evidence, procedural flaws and the outright lies that were presented in court and published in newspapers. They show how there is hardly a single piece of evidence that stands up to scrutiny.

And then, there are even more disturbing questions that have been raised, which range beyond the fate of Mohammad Afzal. Here are thirteen questions for December 13th:

Question 1: For months before the Attack on Parliament, both the government and the police had been saying that Parliament could be attacked. On 12 December 2001, at an informal meeting, Prime Minister Atal Bihari Vajpayee warned of an imminent attack on Parliament.[5] On 13 December Parliament was attacked. Given that there was an 'improved security drill', how did a car bomb packed with explosives enter the parliament complex?

Question 2: Within days of the Attack, the Special Cell of Delhi Police said it was a meticulously planned joint operation of Jaish-e-Mohammad and

Lashkar-e-Toiba. They said the attack was led by a man called 'Mohammad' who was also involved in the hijacking of IC-814 in 1998. (This was later refuted by the CBI.)[6] None of this was ever proved in court. What evidence did the Special Cell have for its claim?

Question 3: The entire attack was recorded live on Close Circuit TV (CCTV). Congress Party MP Kapil Sibal demanded in Parliament that the CCTV recording be shown to the members. He was supported by the Deputy Chairman of the Rajya Sabha, Najma Heptullah, who said that there was confusion about the details of the event. The chief whip of the Congress Party, Priyaranjan Dasmunshi, said, 'I counted six men getting out of the car. But only five were killed. The Close Circuit TV camera recording clearly showed the six men.' If Dasmunshi was right, why did the Police say that there were only five people in the car? Who was the sixth person? Where is he now? Why was the CCTV recording not produced by the prosecution as evidence in the trial? Why was it not released for public viewing?

Question 4: Why was Parliament adjourned after some of these questions were raised?

Question 5: A few days after 13 December, the government declared that it had 'incontrovertible evidence' of Pakistan's involvement in the attack, and announced a massive mobilization of almost half a million soldiers to the Indo-Pakistan border. The subcontinent was pushed to the brink of nuclear war. Apart from Afzal's 'confession', extracted under torture (and later set aside by the Supreme Court), what was the 'incontrovertible evidence'?

Question 6: Is it true that the military mobilization to the Pakistan border had begun long before the 13 December Attack?

Question 7: How much did this military standoff, which lasted for nearly a year, cost? How many soldiers died in the process? How many soldiers and civilians died because of mishandled landmines, and how many peasants lost their homes and land because trucks and tanks were rolling through their villages and landmines were being planted in their fields?

Question 8: In a criminal investigation it is vital for the police to show how the evidence gathered at the scene of the attack led them to the accused. How did the police reach Mohammad Afzal? The Special Cell says S.A.R. Geelani led them to Afzal.[7] But the message to look out for Afzal was actually flashed to the Srinagar Police *before* Geelani was arrested. So how did the Special Cell connect Afzal to the 13 December Attack?

Question 9: The courts acknowledge that Afzal was a surrendered militant who was in regular contact with the security forces, particularly the Special Task Force (STF) of Jammu & Kashmir Police. How do the security forces explain the fact that a person under their surveillance was able to conspire in a major militant operation?

Question 10: Is it plausible that organizations like Lashkar-e-Toiba or Jaish-e-Mohammad would rely on a person who had been in and out of STF torture chambers, and was under constant police surveillance, as the principal link for a major operation?

Question 11: In his statement before the Court, Afzal says that he was introduced to 'Mohammad' and instructed to take him to Delhi by a man called Tariq, who was working with the STF. Tariq was named in the police charge sheet. Who is Tariq and where is he now?

Question 12: On 19 December 2001, six days after the Parliament Attack, Police Commissioner, Thane (Maharashtra), S.M. Shangari identified one of the attackers killed in the Parliament Attack as Mohammad Yasin Fateh Mohammed (alias Abu Hamza) of the Lashkar-e-Toiba, who had been arrested in Mumbai in November 2000, and immediately handed over to the J&K Police. He gave detailed descriptions to support his statement. If Police Commissioner Shangari was right, how did Mohammad Yasin, a man in the custody of the J&K Police, end up participating in the Parliament Attack? If he was wrong, where is Mohammad Yasin now?

Question 13: Why is it that we still don't know who the five dead 'terrorists' killed in the Parliament Attack are?

These questions, examined cumulatively, point to something far more serious than incompetence. The words that come to mind are Complicity, Collusion, Involvement. There's no need for us to feign shock, or shrink from thinking these thoughts and saying them out loud. Governments and their Intelligence Agencies have a hoary tradition of using strategies like this to further their own ends. (Look up the Burning of the Reichstag in 1933 in Germany and the rise of Nazi power; or 'Operation Gladio' in which European Intelligence Agencies 'created' acts of terrorism, especially in Italy, in order to discredit militant groups like the Red Brigade.)

The official response to all of these questions has been dead silence. As things stand, the execution of Afzal has been postponed while the President considers his clemency petition. Meanwhile, the Bharatiya Janata Party (BJP) announced that it would turn 'Hang Afzal' into a national campaign.[8] The campaign was fuelled by the usual stale cocktail of religious chauvinism, nationalism and strategic falsehoods. But it doesn't seem to have taken off. Now other avenues are being explored. M.S. Bitta of the All India Anti-Terrorist Front is parading around the families of some of the security personnel who were killed during the Attack. They have threatened to return the government's posthumous bravery medals if Afzal is not hanged by 12 December. (On balance, it might not be a bad idea for them to turn in those medals until they really know *who* the attackers were working for.)*

The main strategy seems to be to create confusion and polarize the debate on communal lines. The Editor

---

*On 13 December 2006, the families, accompanied by M.S. Bitta, returned the bravery medals after a meeting with President A.P.J. Abdul Kalam.

of *The Pioneer*[9] wrote that Mohammad Afzal was actually one of the men who attacked Parliament, that he was the first to open fire and kill at least three security guards. The columnist Swapan Dasgupta,[10] in an article called 'You can't be Good to Evil', suggests that if Afzal is not hanged there would be no point in celebrating Dussehra or Durga Puja. It's hard to believe that falsehoods like this stem only from a poor grasp of facts.

In the business of spreading confusion, the mass media, particularly television journalists, can be counted on to be perfect collaborators. On discussions, chat shows and 'special reports', we have television anchors playing around with crucial facts, like young children in a sandpit. Torturers, estranged brothers, senior police officers and politicians are emerging from the woodwork and talking. The more they talk, the more interesting it all becomes.

At the end of November 2006, Afzal's older brother Aijaz made it onto a national news channel (CNN-IBN).[11] He was featured on hidden camera, on what was meant to be a 'sting' operation, making—we were asked to believe—stunning revelations. Aijaz's story had already been on offer to various journalists on the streets of Delhi for weeks. People were wary of him because his rift with his brother's wife and family is well known. More significantly, in Kashmir he is known to have a relationship with the STF. More than one person has suggested an audit of his newfound assets.

But here he was now, on the national news, first endorsing the Supreme Court decision to hang his brother. Then saying Afzal had never surrendered, and that it was *he* (Aijaz), who surrendered his brother's weapon to the BSF! And since he had never surrendered, Aijaz was able to 'confirm' that Afzal was an active militant with the Jaish-e-Mohammad, and that Ghazi Baba, Chief of Operations of the Jaish, used to regularly hold meetings in their home. (Aijaz claims that when Ghazi Baba was killed, it was he—*Aijaz*—that the police called in to identify the body). On the whole, it sounded as though there had been a case of mistaken identity—and that given how much he knew, and all he was admitting, Aijaz should have been the one in custody instead of Afzal!

Of course we must keep in mind that behind both Aijaz and Afzal's 'media confessions', spaced five years apart, is the invisible hand of the STF, the dreaded counter insurgency outfit in Kashmir. They can make anyone say anything at any time. Their methods (both punitive and remunerative) are familiar to every man, woman and child in the Kashmir Valley. At a time like this, for a responsible news channel to announce that their 'investigation finds that Afzal was a Jaish militant', based on totally unreliable testimony, is dangerous and irresponsible. (Since when did what our brothers say about us become admissible evidence? My brother, for instance, will testify that I'm God's Gift to the Universe. I could dredge up a couple of aunts who'd say I'm a Jaish militant. For a price.) How can family feuds be dressed up as Breaking News?

The other character who is rapidly emerging from the shadowy periphery and wading onto centre-stage is Deputy Superintendent of Police Davinder Singh of the STF. He is the man Afzal has named as the police officer who held him in illegal detention, and tortured him in the STF camp at Humhama in Srinagar, only a few months before the Parliament Attack. In a letter to his lawyer Sushil Kumar, Afzal says that several of the calls made to him and Mohammad (the man killed in the Attack) can be traced to Davinder Singh. Of course no attempt was made to trace these calls.

Davinder Singh was also showcased on the CNN-IBN show,[12] through the by-now ubiquitous low-angle shots, camera shake and all. It seemed a bit unnecessary, because Davinder Singh has been talking a lot these days. He's done recorded interviews, on the phone as well as face-to-face, saying exactly the same shocking things. Weeks before the sting operation, in a recorded interview to Parvaiz Bukhari, a freelance journalist, he said, 'I did interrogate and torture him [Afzal] at my camp for several days. And we never recorded his arrest in the books anywhere. His description of torture at my camp is true. That was the procedure those days and we did pour petrol in his arse and gave him electric shocks. But I could not break him. He did not reveal anything to me despite our hardest possible interrogation. We tortured him enough for Ghazi Baba but he did not break. He looked like a "bhondu" those days, what you call a "chootiya" type. And I had a reputation for torture, interrogation and breaking suspects. If anybody came out of my interrogation clean, nobody would ever touch him again. He would be considered clean for good by the whole department.'

This is not an empty boast. Davinder Singh has a formidable reputation for torture in the Kashmir Valley. On TV his boasting spiralled into policy-making. 'Torture is the only deterrent for terrorism,' he said. 'I do it for the nation.' He didn't bother to explain why or how the 'bhondu' that he tortured and subsequently released, allegedly went on to become the diabolical mastermind of the Parliament Attack. Davinder Singh then said that Afzal was a Jaish militant. If this is true, why wasn't the evidence placed before the courts? And why on earth was Afzal released? Why wasn't he watched? There is a definite attempt to try and dismiss this as incompetence. But given everything we know now, it would take all of Davinder Singh's delicate professional skills to make some of us believe that.

Meanwhile right-wing commentators have consistently taken to referring to Afzal as a Jaish-e-Mohammad militant. It's as though instructions have been issued that this is to be the Party Line. They have absolutely no evidence to back their claim, but they know that repeating something often enough makes it the 'truth'. As part of the campaign to portray Afzal as an 'active' militant, and not a surrendered militant, S.M. Sahai, Inspector General, Kashmir, J&K Police, appeared on TV to say that he had found no evidence in his records that Afzal had surrendered.[13] It would have been odd if he had, because in 1993 Afzal surrendered not to the J&K Police, but to the BSF. But why would a TV journalist bother with that kind of detail? And why does a senior police officer need to become part of this game of smoke and mirrors?

The official version of the story of the Parliament Attack is very quickly coming apart at the seams.

Even the Supreme Court judgment, with all its flaws of logic and leaps of faith, does not accuse Mohammad Afzal of being the mastermind of the attack. So who was the mastermind? If Mohammad Afzal is hanged we may never know. But L.K. Advani, Leader of the Opposition, wants him hanged at once. Even a day's delay, he says, is against the national interest.[14] Why? What's the hurry? The man is locked up in a high-security cell on death row. He's not allowed out of his cell for even five minutes a day. What harm can he do? Talk? Write, perhaps? Surely— even in L.K. Advani's own narrow interpretation of the term—it's in the national interest *not* to hang Afzal? At least not until there is an inquiry that reveals what the real story is, and who actually attacked Parliament?

Among the people who have appealed against Mohammad Afzal's death sentence are those who are opposed to capital punishment in principle. They have asked that his death sentence be commuted to a life sentence. To sentence a man who has not had a fair trial, and has not had the opportunity to be heard, to life imprisonment is less cruel but just as arbitrary as sentencing him to death. The right thing to do would be to order a re-trial of Afzal's case, and an impartial, transparent inquiry into the 13 December Parliament Attack. It is utterly demonic to leave a man locked up alone in a prison cell, day after day, week after week, leaving him and his family to guess which day will be the last day of his life.

A genuine inquiry would have to mean far more than just a political witch-hunt. It would have to look into the part played by intelligence, counter-insurgency and security agencies as well. Offences such as the fabrication of evidence and the blatant violation of procedural norms have already been established in the courts,[15] but they look very much like just the tip of the iceberg. We now have a police officer admitting (boasting) on record that he was involved in the illegal detention and torture of a fellow citizen. Is all of this acceptable to the people, the government and the courts of this country?

Given the track record of Indian governments (past and present, right, left and centre), it is naive—perhaps utopian is a better word—to hope that any government will ever have the courage to institute an inquiry that will, once and for all, uncover the real story. A maintenance dose of cowardice and pusillanimity is probably encrypted in all governments. But hope has little to do with reason.

Therefore, this book, offered in hope.

2 December 2006   ARUNDHATI ROY

Postscript: Custodial Confessions, the Media and the Law

Is the 'collective conscience' that the Supreme Court refers to the same as majority opinion? Would it be fair to say that it is fashioned by the information we receive? And therefore, that in this case, the mass media has played a pivotal role in determining the final court verdict? If so, has it been accurate and truthful?

Now, five years later, when disturbing questions are being raised about the Parliament attack, is the Special Cell, once again, cleverly exploiting the frantic hunt for 'breaking news'? Suddenly spurious 'exposés' are finding their way onto prime-time TV. Unfortunately, some of India's best, most responsible news channels have been caught up in this game in which carelessness and incomprehension is as deadly as malice. (A few weeks ago we had a fiasco on CNN-IBN.)

Last week (16 December), on a ninety-minute prime-time show, NDTV showcased an 'exclusive' video of Mohammad Afzal's 'confession' made in police custody, in the days immediately following his arrest. At no point was it clarified that the 'confession' was five years old.[16]

Much has been said about the authenticity, reliability and legality of confessions taken in police custody, as well as the circumstances under which this particular 'confession' was extracted. Because of the very real danger that custodial torture will replace real investigation, the Indian Penal Code does not admit confessions made in police custody as legal evidence in a criminal trial. POTA was considered an outrage on civil rights and was eventually withdrawn primarily because it made confessions obtained in police custody admissible as legal evidence. In fact, in the case of Afzal's 'confession', the Supreme Court said the Special Cell had violated even the tenuous safeguards provided under POTA, and set it aside as being illegal and unreliable. Even before this, the High Court had already reprimanded the Special Cell sharply for forcing Afzal to incriminate himself publicly in a 'media confession'.[17]

So what made NDTV showcase this thoroughly discredited old 'confession' all over again? Why now? How did the Special Cell video find its way into their hands? Docs it have something to do with the fact that Afzal's clemency petition is pending with the president of India and a curative petition asking for a retrial is pending in the Supreme Court? In her column in the *Hindustan Times*, Barkha Dutt, Managing Editor of

NDTV, said the channel spent many hours 'debating what the fairest way' was to show this video.[18] Clearly it was a serious decision and demands to be discussed seriously.

At the start of the show, for several minutes the image of Afzal 'confessing' was inset in a text that said 'Afzal ne court mein gunah qabool kiya tha' (Afzal has admitted his guilt in court). This is blatantly untrue. Then, for a full fifteen minutes the 'confession' ran without comment. After this, an anchor came on and said, 'Sansad par hamle ki kahani, Afzal ki zubaani' (The story of the Parliament attack, in Afzal's words.) This, too, is a travesty of the truth. Well into the programme a reporter informed us that Afzal had since withdrawn this 'confession' and had claimed it had been extracted under torture. The smirking anchor then turned to one of the panellists, S.A.R. Geelani, who was also one of the accused in the case (and who knows a thing or two about torture and the Special Cell), and remarked that if this confession was 'forced', then Afzal was a very good actor.

(The anchor has clearly never experienced torture. Or even read the wonderful Uruguayan writer Eduardo Galeano—'The electric cattle prod turns anyone into a prolific storyteller.' Nor has he known what it's like to be held in police custody in Delhi while his family was hostage—as Afzal's was—in the war zone that is Kashmir.)

Later on, the 'confession' was juxtaposed with what the channel said was Afzal's statement to the court, but was actually the text of a letter he wrote to his high court lawyer in which he implicates the State Task Force (STF) in Kashmir and describes how in the months before the Parliament attack he was illegally detained and tortured by the STF. NDTV does not tell us that a Deputy Superintendent of the STF has since confirmed that he did illegally detain and torture Afzal (see Appendix III). Instead it uses Afzal's letter to discredit him further. The bold caption at the bottom of the frame read: 'Afzal ka badalta hua baiyan' (Afzal's changing statements).

There is another serious ethical issue. In Afzal's confession to the Special Cell in December 2001 (as opposed to his 'media confession'), he implicated S.A.R. Geelani and said he was the mastermind of the conspiracy. While this was in line with the Special Cell's charge sheet, it turned out to be false, and Geelani was acquitted by the Supreme Court. Why was this portion of Afzal's confession left out? So that the confession would seem less constructed, more plausible? Who made that decision to leave it out? NDTV or the Special Cell?

All this makes the broadcast of this programme a seriously prejudicial act. It wasn't surprising to watch the 'collective conscience' of society forming its opinion as the show unfolded. The SMS messages on the ticker tape said:

> Afzal ko boti boti mein kaat ke kutton ko khila do. (Cut him into bits and feed him to the dogs.)

> Afzal ke haath aur taang kaat ke, road mein bheek mangvani chahiye. (Cut off his arms and legs and make him beg on the streets.)

Then in English:

> Hang him by his balls in Lal Chowk. Hang him and hang those who are supporting him.

Even without Sharia courts, we seem to be doing just fine.

For the record, the reporter Neeta Sharma, credited several times on the programme for procuring the video, has been previously exposed for publishing falsehoods: on the 'encounter' in Ansal Plaza;[19] on the Iftikhar Gilani case;[20] on the S.A.R. Geelani case; and now on this one. Neeta Sharma was formerly a reporter with the *Hindustan Times*. Publishing Special Cell handouts seems to have got her a promotion—from print journalism to TV.

This kind of thing really makes you wonder whether media houses have an inside track on the police and intelligence agencies, or whether it's the other way around.

The quietest guest on the panel was M.K. Dhar, a former Joint Director of the Intelligence Bureau. He was pretty enigmatic. He certainly didn't repeat what he has said in his astonishingly frank book *Open Secrets: India's Intelligence Unveiled*: 'Some day or the other, taking advantage of the weakening fabric of our democracy, some unscrupulous intelligence men may gang up with ambitious Army brass and change the political texture of the nation.'[21]

Weakening fabric of our democracy. I couldn't have put it better.

The postscript was first published in the *Hindustan Times*, 22 December 2006.

PART ONE
THE ATTACK

[1]

THE MANY FACES OF NATIONALISM

Nandita Haksar

You want proof that the sun exists, so you stay up/
All night talking about it. Finally you sleep/ As the
sun comes up.

—Jelaluddin Balkhi 'Rumi'

On 13 December 2001, the entire country watched the
attack on the Indian Parliament on their TV screens.
We all saw the bloodied faces of the five attackers
killed by our security forces. The country went into a
state of shock. No one questioned the government's
story that the attack was the handiwork of Pakistan-
based terrorists belonging to the Lashkar-e-Toiba and
Jaish-e-Mohammad. The media, in a willing suspension
of disbelief, published whatever the police and
investigating agencies put out.

The police completed its entire investigation in a
record time of one week and quickly arrested four
people—three Kashmiri men and a Sikh woman—for

helping the five deceased attackers. The police forced Mohammad Afzal to cooperate with them. He, apparently, led them to the hide-outs of the five attackers and the shops from where they had purchased mobile phones, cash cards and chemicals for making bombs. Under torture, in police custody, Afzal later 'confessed'.

The Special Branch organized a press conference on 20 December at the Lodhi Road Police Station and produced Mohammad Afzal before the national media. In full view of the nation, Afzal confessed to being part of the conspiracy to attack Parliament.[1] One effect of this 'media trial' was that the public no longer felt the need for a 'judicial trial'. Since everyone in the country knew who had attacked our Parliament, where was the need for formal proof?

The media trial also served a political purpose. The government stood vindicated in the world arena with the international community finally forced to admit that India was a victim of cross-border terrorism. Troops were amassed on the India–Pakistan border, war seemed imminent and there was even talk of nuclear bombs.

In the midst of this war against terror, the government arranged a joint meeting of the two houses of Parliament to pass the Prevention of Terrorism Act (POTA).[2] It would require rare courage for anyone to question the efficacy of POTA a few weeks after the attack on Parliament. It would be blatantly anti-national and unpatriotic. And thus India joined the 'war against terror'.

In Delhi University the 'ultranationalist' forces demanded that the services of S.A.R. Geelani, a lecturer at Zakir Hussain College and one of the four accused of being a part of the conspiracy to attack Parliament, be terminated. They said there was no need to wait for the trial to begin. After all, even respectable newspapers had carried screaming tabloid-style headlines that Geelani had confessed to being a part of the conspiracy.[3] Besides, he was a Kashmiri Muslim and taught Arabic. What more proof could anyone want of his complicity in the conspiracy?

The media of course did not carry any report of the fact that despite use of torture by the police to extort a confession, Geelani had refused to admit to his guilt. No one questioned the Special Branch's blatantly false claims that Geelani had made a confession.

In the midst of this environment of prejudice and hatred, a group of Zakir Hussain College teachers worked quietly but consistently to oppose the forces of fascism and prevent Geelani's services from being terminated. Some Delhi University teachers came together to address issues arising out of Geelani's trial. A few visited Geelani in jail, even though they did not know him personally. Others fought long and hard to win the support of the teachers' unions. Unfortunately, the unions even hesitated to issue a statement demanding a fair trial for a member accused of a terrorist act.

There was a small group of citizens, including veteran socialists, civil liberty activists and democratic Indians, who were deeply concerned over the fact that the new anti-terrorist law made it virtually impossible for any accused to prove his innocence. And they believed Geelani when he said he was innocent.

The challenge before this small but committed group of Indian citizens was how to turn public opinion—to make people aware of the dangers of convicting people merely on the basis of police suspicion, without a fair trial—and how to create a climate where the life and liberty of a fellow citizen could not be sacrificed at the altar of national chauvinism. This appeared an impossible task even when some of the country's most prominent citizens formed themselves into the All India Defence Committee for S.A.R. Geelani.

We will leave it to history to judge whether Geelani and the other three accused were given a fair trial in the designated court. In the defence committee's view the judge, S.N. Dhingra, made no effort to mask his prejudice, forcing teachers of Delhi University and Jawaharlal Nehru University to write an open letter to the Chief Justice of the Supreme Court to ensure a fair trial for Geelani.

The designated court sentenced Geelani and two of his co-accused to death even as the fourth accused, Navjot (Afsan) Guru, was given five years.[4] A mob burst crackers outside the courtroom to celebrate the event. The members of the Special Branch, in pressed suits and polished shoes, could not stop smiling; they had become national heroes.

At the time it seemed virtually certain that an innocent citizen would hang. Could there be any greater shame for a country that called itself the largest democracy in the world? The trial exposed how easily patriotism could be twisted to serve the needs of those who wanted fascism to triumph in this country, my country.

I felt a deep, burning shame when I heard how members of the Special Branch had urinated on Afzal and Shaukat, how the lower court judge had mocked the pregnant Navjot, and that the jail authorities had prevented Geelani from offering namaz during Id. What greater proof of our dehumanization than when a man condemned to death is denied even his right to worship? Surprisingly, the National Human Rights Commission did not react. The media indulged in defamation with impunity, throwing all journalistic ethics to the wind. Political parties committed to democratic and secular values of our constitution did not raise their voice against the denial of fair trial to the four accused; they did not even react when an attempt was made on Geelani's life in jail. All this in the name of nationalism.

Geelani heard the death sentence on 18 December 2001. When asked for his reaction, he responded quietly, calmly, with great dignity and political clarity: 'By convicting innocents you cannot suppress feelings. Peace comes with justice. Without justice there will be no democracy. It is Indian democracy that is under threat.'

The death sentence for Geelani shocked the people of Kashmir and they declared a bandh for three days. Hundreds in Kashmir sent postcards to the home minister and the National Human Rights Commission demanding a fair trial for Geelani and the other three accused, insisting that if Geelani got a fair trial he would be acquitted. In the rest of the country too people demanded a fair trial, even if ambivalent about Geelani's innocence.

The media neither supported this campaign nor reported on its growing momentum. For them, the fact that more than 50,000 postcards had been sent from across the country demanding a fair trial was not news. Apart from the three universities in Delhi, the Defence Committee for S.A.R. Geelani got support from the university community of West Bengal.[5] The All Bengal University Teachers Association, representing nine universities, passed a resolution in Geelani's support. With the help of our website, pamphlets, posters, meetings and alternative media in regional languages we reached more than 100,000 people. The campaign also got the support of individuals and organizations abroad—from Amnesty International to Noam Chomsky.[6]

The fact that Ram Jethmalani, senior counsel and former union law minister, offered to defend Geelani pro bono greatly boosted our campaign. Ram Jethmalani argued with passion and conviction. He told the high court judges hearing the case that Geelani did not get even a moment's fair trial in the lower court, that he had taken up the case because he was morally convinced that Geelani was innocent and there was no evidence against him. The campaign for Geelani's release, along with Ram Jethmalani's passionate defence, succeeded in getting Geelani's acquittal.

The acquittal was hailed as a triumph of Indian democracy. Newspapers across the country carried editorials proclaiming that justice had been done. For some, the judgement reflected the competence and independence of our judiciary. Others, who had lost hope in Indian secularism in the aftermath of the Gujarat riots and the rising tide of communal prejudice, felt that this judgement of the Delhi High Court had vindicated their faith in Indian secularism. Still others felt that it reflected the vibrancy of our democratic institutions.

There were those who read the news of the acquittal with an indescribable happiness, similar to what one experiences after a miracle. Friends who had lost touch with me for more than fifteen years called to express their joy. In a manner of speaking, the judgement is a miracle. How many of us really believe that a Kashmiri Muslim sentenced to death for conspiring to attack the Indian Parliament can be acquitted, even if absolutely innocent?

And then our 'patriotic' celebration seemed to have been abruptly sullied by a statement made by Geelani at a press conference immediately after his release from jail. Instead of praising Indian democracy, or at least the judiciary, he expressed concern about the politicization of our courts and the criminalization of the police. Also, that a lasting solution to the Kashmir conflict could emerge, only if the aspirations of the people of Kashmir were taken into account. He added that he wanted to help other prisoners, especially the Kashmiris in Tihar jail, who had been denied a fair trial.[7]

It is true that a few thought Geelani's statement reflected a rare courage. Even at the press conference his colleagues, including senior professors, endorsed his statement by clapping and cheering. But there were many others who felt he was being rash and foolhardy by making such statements, especially since the police had already announced that they would appeal in the supreme court against his acquittal. Geelani's supporters advised caution and self-restraint. Other friends advised him to return to normal life, begin teaching and resume research.

Many who advised caution were worried not only about Geelani's personal safety but that the Kashmiris may draw wrong conclusions from his statement. Kuldip

Nayar, one-time Emergency victim and a prominent voice of democratic India, reflects this opinion. Writing in the *Indian Express* on 4 November 2003, Nayar castigated Geelani: 'For Geelani to mix the Kashmir question with the attack is to politicize a heinous crime . . . I hope Geelani's statement does not become grist for the propaganda mills. A favourable ground for talks between Deputy Prime Minister L.K. Advani and the Hurriyat is being prepared.' He added that Geelani's 'only claim to fame was the police case against him which it could not prove in the court.'[8]

Such 'democratic minded' Indians hope that the people in Kashmir will see Geelani's acquittal as a testimony of the democratic credentials of our country. They think that Kashmiris will forget their history and bitter experience of the past decades only because a high court has acquitted an innocent Kashmiri against whom there was not an iota of evidence in the first place and who had been condemned to death by a POTA court.

It is undeniable that the two high court judges who acquitted Geelani, Justices Usha Mehra and Pradeep Nandrajog, showed rare courage and integrity. The acquittal of Navjot was simpler because there is no constituency that could make political capital out of her release. But we need to take a closer look at the high court judgement in order to analyse how far it helped open up space for future democratic struggles for fair trial of accused in cases of terrorism.

Justice Pradeep Nandrajog's judgement raises many vital questions. The most important relates to the role of media trials. The judge has held that media trials do not vitiate the trial itself because, unlike with a lay jury, propaganda or adverse publicity does not influence professional judges. In this he seems to echo the Supreme Court judgement in the Zee News case. Therein, the defence lawyers for the Parliament accused had managed a stay from the Delhi High Court restraining the broadcasting of Zee TV's film *December 13*. Though the film claimed to be based on the charge sheet, it in fact made allegations against Geelani that went far beyond the prosecution case. The Supreme Court, however, vacated the stay on grounds that judges could not be influenced. It failed to appreciate how such films are responsible for creating a climate of fear and mistrust. Today, even post acquittal, Geelani cannot get a house on rent. His children find it hard to lead normal lives.

Though Justice Nandrajog was bound by the Supreme Court judgement on the question of what effect media trials have on judges, there was also the question of police organizing media conferences. The judge made observations against the practice of allowing the media to interview the accused persons when they are in police custody under orders of the court. But neither did he lay down any guidelines, nor did he pass any strictures against the policemen who organized the press conference and forced Afzal to incriminate himself in full view of the national media. The judge did not even reprimand the senior officers who denied—on oath—any knowledge of the press conference in the court.

The 392-page judgement contains many observations on the disturbing trends in police investigation. The judge asked whether there was a breach of statutory safeguards during investigation. If yes, what are the consequences thereof? After a detailed examination of the facts, the judge found that the 'prosecution stood discredited qua the time of arrest of the accused, S.A.R. Geelani.' He also found that the arrest memos had been forged. The police forged documents, lied on oath, failed to follow even basic rules of criminal procedure and violated the letter and spirit of the Indian constitution. Despite all this, the Delhi High Court failed to pass any strictures against the police officers of the Special Branch.

Perhaps the weakest part of the judgement is that the judge did not make any adverse observations against the designated judge, S.N. Dhingra, who showed his hostility and prejudice against the accused by routinely denying their counsel the right to cross-examine the prosecution witnesses. Further, he behaved like the prosecution by cross-examining defence witnesses and the accused when they gave their statements to the court.

At best the high court has created only partial space for further struggles to protect people who are similarly framed. It does not restrain the media from irresponsible reporting, nor the police from using the media in the war against terrorism, unmindful that in the process the police acquire powers without being accountable. They seem to have the power to violate rules, regulations, procedures, laws and even the constitution—with impunity. The media failed to point out that one of the officers in charge of the investigation is accused of being involved in false encounter deaths in Delhi and another is in Tihar jail on corruption charges. If such policemen have power of life and death over citizens, the future of our democracy is bleak indeed.

Even those who campaigned for Geelani's acquittal are now hesitant to address the uncomfortable questions which have arisen in the course of the trial of the four accused of conspiring to attack Parliament, questions which have a bearing on our future as a democratic country. We knew that the trial would raise such questions, which is what prompted us to form the All India Defence Committee for S.A.R. Geelani. We were aware of defending more than the civil liberties of an individual citizen. We were expressing our concern about the erosion of civil liberties in the name of national security and the war against terrorism.

The acquittal has raised even more questions, but few seem to be willing to publicly debate them. It seems that we are satisfied that the Delhi High Court has redeemed our faith in the judicial process, that we should not expect anything more from this system. Rather, we should just celebrate the miracle and Geelani should get back to normal life.

Has our society become so dehumanized as to lose its capacity to feel moral outrage for a human being who has been wronged? I have watched Geelani right from the time he stepped out of the jail gates. He has not had a minute's reprieve. The media has not stopped vilifying him. Even when he sent a rejoinder, at least one paper refused to publish it and an advertisement had to be inserted giving Geelani's clarification. He is expected to step out from months of solitary confinement where he was denied access to books, walk into class and start teaching for three to four hours every day.

In addition, he must look for a new house to rent and deal with the fear and insecurity afflicting his children. They had spent the past two years regularly visiting him in jail, seen him in handcuffs in court, and they cannot forget the sight of their father at the police station on the night of 14 December 2001. True, never for a minute did they lose hope of his ultimate release. Perhaps children have an inherent belief in justice, in the ultimate victory of good over evil. They waited for the nightmare to end as suddenly as it had begun. But the nightmare has not ended. They do not know why their beloved Abbu was wrongfully arrested and can never be sure that it might not happen again—to him or to someone else they love.

The high court judgement will not restore the lost childhood of Geelani's children; nor will it restore the faith of other Kashmiris in Indian democracy. As much as the judgement reflects the integrity of two judges, it also reflects the success of our campaign which proves that there is democratic space for struggle in our country. The struggle opened up spaces for us to expose the injustice in one particular incident. But how many innocent Kashmiris languishing in jail can expect such campaigns in their support? How many will be defended by lawyers of the calibre of Ram Jethmalani?

It would only be self-delusion to expect the Kashmiri people to be bowled over by Indian democracy merely because the judges acquitted one innocent Kashmiri after keeping him in death row for nearly a year. However, perhaps our campaign may persuade some Kashmiris that Indians are willing to fight against human rights violations even in the midst of the 'war against terror'. But how many of us are willing to confront the real problem, the question of the right to self-determination of the Kashmiri people? Even Geelani's mild statement that the aspirations of the

Kashmiri people must be taken into account if we want a resolution to the conflict aroused so much hatred.

Of course we have a right to celebrate Geelani's acquittal. It deserves to be celebrated for what it is: a successful struggle for justice in rather difficult times. But the struggle is far from complete; the task ahead is even more difficult than ensuring a fair trial for one individual. Our task is to create a political climate where all issues, including the demand for self-determination in Kashmir, can be fairly discussed. The struggle for a fair trial is a part of that struggle.

The state has not given up its attempts to convict Geelani. The media has not stopped its vilification campaign. It is true that the *Hindustan Times* in its editorial of 31 October 2003 admitted: 'When the Delhi Police announced that they had come across vital evidence beyond doubt [that] Geelani was guilty, many, including this paper, made the mistake of believing them.' Nevertheless, many of the reports continue to portray Geelani as a guilty man who has escaped through some legal loophole. Why, even Kuldip Nayar thinks the acquittal is a result of the inability of the police to establish their case.[9]

There is no media report that captures the really extraordinary feature of this case: that Geelani, from the very beginning, asked the court to put all the evidence on record. And the prosecution refused to do so. First, there was the intercepted conversation between his younger brother and him on 14 December 2001. It was the main prosecution evidence against Geelani. The police informed the court that they had started tapping his phone from the night of 13 December to the afternoon of the next day. All the conversations were in a cassette marked Cl. These included many conversations between him and other family members in Kashmir. Geelani asked the court on several occasions to put the entire cassette on record. However, the police only produced the 2.16-minute conversation between him and his brother on the afternoon of 14 December 2001.

In the high court, Geelani filed an application requesting permission to explain each telephone conversation. The prosecution had placed the Airtel record of 521 calls made between October and December 2001. Geelani said the sessions court had denied him an opportunity to explain these calls when he made his statement to the court under section 313 of the Criminal Procedure Code. He was willing to do so during the appeal.

Second, Geelani asked the court to arrange a transcript of the conversation by someone conversant with the Kashmiri language. He even suggested that the court appoint an IAS or IPS officer. The sessions court refused to direct the prosecution to do so. To date, the prosecution has not put on record a Kashmiri transcript of the conversation, even though it claimed that this was the main evidence against Geelani to establish his complicity in the conspiracy to attack Parliament. Two expert witnesses produced by the defence, Sampat Prakash and Sanjay Kak, put the transcript and translation on record in the court.

Third, Geelani admitted the conversation even though the tape was inaudible. The Central Forensic Laboratory in Delhi returned a finding that it could not conduct a voice sample test since the tape was inaudible. And yet the prosecution witness, Rashid the vegetable vendor from Azad market, claimed to have deciphered it after hearing it a few times.

Fourth, the interception of the conversation was in violation of the procedures laid down under the Indian Telegraph Act and POTA. Although Geelani's lawyers did challenge the procedures, they did not make it their main defence. And at the high court they did not even argue the point.

Fifth, the prosecution failed to produce Geelani's brother as a witness. If the conversation showed complicity, then clearly the younger brother knew of Geelani's role in the conspiracy. The police told the court that on questioning the younger brother they found he was innocent. Consequently they did not bother to take down his formal statement under Section 161 of the Criminal Procedure Code, even for the record.

The Delhi High Court has held: 'Prosecution had relied upon the conversation between Geelani and his brother in the afternoon of 14th December 2001 and had contended that the talk was incriminating, in that it showed Geelani's participation in the attack on Parliament House. We had, while discussing the taped conversation, even assuming the prosecution version to be correct, come to the conclusion that there was nothing which could incriminate Geelani as far as the conversation is concerned.'

Finally, the only other evidence against Geelani was his acquaintance with the co-accused. Geelani has never once attempted to deny this, admitting he knew them from well before the period of the conspiracy. The Delhi High Court judgement stated that the record of telephone calls between him and his co-accused is the only other evidence: 'We are, therefore, left with only one piece of evidence against S.A.R. Geelani, being the record of telephone calls between him and the accused Mohd. Afzal and Shaukat. This circumstance, in our opinion, does not remotely, far less definitely and unerringly, point towards the guilt of the accused S.A.R. Geelani.'

There was no other evidence against S.A.R. Geelani. He was acquitted *not* because the prosecution could not produce evidence, but because there *was* no evidence to produce.

And so the inevitable question: Why was Geelani arrested? Why should the police want to frame an innocent man? Suddenly our usual scepticism about the police dissolves in the face of our suspicions about Kashmiri Muslims. Instead of asking why the Special Branch carried out such a shoddy investigation, we start doubting the innocence of a 'blameless citizen' who has been victimized by a 'corrupt and communal' police and a 'prejudiced' designated judge.

Let us examine the facts relating to the actual attack that have emerged in the course of the trial of the four accused in the Parliament attack case, facts that the media has refused to publish, facts that raise uncomfortable questions that must be answered if we want to protect Indian democracy.

At first the government told us that the attack was the handiwork of the Lashkar-e-Toiba and Jaish-e-Mohammad and that the five attackers were Pakistanis. L.K. Advani, our home minister at the time, announced in Parliament that they 'looked Pakistani'. However, in the course of the trial, not one of the prosecution's eighty witnesses ever alleged that any of the four accused belonged to any terrorist organization. Even the designated court was hard put to find a way of convicting the accused of belonging to any terrorist organization. As for the five men who actually attacked the Parliament, the only 'evidence' that they were Pakistanis was that no Indian came forward to claim their bodies.

The main accused, Mohammad Afzal [who has, since this essay first appeared, been sentenced to death by the supreme court, and whose clemency petition lies with the President of India], is a self-confessed surrendered militant—a renegade in the eyes of militants. Besides, he is a surrendered militant of the JKLF, a group that has already laid down arms. Why would a Pakistan-based militant organization trust a renegade, that too of the JKLF, with such an important job? Especially when the man had been working in Delhi for the past ten years and his entire motivation seemed to have been money.

Afzal has admitted to playing an inadvertant peripheral role in the conspiracy. He said he brought one of the attackers, Mohammad, from the Special Task Force (STF) camp. However, he also insisted that he did not know the other four attackers who were killed during the attack. If he can be sentenced to death on three counts on the basis of his own confession, why can we not believe the other part of his story recorded in the court under Section 313 of the Criminal Procedure Code?

We must demand that the government table a full report on the facts relating to the attack on Parliament. We have a right to know who actually attacked our Parliament. Why have we not made this demand? Out

of a sense of nationalism? Are matters of national
security best left to the state, no matter what its
character? Do we seriously believe any government can
bring about a lasting solution to the Kashmir question
if only Geelani keeps quiet and we refuse to raise
awkward questions?

Only when we have real democracy in India can we
expect others to respect us.

January 2004

* * *

Postscript, 25 November 2006

On 8 February 2005, there was an attempt to assassinate
S.A.R. Geelani. Someone tried to kill him right outside
my home. Within a few hours the news spread and his
students, colleagues, friends, civil liberty activists and
other concerned citizens gathered outside the hospital.
So did the media. Restless with the waiting as Geelani
was being operated upon, the media asked for reactions.
Who could have shot Geelani? Without exception
everyone responded: 'Special Cell, Delhi Police.'

There was good reason to suspect the Special Cell,
because no one else could have known that we had
decided to meet at my house that night. In fact, after
the day's hearing at the Supreme Court we had decided
we would not meet and he went to take classes and I
went home to prepare for the next day. But suddenly I
realized I needed to ask him some questions and
phoned around five in the evening to ask whether he
could come over on his way back from college. He
arrived at 8.45 p.m. He parked his car and was

checking whether the car doors were locked when he saw a man raise his hand and fire.

The police desperately tried to put out various theories on the assassination attempt. These included: road rage (no details given), an irate lover (never named), Naga insurgents (including my husband who is a Naga), a Kashmiri militant (one was arrested and tortured and when he refused to confess that he had tried to assassinate Geelani he was booked under the Official Secrets Act and is in jail). Very few noticed a story from an unnamed source in a Hindi newspaper. The story was that the intelligence agencies had used the services of the Chhota Rajan gang for the assassination. But who was going to ensure an investigation into the workings of our investigation agencies? And so Geelani is guarded by the Central Industrial Security Force with three bullets still lodged in his guts. The intelligence agencies continue to find new ways to vilify him and those who support him.

This time the intelligence agencies have found a new tool. It is Aijaz Guru, Mohammad Afzal's elder brother. On 3 October 2006, outside the gates of Jail no 3 of Tihar jail, the media waited for Mohammad Afzal's family to come out after meeting Afzal for what could be the last time. It was an emotionally charged atmosphere. Afzal's widowed mother Aisha Begum, his young wife Tabassum and seven-year-old son Ghalib, his younger brother Hilal and his elder brother Aijaz had all rushed down from Kashmir after seeing the report on television that Afzal's execution had been fixed for 6 a.m. on 20 October 2006. The execution was to be in the month of Ramzan, one day before Diwali.

As the family stepped outside the jail gates, in full view of the national media, Afzal's elder brother created a scene he had probably planned and rehearsed that day. He shouted, screamed and tore off his shirt and said that Geelani and I and other unnamed supporters who were campaigning for clemency for Afzal were using Afzal to make money. Two or three anonymous men stood around prompting him in case he forgot some important lines of his solo melodramatic act.

We waited for the next day's newspapers and watched the TV channels. The media on the whole did not report or broadcast the scene. But one Hindi newspaper did think it was its nationalistic duty to print the story. And now I have news that a television channel is making a telefilm with Aijaz starring in it.

Of course it is despicable that an elder brother should sabotage a campaign aimed at saving his younger brother from the gallows. And the journalists could see through the whole drama. But the question is why no one has bothered to find out who is using Aijaz and what are his motives for behaving in this manner.

If any journalists had tried to find out they would have discovered that Afzal's family has a terrible fear that the STF will eliminate them if our campaign succeeds in exposing the role of the STF in the Parliament attack case. Afzal has from the beginning maintained that his involvement in the conspiracy to attack Parliament was 'unknowing, unwilling and unintentional'. He had told the designated court that the STF had told him to bring one Mohammad to Delhi and he admitted that he had even helped this Mohammad to buy a car. But he has also maintained that he did not know any of the other four men who actually attacked Parliament.

Afzal's family has good reason to be afraid of the STF.

Mohammad Afzal comes from a very poor family. His father died when he was young and his elder brother, Aijaz, brought him up. Aijaz himself could not study very much but he supported his younger brother who had a passion for learning and wanted to be a doctor. It was Afzal's dream and Aijaz supported him.

Afzal was in his first year of MBBS when the youth in Kashmir rose up in revolt against the farcical elections of 1987 when the candidates who had won were put into jails and those who had betrayed their people were put in the assembly. It was a tidal wave of resistance to decades of oppression. The processions in the Valley were kilometres long. The youth in their thousands gave up their dreams of secure careers and the warmth of their homes and crossed steep, dangerous icy passes to take armed training in Pakistan Occupied Kashmir (POK). Afzal was one of them.

However, he came back after three months because he was disillusioned by the fact that Pakistan too was using Kashmiris for its narrow politics. He returned and surrendered to the Border Security Force. The condition of surrender is that the militant has to motivate two others also to surrender and he did that as well.

Afzal got a job selling medical and surgical instruments. It was the closest to his dream of becoming a doctor. He earned some five thousand rupees a month and he got married. Two days after his marriage, the STF men came to his home and took him to their camp. They kept him there for nearly a month and every day he was brutally tortured. They poured petrol into his anus, they kept him in freezing water and they beat him.

The family managed to rescue him only after they raised one lakh rupees to satisfy the greed of the STF who are known to be extortionists. Tabassum, a new bride, sold all her jewellery, his mother sold his scooter and finally Afzal was handed back more dead than alive. No one in the family can forget the terror of those days.

Aijaz is wild with fear that the STF will pick him up if Afzal expose's the STF. The irony is that Aijaz seems to have more faith in the media and Indian democratic institutions than is merited by the facts. Despite the fact that Mufti Saeed came to power in Kashmir with the promise to dismantle the STF, and that innumerable international and Kashmiri human rights groups have demanded that these illegal torture centres be dismantled, they continue to exist and the officers continue to torture and extort with impunity.

In India, even the human rights groups have not taken up the demand for the dismantling of these mini-Abu Ghraibs. Perhaps it is an unwritten rule of our patriotism that we are silent about torture if it is the torture of Kashmiris.

It was the harassment and threat of the STF camp that brought Afzal to Delhi in the 1990s and he graduated from Delhi University while continuing his business. He already had a son and now he dreamt of living a normal life. He rented a room in Indira Vihar in 2001 and had planned to go home for Id and then bring his wife and son to Delhi.

But even this small dream was cut short when he was arrested from the Srinagar bus stop and framed in the conspiracy to attack the Indian Parliament. He was sentenced to death by all three courts and is now on death row. The special rope for the gallows has been bought from Bihar. The hangman from Meerut found. The date and time for his execution set.[10]

The news was greeted with widespread protests both in Kashmir and in Delhi.

Every television channel organized heated and passionate debates on whether Afzal should hang or should the death sentence be commuted into life imprisonment. Legal luminaries voiced their opinions, politicians made it a political issue and civil rights activists protested.

And then the execution was stayed when his wife Tabassum filed a petition for justice (she did not want to call it a petition for clemency).

The media made it a national issue. But what is the issue? The ultra-nationalists wanted the government to hang Afzal immediately so as to demonstrate to militants and the Kashmiri people that India would not tolerate terrorism. Members of the BJP argued that Afzal must be hanged so as to give justice to the families of security men and women; as an assertion of our national strength in the face of terrorism and as a way of upholding law and order. The BJP was supported by policemen, intelligence agents and those concerned with national security. Although one expert on national security who appeared along with me did say that an assessment of the situation in Kashmir could lead to the decision that Afzal was not hanged as a measure of counter insurgency. In another programme, hosted by Karan Thapar, the show ended with the BJP leader and Congress spokesman giving the same kinds of arguments.

A section of the media tried to portray the protests as a reflection of the division between the Indian people and the Kashmiri people. But the media does seem to get facts wrong when it comes to certain issues. All those who are protesting against the death sentence for Afzal are doing so because they know that he has not been given an opportunity to defend himself. Even the so-called separatist Kashmiri leaders are not saying that Afzal should not be hanged merely because he is a Kashmiri. They are saying that he should not be hanged because he was never given a fair trial.

In a resolution passed on 24 September 2005 in Srinagar, Syed Ali Geelani, Shabir Shah, Mohammad Yaseen Malik, Main Abdul Qayyoom and Nisar Ali said:

> The judgement of the supreme court states that the attack on the Indian Parliament resulted in heavy casualties and has 'shaken the entire nation and the collective conscience of the society will only be satisfied if capital punishment is awarded to the offender.'
>
> We the people of Kashmir ask why the collective conscience of Indians is not shaken by the fact that a Kashmiri has been sentenced to death without a fair trial, without a chance to represent himself? Throughout the trial at the sessions court Mohammad Afzal asked the judge to appoint a lawyer. He even named various lawyers but they all refused to represent him. Is it his fault that the Indian lawyers think that it is more patriotic to allow a Kashmiri to die than to ensure he gets a fair trial?[11]

So what are the facts? I mean the facts on record before the courts?

First of all, Mohammad Afzal did not have a

lawyer to represent him at the stage of trial. He knew his family could never raise the exorbitant fees demanded by professional criminal lawyers, that if he asked his family to engage a lawyer it would ruin them. However, he was happy to accept a lawyer appointed by the court. The judge appointed one lawyer who never appeared. Then another was appointed and she appeared without taking instructions and even agreed to admission of documents without formal proof. In other words, she admitted on Afzal's behalf the identification of the deceased terrorists when Afzal has always maintained he knew only one of them and not the other four.

Afzal himself gave the names of four lawyers but they also refused to represent him and finally the designated judge who was in a hurry to start the trial appointed Neeraj Bansal as amicus curiae. Neeraj Bansal stated that he did not want to appear for Afzal and Afzal also expressed a lack of confidence in the advocate. But the judge wanted to get on with the trial and so insisted that Neeraj Bansal continue. However, the judge gave Afzal the right to cross examine the witnesses if he wished.

Thus the lower court records show that Judge S.N. Dhingra passed the following order on 12 July 2002:

> I consider that irrespective of accused saying that he does not want amicus curiae, the court has the duty to seek the assistance of an amicus curiae in such cases where the accused is not cooperative. Mr Neeraj Bansal has requested for withdrawal from this case, but is requested to assist the court during trial.
>
> Accused Mohd Afzal has requested to cross examine the witnesses himself. He is given the liberty to cross-examine the witness.

The result of this decision was that of a total of eighty prosecution witnesses only twenty-two witnesses were cross examined by Neeraj Bansal—all of them insufficiently—and Afzal put a few questions to three witnesses. (In his petition before the President of India Afzal has produced a long chart—reproduced here as Appendix 1—with exact details of the cross examination.)

Afzal has written to the President:

> The Supreme Court held that no prejudice was caused to me even though I did not have a lawyer to represent me and my lawyer at one point told the court he did not wish to represent me. The Supreme Court states that it was not demonstrated by my counsel how the case was mishandled. Supreme Court was of the view that cross examination of the witnesses on behalf of me was not faulty. But the very basis of my conviction is founded on the facts that the material witnesses were not challenged in cross examination or no suggestion was put to them to disprove their allegations against me. I would like to show that the Supreme Court's own judgement shows how the fact that I was deprived of a counsel affected me.

The second argument for not hanging Afzal is that the investigation was full of illegalities and the courts noted with concern that evidence was fabricated; the police officers of the Special Cell told lies on oath in court and the supreme court has observed that the police had got false confessions from Afzal by torturing him.[12] Criminal law prescribes the death penalty for anyone who fabricates evidence with a view to getting someone death penalty. But the courts did not even pass a stricture against DCP Ashok Chand for denying any knowledge of the media conference held on 20 December at the police station of the Special Cell in which Mohammad Afzal was made to incriminate himself before the national media.

Third, Mohammad Afzal was not responsible for anyone's death or injury. He did not mastermind the attack. In fact, he was acquitted of charges of belonging to any terrorist organization even by the POTA court because none of the eighty prosecution witnesses even alleged that he belonged to any such organization. Even according to the police charge sheet, the real masterminds were three Pakistanis—Masood Azhar, Tariq Ahmed and Ghazi Baba. None of the three were arrested or brought on trial. Even if Pakistan were to extradite them they would be protected from the death penalty, as in the case of Abu Salem.

The ultra-nationalists do not care to know these facts. They want Afzal hanged. But there are a growing number of Indians who have informed themselves of the real facts and are doing their best to ensure that he is saved from the gallows. They believe that hanging Afzal would be a stigma on Indian democracy.

Afzal has been moved by the growing support and solidarity and now once again hopes for justice. He has sent his petition to the president in which he has said . . .

> . . . records clearly show that I was not involved in the actual attack on the Indian Parliament. I did not murder anyone and I did not injure anyone. I do not think that the attack on Parliament served the cause of the Kashmiri people and I am genuinely sorry for the family members of those who died doing their duty. I feel no personal enmity towards the nine persons killed or the sixteen injured. It is unfortunately

the poor and the vulnerable who suffer. Even if no one believes me I can honestly say that I do not justify or rationalize the pain of the children who lost their fathers on that day as I feel the pain of the seven year old son who is living with the nightmare that his father may be hanged any day.

I met Afzal a few days ago. He is now not allowed to go out of his cell and he is deprived of even half an hour of sunshine. The Red Cross is being denied access to him even though they have a right to visit Kashmiri prisoners. But Afzal is full of hope that he will live to see his son grow up. I asked him whether there was anything he needed. His immediate reply was, 'Books.' I asked him if there was any particular book he wanted, and he hesitated and rather shyly asked for Noam Chomsky and Arundhati Roy.

A version of this essay, except the postscript, first appeared in the January 2004 issue of *Seminar*.

MEDIA TRIALS AND COURTROOM TRIBULATIONS

A BATTLE OF IMAGES, WORDS AND SHADOWS

Shuddhabrata Sengupta

'The acquittal of an innocent man is not an occasion for celebration, but a cause for reflection.'

—Syed Abdul Rehman Geelani, on his being acquitted by the Supreme Court on charges of conspiracy in the Parliament attack case

On 4 August 2005 the Supreme Court of India gave its verdict on the 13 December 2001 'Attack on Parliament' case, acquitting two of the original accused, S.A.R. Geelani, lecturer in Arabic at Zakir Husain College, Delhi and Afsan Guru (aka Navjot Sidhu), wife of one of the accused Shaukat Husain Guru, and upholding the death sentence pronounced by the Delhi High Court and the Special POTA court on Mohammad Afzal. The high court's pronouncement of a death sentence on Shaukat Husain Guru was commuted to ten years imprisonment. In announcing this verdict, the Supreme Court of India upheld the Delhi High Court's acquittal of S.A.R. Geelani and Afsan Guru. Geelani had been sentenced to death, and Afsan Guru awarded five years of rigorous imprisonment by the judge of the special POTA court, S.N. Dhingra, on 18 December 2002.

The justices P.V. Reddy and P.P. Naolekar, while acquitting S.A.R. Geelani on the grounds that the prosecution was not able to present adequate evidence against the accused, maintained that there was still a 'needle of suspicion' against S.A.R. Geelani, but that suspicion alone could not form the basis of a sentence in the absence of robust evidence.

With the pronouncement of this verdict by the highest judicial authority of the Republic of India, a sordid chapter in the history of this republic came to a provisional and uncertain conclusion. One hesitates to use the term 'end' because the unpredictable nature of events as they unfold, perhaps in the immediate future, perhaps due to a random discovery in the archives many decades hence, may yet deliver us another 'turn' in the unravelling of this story which might still give cause to startle us all.

Or it might not, and as in what befalls many unexplained twists and turns in the script of our times, we may learn to become inured to the tug of an uncomfortable and persistent memory of things and people that went amiss. Like the 'out-takes' in footage that never quite made it into a film, about which we can say that we have a memory of being present as witnesses at the shooting, but little or no recall of ever having seen them on screen, like papers, documents, transcripts, bodies and memories that turn to dust and are scattered, the history of the attack on the Parliament of India too will in all likelihood become a hazy recollection with only the words and images of 'terrorists' and 'martyrs' and 'threat to national security' thrown up in bold relief, and with all else obscured within a labyrinth of shadows.

Some people call this forgetting, others call it history. The history of the Republic of India could fill an archive of lost memories. Perhaps there needs to be, somewhere near India Gate, not far from the present 'National Archives' and the Parliament, a site earmarked for a building to house a 'National Archive of Forgetting'. A building—part Lutyens, part Le Corbusier, part Raj Rewal, part Kafka and part Borges—that in its architectural imagination would do true justice to the delicate combination of pomp, paranoia and amnesia that buttresses the foundations of the republic.

While there may be widespread relief in the knowledge that S.A.R. Geelani and Afsan Guru are now acquitted (if not unconditionally exonerated) by the judicial apparatus, the turn of events does not give anyone any cause for celebration. Neither the Delhi Police and the prosecution, who have seen their arguments fall like so many dead birds from the judicial sky. Those who have stood by Geelani and sought to defend him can breathe easier, and pause at the end of the maelstrom that has occupied their sleeping and waking hours, but there is little cause to rejoice. The court has maintained that there is a 'needle of suspicion' even as it has not been able to show any evidence to substantiate this charge. We need to ask how this 'needle of suspicion' got created, and why it continues to persist, quivering in the minds of the judges even as they comb swathes of missing and faulty and forged evidence. As Geelani' himself said in a press conference immediately after the pronouncement of the verdict, 'the acquittal of an innocent man is not an occasion for celebration, but a cause for reflection'. Why, after all, did the police and concerned security agencies, and large sections of the 'independent' media have to go to such lengths to frame a man against whom they could not provide a shred of quality evidence in the special POTA court, in the high court, and in the Supreme Court? Now that at least two of the accused can walk free, and one other can live (albeit in prison), we need to begin to ask what really happened. Some others may have to do whatever is necessary and permissible under the law to ensure that Shaukat Husain too is able to leave prison sooner and that Mohammad Afzal does not take the final walk to the gallows.

The doubts about the circumstances that led to the attack on the Indian Parliament will persist as long as the primary actors in the case do not reveal, or are not compelled to reveal, through the process of an independent and impartial inquiry, the roles that they have played. A committee to demand precisely such an enquiry has indeed been constituted by a group of citizens, but as of now, no agency of the state, or civil society, and no voices of substance in the media have either endorsed or echoed their demand.

If Mohammad Afzal is indeed executed, then some of the truths that he alone (barring some of his handlers and interrogators) has access to, will follow him to his grave. In the event that the spin doctors of the media continue to play the role that they have played so

honourably in the duration of this entire set of trials, it
is unlikely that anything approximating the truth will
ever be made available to the public in India, or indeed,
anywhere in the world. The gentlemen and women of
the fourth estate, the shining knights of the free press
and electronic media of India will once again have
demonstrated their willingness to construct an elaborate
machine made out of smoke and mirrors that does
more to conceal than to reveal. For an alternative
version of the events to eventually emerge, it is crucial
that Mohammad Afzal's death sentence be challenged,
and that S.A.R. Geelani (on whose life there have been
two extra-judicial attempts, once while he was in
prison, and again outside his advocate Nandita Haksar's
residence by an as yet unidentified assailant in February
2005) survives. Both Geelani and Afzal need to live if
we are to get any closer to the truth of what happened
on 13 December 2001, and why Geelani was framed.
It is vital to understand that the 'climate of suspicion'
that has led to Afzal's conviction, and to the Supreme
Court's unwarranted remark that a 'needle of suspicion'
still points at Geelani, are a product of more than four
years of consistent information management and the
production of images. Judges, like the rest of us, are as
likely to be swayed by these images and processed
bodies of information in the media, and we need to be
sharply aware at least of the fact that the management
and processing of information is a key element in the
realpolitik of 'terrorism and counter-terrorism' before
we jump to any conclusions about apportioning guilt
and innocence. My hunch is that the critical media
literacy of the highest judiciary of the Republic of India
is not so immaculate at the present as to render it

immune to prejudice. The role played by the production of moving images, in film and video, in cinema and on television is particularly pertinent here, and I will attend to this in some greater detail later in this essay.

As of now, barring a presidential pardon, or the unlikely re-opening of the case, Afzal will hang. One hopes, for all our sakes, that it is otherwise, and that the circumstances that led to the alleged 'terrorist' attack on the parliament of what is sometimes loosely called the 'largest democracy in the world', to the passing of the most draconian preventive detention law by the legislature of the same 'largest democracy' (the now thankfully repealed POTA), and the situation of near war that lasted for more than a year between two nuclear weapons states who are also neighbours, will one day become available in the public domain. Until then, the delicate combination of secrecy and hyperbole, of understatement and exaggeration, of straight lies and half-cooked truths, of skulduggery and sentimentality, will continue to taint the history of communication practices in our republic of forgotten truths and remembered illusions, where (as elsewhere) the 'media', the 'television and film industries' and the 'intelligence community' dance an elegant tango in which it sometimes becomes difficult to discern who leads whom on the dance floor.

This text is only a call for a sustained meditation on this condition. And an attempt to account for and ask some questions about the overproduction of images and the aporiae within them that surround the representations of what is called 'terrorism', the events of 13 December, and the trials that followed. I do not pretend to give a comprehensive account of what happened, because I do not possess the necessary critical forensic-legal apparatus by way of training, nor am I an expert media 'analyst'. I am a media practitioner, and I write this from the standpoint of someone who practises media and who observes what others practise. I do hope, however, that reading this might prompt those who have the necessary legal–forensic apparatus, or who may lay claim to being expert media analysts, to ask some hard questions on the role that the media have played in this case, and with regard to the representation of 'terrorism and counter-terrorism' in general, and provoke some reason for introspection within the community of media practitioners.

A thorough enquiry into these matters will make it necessary for us to examine a whole range of materials—charge sheets, court records, depositions, defence and prosecution arguments, judgements as well as news reports, television news and current affairs programmes, televised enactments or dramatizations and feature length fiction films.[1]

This text is culled from preliminary notes towards such an exercise, but even in making these notes I have become aware of the fact that the task of reflection on the media requires us to consider media materials, not as isolates, but as elements in a networked reality, where cinema, television, newspaper reportage and even public service messages enter into elaborate interweaving feedback loops that reinforce and sustain each other, either through direct quotation, or through narrative 'enhancements' that create a situation where each message enhances its claim to credibility by relying on the credentials of the other. Thus, when hearing a voice say authoritatively on a televised commentary accompanying a visual of a slain man's visage that the face belongs to a 'terrorist', we are implicitly being asked to invoke 'images' of terrorists' faces that we may have seen in fiction films. Conversely, when a fictional film consciously evokes the aesthetic register of the rough-hewn 'documentary' look and feel of news reportage when invoking terrorism, it is doing so in order to buttress its own claim to credibility. Events and processes such as the 'reading' of 13 December and its aftermath take place at the intersections of a densely networked media space, where messages, memories, events and mediums relay and overlay each other. These realities make the task of sophisticated and sensitive readings of media not an academic excercise but an urgent political task, that has bearings not only on the destinies of our polity but also, as in the 13 December case, on the life and death of individuals. The galling neglect, incapacity or unwilllingess, on the part of a vast majority of media scholars and critics in India to undertake this excercise, and the lax ethical standards of many media practitioners has in the final analysis to be read against what happens to us as a polity, and what happens to the lives of individuals and to those close to them.

For too long we have looked at media materials— be they film, or television, or print, as if they exist in isolated, hermetic universes. This mode of analysis that sees 'cincma as cinema alone' and that does not take into account the networked information world inhabited and created by viewers, readers, audiences and producers of media materials through a constant process of interactive, cross-referential and self-referential iteration of media objects, is totally inadequate when it comes to the task of understanding the place of images, sounds, words and information that attempt to express the contemporary realities we live in.

It is important to remember that on seeing the pictures of the bodies of the slain alleged 'terrorists' who entered the precincts of the Parliament building on the morning of 13 December, the then home minister Lal Krishna Advani is said to have remarked that the assailants 'looked like Pakistani terrorists'. Advani must have known what he was talking about (at least the part about their looking like 'Pakistanis') since he looks a lot like a Pakistani himself (as do many North Indians and migrants to India—like Advani—from the provinces of British India that became West Pakistan in 1947). But more importantly, he was able to assert the fact that they looked 'like . . . terrorists'. It is important to pause and consider how exactly we know that someone looks like a 'terrorist'. The Delhi Police, which has had considerable experience in handling 'terrorists' and 'terrorism' over the years, has reminded us in a series of thoughtful public service advertisements that 'terrorists' are suspicious because they stand out by virtue of their somewhat unusual appearance and behaviour (they wear clothing unsuited to the weather, etc.), and that simultaneously they are suspicious precisely because they blend in so easily with the general population. It is this combination of 'standing out' and 'blending in' at the same time that causes alarm. It is possible to say that one can't quite make out if a person 'stands out' if he/she 'blends in' at the same time. But to this, like Advani, we know that we can respond with certainty, because we feel we know that when we see a 'terrorist' we will be able to recognize one. After all, we have 'seen' people who convincingly embody 'terrorism' many times. We have seen them on identikit photographs pasted on to walls and street corners, we have seen their disfigured, hooded and blurred faces in newspaper and magazine photographs and television reports, and we have seen them up close countless times in mainstream cinema. We have seen the face of the terrorist so often, and so intimately as a moving image, that in a sense the terrorist actually lives in our own heads, and were we to ever come across his body, living or dead, or his image, we would be immediately in a position to cross-check his features against the indelible impress of those features in our nervous systems.

The production of terrorism is not something that happens sui generis. The production of terrorism is almost always, in every society, also a production of images of terror. In fact the fear that terrorism induces in general terms is not so much by way of the actual impact of explosives, gun shots and incendiary or lethal materials but by way of a circulation and amplification of images and their effects. We know this from every instance of spectacular terrorism that we have witnessed in the last hundred years or so. So much so that even more or less arbitrary calendrical notations like 9/11, 12/13 or now, more recently, 7/7, become indexical images of terror. All we need to do is to see a particular alphanumeric arrangement to experience at the very least a twinge of the recognition of the feeling that terror induces. If the production of terrorism is so interlaced with the production of images, we can also say that the production of certain images is also linked to a climate that gives credibility to the production of a certain set of seemingly self-evident truths about terrorism. Sometimes, to create the consequences that a terrorist incident produces, it is necessary to create a strong body of images that will serve the necessary purposes in a focused way.

The tried and tested tactics of infiltration into existing terror cells or political groups, or the creation of such cells where none exist, or when those that exist are too weak to perform a spectacular act of terror, are well documented in the extant literature on the work and function of intelligence agencies of various states. The MI6's murky relationships with the IRA, and later, the provisional IRA, Mossad's successful infiltration of the Palestinian Abu Nidal group, and the Italian and Belgian intelligence agencies' dealings with the mafia, ex-Nazis, far right militias, fascists and secret societies in setting off a chain of spectacular terrorist incidents in the 1980s (including the Bologna train station bombing of 1974 and 1980 that killed 113 people and wounded 180) that could later be attributed to 'left wing' terrorists is very well documented, as is the history of the infiltration of the 'Naxalite' movement in India in the 1970s by the Indian intelligence bureau and special police operatives. The picture of a shadowy dalliance between 'terrorism' and 'counter-terrorism', between 'militants' and 'surrendered militants', between people in and out of different kinds of uniform is also beginning to emerge from the battlegrounds of Kashmir, Assam and the rest of the North East. Military intelligence officers, 'special task force' personnel, intelligence bureau operatives and a host of 'freelance' professionals occasionally masquerading as 'insurgents' to give effect to 'special operations' are freely written about in magazines like *Force*—a journal specifically catering to the professional needs and realities of 'armed forces and security personnel' in India.

There is no reason to suppose that the tacticians and strategists of the 'intelligence community' that owes its fealty to the Indian state do not, from time to time, have to consider it necessary to 'create' or manufacture instances of terrorism, when it suits the purposes of the state to do so. This is standard practice worldwide, especially under the conditions of the 'global war against terror', and there is no reason to suppose that Indian intelligence professionals are anything but abreast of key global trends in this regard.[2]

This 'creation' of terrorism is something that generally requires a calibrated media strategy and information management such that the bodies and actions that characterize a particular operation can be 'rendered' in a manner that is convincing and useful. The overproduction of enthusiastic and detailed reports on the supposed backgrounds, past lives and actions of the primary accused in the 13 December case bear an overwhelming stamp of such a close alignment between the need to create a body of convincing 'evidence' on the part of the security and intelligence community and the media's thirst for a meaty story. Television channels and newspapers routinely projected the accused and arrested as 'terrorist masterminds and co-conspirators' without even the caveat that this was as alleged by their captors.

The enthusiastic reportage of the 'arrest' of the prime accused Afzal, Shaukat Husain and Geelani, which in some instances bordered on the hysterical, particularly in the week following 14 December (when

Geelani was detained under POTA), is particularly noteworthy. In the stories that began to make their appearance, the swoops were a result of the brilliant investigations carried out by the police on the mobile phone records of the phones and sim cards found on the bodies of the alleged slain terrorists. Not one newspaper or television channel paused to ask why a group of terrorists going on what could clearly be a 'suicide mission' or one in which the chances of their being captured was very high, should carry identity cards, diaries detailing their actions and plans and mobile phones that could be made to yield entire directories of their contacts. No one paused to ask what can only be very reasonable questions about the veracity and provenance of these records and documents, nor were any questions raised about the absence of stringent forensic procedures and criteria pertaining to the recovery of data from these documents. Court records show that the phone records relevant to the conversations between Afsan Guru and Shaukat or to certain conversations that Geelani is said to have had that were produced by the police as evidence (after much dithering) are actually of the days 'after' they were detained. Not a single newspaper or television news programme in those days, or in the early days of the trial in the special POTA court, could exhibit the necessary degree of reticence or patience required in the handling of a case as sensitive as this one. If the investigating authorities or the prosecution or the police said that phone records said something, no one actually asked to see the phone records, or to examine the dates, let alone the content of what transpired. The fact that the death sentences handed out by the POTA court were on the basis of false, forged, or inadmissible or absent evidence was not remarked upon by any news channel. A notable exception, however, which should not go unremarked is the reportage of the case in the *Hindu*, which, barring a stray story in the early days, was marked by balanced and fair reporting, especially the reports filed from the court by Anjali Mody which even subjected other media reports of the case to some degree of critical scrutiny.

Finally, when the defence asked for the phone records to be produced and examined by independent and knowledgeable witnesses, what came to light were discrepancies in translation and transcription. The fact that the translated sentence 'It becomes necessary sometimes' ('*yeh kabhi kabhi zaroori hota hai*'), apparently said in response to a question about 'what has happened in Delhi' , which Geelani said referred to a domestic dispute and which the prosecution claimed was about the attack on Parliament, and on which hinged the entire structure of the case against S.A.R. Geelani, was not found to be audible in the tape of the phone intercept when it was played repeatedly for the benefit of the two independent defence witnesses—a documentary film-maker, Sanjay Kak, and a trade union activist, Sampath Prakash, both native Kashmiri speakers.

It needs to be mentioned that while the media attention on S.A.R. Geelani, as the 'intellectual preceptor' of the terrorists, was particularly intense, it was less so with regard to Mohammad Afzal, the man whose 'confession' in detention, an instrument inadmissible in ordinary law as evidence (although permitted in POTA) escaped much by way of scrutiny. The media nailed Geelani on the basis of this confession.

But the media did more. Newspapers detailed property Geelani is said to have amassed as rewards for his labours, as well as the minutiae of his contacts with a student of 'west Asian' origin who must have been an 'Arab terrorist'. But no newspaper or television channel ever mentioned that Afzal, identified as a former JKLF militant and fruit merchant, was in fact a 'surrendered militant' and that he had for seven years been harassed by, and on occasion worked for, the 'Special Task Force', a shadowy counter-terrorism outfit that operates with impunity in Kashmir. The fact remains that in his statement to the court Afzal said unequivocally that he met one Tariq, a trusted lieutenant of the arch-terrorist 'Ghazi Baba', who is said to have motivated him to return to the ways of the 'jihad for azaadi' in an STF training camp in Dral in south Kashmir, and his wife's statement that Afzal was instructed to bring two of the men, later identified as the 'slain terrorists' in the Parliament attack, to Delhi and provide them with shelter while they were in 'transit' by none other than his STF handlers, went unremarked, with one significant exception, to which we will refer later.

It is interesting to speculate as to how some stories made their way into the media, and how some stories remained virtually 'out of bounds' even if they made their appearance sometimes in court documents. It is also interesting to consider whether this pattern of omission and insertion or fabrication pointed to the collaborative authorship (between the police, the intelligence community, and the media professionals and channels/newspapers) of these media materials. It is still not clear as to where the origins of these stories lay, and why they appeared so frequently, and why they were given so much space. One thing is certain, the efficient public relations and media exercises carried out (whether through fear or favour, or simply, access) by the 'Special Cell' of the Delhi Police in order to make the journalist community simply reproduce what was fed to them in routine press briefings seems to have worked well. The operation worked particularly well with television, with several channels broadcasting 'exclusive' interviews with what seemed to be an affable and loquacious prime accused Mohammad Afzal on 20 December.

If media professionals highlighted elements from Afzal's first 'confessions' in custody to substantiate their allegations against Geelani, they also obscured the fact that later, during the filming of the 'broadcast confession' of 18 December, Afzal explicitly denied the fact that Geelani had anything to do with the conspiracy. It was only when footage from this 'interview' was reproduced in a special Aaj Tak ('100 Days After the Attack') programme that it came to light that Afzal had actually explicitly exonerated Geelani. When S.A.R. Geelani's defence lawyers called upon the Aaj Tak reporter who took that interview, Shams Tahir Khan, as a witness, it became clear from his deposition that journalists had in fact been instructed, indeed threatened, by the much decorated Delhi Police 'Special Cell' officer and 'encounter' specialist ACP Rajbir Singh that airing the latter part of Afzal's 'confession' would invite dire consequences on any journalist present who chose to do so.

These developments did not deter Zee News, one of the most zealous extra-judicial prosecutors of the 13 December case, from producing an extensive 'docudrama' on 13 December which it aired on more than one occasion even as the trial progressed, including in the countdown to the final hearings in the special courts.

This television programme has an interesting and chequered history. Its premiere screening took place in the august presence of the then home minister and dead Pakistani identification expert, L.K. Advani. Advani praised the film as an excellent example of investigative journalism and in fact even compared it favourably to a subsequent Zee TV expose (on the attack on 'Akshardham' in Gujarat) saying that the former was much more meticulously and thoroughly produced. The film, which relayed and re-presented news, was itself news on the Zee News channel, and its making was featured as a lead story on the Zee News network. The film, with a stentorian commentary by the Bollywood 'B' movie star Raza Murad, featured a troupe of actors, enacting the 'conspiracy'. The script of this television programme, as stated in a text insert at the beginning of the programme, is based on the charge sheet of the Delhi Police in the case. What is particularly interesting are the many parallels, both in plot, mise en scène and narrative detail, between the charge sheet, the Zee TV film and the Shahrukh Khan–Manisha Koirala-starring film by Mani Ratnam—*Dil Se*.[3] We see the same procedures—procurement and manufacture of identity cards, the reconnaissance of the landmarks of Lutyens' Delhi on winter days, the listening to Hindi film music as terrorists work (on radio in the film, downloaded from computers in the TV programme), the hint of romance, the presence of a hard-line intellectual ideologue, the same locale—the alleyways of Old Delhi, around Karim's—and the same method of masquerade as security 'personnel'. There is an uncanny similarity between the plots, almost as if the 'terrorists', the police investigators, and the producers of the docu- drama had seen the film together and discussed its merits in a film analysis class before going their separate ways to give form and shape to their different agendas. Or, could it be, that the police genre of literature and film-making, which often shapes the trajectories of alleged 'terrorist' incidents, found in 'Dil Se-13 December' a suitable vehicle for the execution of one of their most complex plots till date? We will never know whether or not this is indeed the case, until some of the key actors in this 'film' decide to speak. But it is self-evident that a private news network gaining access to the highest echelons of the home ministry in order to be able to re- enact and shoot on the grounds of Parliament, with the extensive operational cooperation of police and security personnel, points to a close embrace between the security apparatus and a media agency. And just as the justices of the Supreme Court may well have their reasons to continue to point their 'needles of suspicions', we too will have reason to begin looking for, and pointing, our needles of suspicion in the directions that they lead us. We will need to continue to ask questions as to why the events of 13 December and their aftermath needed the extent of 'spin doctoring' that we have seen? We will have to continue to ask why the prosecution's case in the 13 December case had to be argued, not only in the court, but also on air, in living rooms, between commercial breaks. There are no doubts left any more about the fact that the arguments were flimsy and untenable, that they were bad in law, and that they could not be sustained under cross-examination. This is perhaps why they had to be buttressed with so much media hype, in the hope that TRP ratings would work where forensic evidence may fail.

The dense tangle of film and reality in the 13 December case does not begin and end with *Dil Se*; there are two other films that bear looking at as well (and there may well be more to come), one being 26 *December*, and the other *Khakee*. The two films have two distinct approaches, and are noteworthy not because I think they influenced what I think is the 'scripting' of 13 December, but because they are mirrors through which 13 December can be read. *16 December* (titled so because it happens to be the date on which India won the 1971 war against Pakistan, and so is the date when in the film, a Pakistani soldier turned terrorist wants to unleash a nuclear attack on Delhi as an act of vengeance). As can be expected, the film features a dedicated bunch of Indian intelligence operatives (including the model turned actor Milind Soman who portrays a surveillance expert, with a special fondness for mobile phones) who foil the plot and save Delhi, India and the world from nuclear Armageddon. What is interesting about *16 December* is the way in which it 'naturalizes' surveillance technologies (CCTV cameras, satellite-based video surveillance, human surveillance through street based 'agents' who happen to be an army of blind beggars with sharp ears, and mobile phone interception), to produce a seamless evidentiary narrative. Mobile phones are high technology, the capacity to tap mobile phones is still higher technology and truth flows out of higher technology. What is even more interesting is a remarkable sequence in the film when the entire intelligence apparatus connives to create a 'simulation', an image of a location in far away Afghanistan on the floor of a 'film studio' so as to hoodwink a drugged and captured 'terrorist' into talking. This tacit admission of the practice by intelligence agencies of 'staging' incidents relating to 'terrorism' as a measure necessary in order to combat terrorists is almost like a sudden revelation of the 'repressed' narrative of how intelligence agencies actually create the realities that we think they are combatting. One might recall also the climactic revelation in the Sanjay Dutt–Jackie Shroff–Hrithik Roshan starrer *Mission Kashmir* (with its own oblique references to the enigmatic figure of 'Ghazi Baba') of how a 'video simulation' of 'terrorists in Indian Army uniforms' (found during the course of a raid by Indian military personnel dressed as 'terrorists' on a 'terrorist hideout') blowing up a Muslim holy shrine in Srinagar in Kashmir is yet another instance of the way in which the 'production of images' is seen as key to the 'production of terror'. The deliberate confusion in the appearance of combatants in and out of uniform, of masked men who appear in the middle of the night and wreak devastating violence, in the pursuit of an 'image', who could be 'militants' or 'soldiers' or 'both', is a reflection of the shadowy realities that have overtaken Jammu and Kashmir. Here, as we observed earlier, we know who is who, even though the 'terrorist' both 'stands out' and 'blends in' at the same time. It is as if the apparatus of illusion that is the cinema had taught many lessons to the secondary art of the moving image of statecraft, at least in its 'terror/counter-terror' avatar.

Seen in the light of the extraordinary 'entente

cordiale' between security and intelligence agencies and the image-producing agencies of the media in India, the film *16 December* becomes an interesting if unwitting source for the making of an oblique comment on the reality of '13 December'.

In a similar, though perhaps more conscious vein, the film *Khakee* (starring Amitabh Bachchan, Akshay Kumar, Ajay Devgan, Atul Kulkarni and Aishwarya Rai) actually invoked the figure of a 'rogue security agent' acting to protect what he thinks are the interests of the nation state, by seeking to eliminate what we are at first led to believe is a 'suspected terrorist mastermind'—a Dr Ansari, whose appearance, demeanour and dignified silence, particularly in the first half of the film, cannot but fail to bring to mind what we know of S.A.R. Geelani. Ansari is later revealed to be someone who knows 'vital information' about the engineering of a communal riot by corrupt politicians (shades of 'Gujarat 2002' here) and his silence is an effort to protect what he knows so that he can reveal it at the most appropriate moment. Although the film follows the formula of good cops versus 'rogue' cops (not exactly 'bad' cops, but cops used by shadowy forces within the state beyond their control), it again points out the macabrely pantomimic character of 'war against terror'.

What do *Dil Se, Mission Kashmir, 16 December* on the one hand, and the Zee TV docu-dramas add up to? They add up to the metaphorical identikit photograph of the terrorist in our heads whom we can recognize when we look at almost anyone's face, regardless of whether they 'stand out' or 'blend in'. This is the terrorist writ large as 'everyman', so much so that Zee

TV can use the footage from the 're-enacted' scenes of the '13 December' film even in another programme, an 'Inside Story' special broadcast on 'the Al Qaeda Terror Manual' on the evening of 24 July 2005, in the wake of the London bombings of 7 July and barely days before the final Supreme Court verdict on the 13 December case on 4 August. This programme, which can be seen as a sort of do-it-yourself 'how to become a terrorist even if you never thought of becoming one', with details of how to obtain and mix chemicals to make bombs, the details of poisoning drinking water systems, how to form cells and conduct communications using codes, etc. (in a classic example of the 'system' actually egging people on to become the 'terrorists' that it can then frighten the rest of us with) again used the same scenes of the actors playing Geelani, Shaukat, Afzal and the five dead men, though this time it did not name them. But anyone who had seen the earlier '13 December' film would immediately recognize once again the fictionalized S.A.R. Geelani hectoring his cell comrades in the sequence on 'organization of terrorist cells'. Just as anyone who had seen the '13 December' film would have seen the gratuitous and grainy images of 'terrorists' training under pine trees and of a televised 'encounter' with the late and larger-than-life 'Ghazi Baba' caressing a strangely shaped 'Scorpion' pistol in what was marked 'file footage'. Like a nightmare or a bad B movie that condemns its audience to constant re-runs, the 'images' of the Zee News–Delhi Police Special Cell co-production collaborative genre of 'terrorism' refuses to give up its ghost. It returns to haunt our television screens, back-to-back with 'Crime Reporter' and a host of other sensational programmes that can only be described as a sad case of police-porn-snuff movies on late night but prime time television.

It returned to our screens momentarily when Geelani was shot by an unidentified gunman in Delhi on 9 February 2005. When earnest reporters and television news anchors across channels, for several days following the incident, instead of asking why the police were constantly shadowing Geelani, his brother, his friends, asked why his advocate had thought it wise to save his life by taking him immediately to hospital, and not waiting for him to succumb to his injuries as she went through the process of filing, first and foremost, a 'proper FIR (first information report) as per procedure, with the Delhi Police'.

The night of 4 August 2005 was occasion for broadcasts on the final Supreme Court judgement on the 13 December case. These broadcasts, produced once again the latest (and perhaps last) episode in this continuing 'B' series TV show. Zee News produced yet another 'special' dovetailed into its prime time news show at 9 p.m. This time it was titled '13 December: Ek Saazish'. The news report showed a high-ranking Delhi Police Special Cell officer Ashok Chand (in a split screen with the first-ever viewing of surveillance camera footage from the Parliament on 13 December) offering an explanation of the splendid conduct of the Delhi Police in the case; after all, Afzal had been convicted as a result of the investigation. The others could not be convicted, because, as the reporter explained to the anchor in the studio, the terrorists had used high technology—mobile phones and laptops. And what this implied was that we need better and stricter laws to deal with such high-tech terrorists, so that no one would be able to get away. There is some irony in the fact that the very 'high techonology' which had helped the police write their charge sheets in the first instance, was now being blamed for their inability to fix the blame on say, a Geelani, on whom, the report continued to assert, the 'needle of suspicion' stayed firm and unwavering, though somewhat unsubstantially. So, mobile phones help catch 'terrorists', mobile phones are also so high-tech that they can be used by those 'terrorists' and their advocates to subvert the commendable work done by hard-working police officers. Therefore bring back laws, or make new laws that can make the task of using evidence from mobile phones and other high-tech devices 'easier' for the prosecution. In other words, bring back or make laws that enable phone tapping and surveillance on a generalized scale, that facilitate the faulty transcription and translation of tapped conversations, that enable the manipulation or obfuscation of phone records, and that do not have to produce the taped evidence in court in order to obtain a necessary conviction, and that enable the airing and unofficial pre-censoring of 'interviews' of the accused in detention in the media while a trial is in process, so that television network news executives can have an easier night's sleep and count their takings.

In a remarkable admission, while playing once again the 'dramatization' of Afzal's indoctrination (once again from the '13 December' film) the Zee News broadcast commentator said in passing what was to the effect—'Afzal was a surrendered militant, he had worked off and on for the STF for seven years, and he had met Tariq in an STF camp in Dral.' Why was this piece of information which had been available in the court

records, like everything else in this case, since 21
September 2002, not made public knowledge either in
the previous Zee News programmes, or in any
programmes thereafter to inform the public? Any
reasonable person would surmise that a person who
has been in regular contact with intelligence operatives
of the Indian state, who has been harassed by them,
who has had money extorted by them (as per his wife's
statement made to a newspaper), must also be asked
what relationships these operatives had to the sequence
of events leading up to 13 December. If one needle of
suspicion points at 'militants' and their handlers, whether
local or across the border, then, clearly, another 'needle
of suspicion' (which looks stronger, at least,
circumstantially) also points to the activities and
personnel of the shadowy agency or cluster of agencies
called the 'Special Task Force'. Until these details are
investigated, we cannot come to any certain conclusion
about who Afzal is, what role he played, and why he
has to die.

Why also were the surveillance camera footage of
the vehicle seen proceeding towards the Parliament
building about as far as the 'Red Cross Road–Sansad
Marg' roundabout not ever made public before? Was it
because the channel had to 'wait' until the case was
satisfactorily 'closed'? Surely any journalist or television
producer would know that the vicinity of the Parliament
and other sensitive government buildings have been
photographed on CCTV cameras for a long time.
Surely an analysis of the movement of the car, as seen
in this footage, would be able to tell us something
about how the car approached, which barriers it crossed
and how.

In the end, more questions than ever remain unanswered, about the conduct of the intelligence and security agencies, about the conduct of the media and about our gullibility as citizens to be quick to condemn, first S.A.R. Geelani, and now Mohammad Afzal. Questions remain about the fact that news channels and papers can see it fit never to apologize either to S.A.R. Geelani or Afsan Guru for the deliberate distortions of the truth that these organs of the media were party to, throughout the course of the trials. Not once did Zee News or any other news channel offer an apology to any of the accused, or to the public, for the emotional stress that their broadcasts may have caused, even as they continued to highlight the 'plight' of the families of the 'martyred' security and other personnel who fell in the line of duty on 13 December 2001. Even in the telecast of 4 August 2005, Zee News considered it necessary to provoke the family members of one of the 'martyred' security personnel into an outburst demanding death for all the accused. It did not however deem it necessary to reflect on the fact that the families of S.A.R. Geelani, Afsan Guru, Shaukat Husain or Mohammad Afzal too had had to suffer, knowing that their loved ones were in prison, that they were brutally tortured, and had to go through the trauma of hearing that they had been awarded death sentences. Not once did any news channel ever apologize for creating and sustaining the climate of suspicion against people who were ultimately acquitted; they did not see it necessary to issue a single note of regret to their viewers for having failed to live up to their stated claims of providing free, fair, fearless and objective reportage. The events of 13 December and their aftermath, along with the sad episode of the Kargil War, are probably the nadir as far as a deviation from media ethics and professional standards are concerned for a vast swathe of the 'free and independent media' in India.

In the end, the truth, or the truths (there may be many and conflicting truths) may yet turn out to be more complex and disturbing than either Zee News or the Supreme Court of India can permit themselves to imagine or ask. Zee News, or 'any other alphabet News' is not asking, at least not yet, any of those slightly difficult questions. And if the Supreme Court of India is to have its way, Afzal is going to hang some day. Some of the answers will die with him. S.A.R. Geelani remains alive, and we hope he lives long, but as he has himself said—let us not celebrate the acquittal of the innocent, let us instead pause to reflect on where we are and how we got here. Geelani has reminded us that his fate is not special, that there are many in his generation, in Kashmir and elsewhere, who have had to go through things that are as bad, or worse. And few have had his good fortune, to come out of it alive and sane. For their sake, and so that Geelani's quiet and dignified fight for justice for those still in prison, or are facing the gallows, or have 'disappeared', or have turned up with bullets in their heads, we must all continue to ask some very hard questions, for a very long time. It is possible that the mainstream media will be a weapon in the process of silencing such questions. It is also possible that professionals in the mainstream media will become more aware and sensitive to the ethical and professional demands associated with their practice, and will occasionally refuse to toe the lines dictated in smoke-filled backrooms where channel executives, editors, senior correspondents and intelligence agents gather for quiet chats. We hope for the latter, the demands of justice, and freedom in South Asia, will depend on such acts of refusal to 'spin' stories out of blood and smoke.

This essay has been adapted from a posting made on the Sarai Reader List on 5 August 2005.

[3]

THE MEDIA CONSTRUCTS A KASHMIRI TERRORIST

Syed Bismillah Geelani

Between 16 December and 23 December 2001, the investigating agencies and the media constructed an image of my brother as an archetypal Kashmiri terrorist. This is the image that I believe condemned him to death even before the sessions court trial began. That is the image that has come to stay, even though the Delhi High Court and the Supreme Court have acquitted him.

The *Hindustan Times* announced on 16 December 2001: 'Case Cracked: Jaish behind attack'. The story was written by Arun Joshi and Neeta Sharma from Jammu and New Delhi.

I quote verbatim the first three paragraphs of the report:

> The Delhi police have claimed that Special Cell investigators probing Thursday's attack on the Parliament House Complex have cracked the case.
>
> In Delhi, the Special Cell detectives detained a lecturer in Arabic, who teaches in Zakir Hussain

(evening) College of Delhi University, after it was established that he had received a call made by the militants on his mobile phone (cash card no. 0811641893). The lecturer, Abdul Ahmed Jelani, allegedly also spoke to some people in Pakistan. The agencies believe that he spoke to militants belonging to the Jaish-e-Mohammed. They also claim that Jelani is related to a Kashmiri separatist leader based in London.

Under interrogation, Jelani named two people in Kashmir—Ashfaq and Shaukat—as the two key planners of the operation. Police sources say that the explosives used in the operation were transported to Delhi in trucks owned by them.[1]

In this six-column bottom-spread there is a small box entitled 'The Usual Suspect', with a photo of Maulana Masood Azhar and a line on my brother: 'A Delhi lecturer, who spoke to militants, also called up Jaish militants in Pakistan.' In another news item (in a long single column) entitled 'Past 24 Hours', the first item is again on Geelani:

A Zakir Hussain (evening) College lecturer, Abdul Ahmed Jelani, detained after a call from the militants' mobile phone is traced to his mobile. Terrorists spoke to him before the attack and the lecturer made a phone call to Pakistan after the strike.[2]

It is astonishing that the journalist states that 'it was established'[3] that Geelani received a call from militants. This is a very grave allegation. In addition it is totally false on several counts, making it a highly defamatory statement.

1. Geelani was the only one who did not use a cash card. He had a regular phone connection

and his bills were paid through his bank account in the State Bank of India. It was because he had a regular connection that the police were able to trace his name and address. He was the only one accused who did not use cash cards, and the police were therefore able to get all his call records from the Airtel company. The charge-sheet filed on 12 May 2002 states: 'Out of all the prominent numbers only one mobile number 9810081228 was found to be a regular mobile card of Airtel which stood in the name of Sayed Abdul Rahman Geelani, resident of House No. 535, Mukherjee Nagar, Delhi. The subscriber was also found to have made the payments to the mobile company through his SBI card which also had the same address as revealed from the report received from the SBI.'

2. The call records from October to December 2001 list more than 500 calls; not a single call was made to or received from Pakistan, Dubai or anywhere abroad.

3. The charge-sheet filed five months later did not even allege that my brother received any calls from Pakistan or that he was ever in touch with the militants who attacked Parliament.

4. Even the so-called disclosure statement fabricated by the police (which claimed that Geelani had confessed to various crimes) did not state that he was ever in touch with anyone in Pakistan or with the dead militants.

5. The prosecution produced eighty witnesses but not a single witness even alleged that my brother (or the other three accused) was a member of

any militant organization. The sessions judge could not convict any of the four accused of belonging to any terrorist organization.

6. The court records show that the SIM Card number 8991100108011641893 was recovered from the hand-set of one of the militants called Raja on the day of the attack. Therefore the police knew that this had nothing to do with Geelani; yet they deliberately fed journalists with false information.

On 17 December 2001 there was a six-column headline in the *Times of India:* 'DU lecturer was terror plan hub'. Let me quote the relevant paragraphs. The story begins thus:

> The attack on Parliament on 13 December was a joint operation of the Jaish-e-Mohammad (JeM) and Lashkar-e-Taiba (LeT) terrorist groups, in which a Delhi University lecturer, Syed A.R. Gilani, was one of the key facilitators in Delhi, Police Commissioner Ajai Raj Sharma said on Sunday.[4]

In a single-column article, entitled 'The People', there is another paragraph in the same newspaper:

> Sayed Abdul Rahman Gilani. He is a lecturer in Arabic at Zakir Hussain College in Delhi University. Gilani is a resident of Mukherjee Nagar and was the key person in the plan. He met with the others, stayed in touch with the mastermind. He has been arrested.[5]

Geelani is now being described as the 'key' person who is in touch with the 'mastermind'!

The same day, on 17 December 2001, the *Hindu*

carried a story entitled 'Varsity don guided "fidayeen"', and above the headline is a sub-headline: 'Delhi/well-qualified logistic support.' This story is by Devesh K. Pandey. He does not bother to quote the source of his information and we can only presume it is the police, especially since there is a photo of the police commissioner of Delhi addressing a press conference. It is not at all clear whether all the 'facts' were given at the conference. But here is the story:

> Three of the four persons who supplied logistic support and provided a safe haven to the five 'fidayeen' to mount a daring attack on Parliament here on December 13, studied at the prestigious Delhi University; one even turned out to be a highly-qualified lecturer.
>
> Sayed Abdul Rehman Geelani, an Arabic lecturer at the Zakir Hussain (evening) College was arrested by the special cell of the Delhi Police for his role in the conspiracy hatched by Pakistan-based terrorist outfits Jaish-e-Mohammad and Lashkar-e-Taiba.
>
> Born in Baramullah in Kashmir, Geelani came to Delhi after completing his graduation from Lucknow. He did his Master's and M.Phil in Arabic from Delhi University. He had his primary education and studied the Quran and Arabic from a 'madrasa' at Muzzafarnagar, Uttar Pradesh. Later he joined the Zakir Hussain College here in 1997.
>
> During interrogation, Geelani disclosed that he was in the know of the conspiracy since the day the 'fidayeen' attack was planned. Sources said intelligence agencies had been tapping Geelani's phone for some time as he had contacts in Pakistan. Geelani revealed that he became part of the conspiracy due to his ideological leanings. He was closely related to the

main Jaish-e-Mohammad co-ordinator in Delhi, Mohammad Afzal, and his cousin, Shaukat Hussain Guru, who have also been arrested. He also knew the terrorist who came to the capital to execute the plan.

The cousin-conspirators, Afzal and Hussain Guru, hail from Sopore in Baramullah, and had their higher education from Delhi University.[6]

We can see how the police are now slowly constructing Geelani's image. In this item he has become a 'highly-qualified' lecturer who has a background in a madrasa and studied the Quran. A little later the journalist states that Geelani has 'ideological leanings'. Here are the bricks with which the image of a Kashmiri terrorist are constructed: 'madrasa', 'Quran', 'teaches Arabic', and, finally, 'ideological leanings'.

The police continue planting totally false stories and the journalists reproduce them, without attempting to cross-check. Consider the following points:

1. There is no evidence that Geelani knew the five militants who attacked Parliament. Even the prosecution did not allege that he either called or received a call from the deceased attackers.
2. Geelani is not remotely related to the co-accused.

The daily *Rashtriya Sahara* in its Hindi edition on 18 December 2001 carried a report titled *'Rajdhani Mein Ek Nahin Kai Thikane The Geelani Ke'* (Geelani had not one but many places to reside in in the capital):

Sansad Bhawan par hue aatankwadi hamle ki koshish ke shadyantrakariyon mein se ek Dilli Vishwavidyalaya ke shikshak Syed Abdul Rahman Geelani ke Dilli mein ek nahin, kai thikane the. Pitampura Mukerjee Nagar sthit Dilli

Vishwavidyalaya transit hostel aur isi ilaake mein ek aur makaan se weh apni gatiwidhiyan sanchaalit karta tha. Waise Zakir Hussain College ke record mein uske awaas ke roop mein Pitampura ka ullekh hai. Geelani aam taur par apne sehkarmiyon se kata-kata rehta tha aur uska jyadatar wakt Dilli Vishwavidyalaya parisar mein hi gujarta tha.

[One of the conspirators in the attempt to attack Parliament House is Delhi University teacher, Syed Abdul Rahman Geelani, who has many places of residence in Delhi. Pitampura, Mukherjee Nagar, Transit Hostel of Delhi University, and another house in that vicinity are the places he carried out his activities from. According to Zakir Hussain College records, he lives in Pitampura. He stayed aloof from his colleagues and spent most of his time in the University.]

Here the journalist does not even state the source of information, except towards the end when the report quotes a teacher and student. The allegation here seems to be that Geelani spent more time on the campus than in the college. I wish the journalist had checked his facts because he would have found that Geelani was teaching MA classes in the campus and also working in the University library since he was in the midst of finishing his thesis—the thesis which the police took away without any record on the day they arrested him.

As for Geelani having more than one place to live, I wish that had been true—it would have saved us all a lot of time looking for a rented place after he was arrested. Even after his acquittal at least thirty-five landlords refused their houses to us on rent. I can only say that the journalist was just trying to mystify Geelani's image and feed the public sensational tidbits.

The *Hindustan Times* of 17 December 2001 carried a four-column story: 'Don lectured on terror in free time'. The story is by Sutirtho Patranobis and has a photo of Geelani with the caption 'The Ideologue', and a picture of Afzal with the caption 'The Mastermind'.

This is a story based on an interview with the principal of Geelani's college, Prof. Riaz Umar. The principal testified that Geelani was a conscientious teacher and that he took his classes regularly. The journalist quotes Prof. Umar:

> He mixed around in the college as any other professor and spent time in the staff room as well. Students liked him and I have also not heard any colleague complain about his behaviour. But he became reserved after a point. There was nothing extraordinary in his character either.[8]

The entire story is a positive image of a good teacher but the headline is taken from the last paragraph and I quote that in its entirety:

> Investigations have revealed that by evening he was at the college, teaching Arabic literature. In his free time, behind closed doors, either at his house or at Shaukat Hussain's, another suspect to be arrested, he took and gave lessons on terrorism. Gilani, Shaukat and Mohammad Afzal, the third person to be arrested, were long-time friends sharing similar views.[9]

The journalist quotes police sources on matters which go against his own investigation. The police were desperately trying to construct an image of the 'ideologue',[10] and the journalists had suspended all their usual disbelief and scepticism and were swallowing the police stories whole.

The same day, the *Hindustan Times* carried a story by Rajnish Sharma entitled 'Hunt for Teacher's Pet in Jubilee Hall':

> Investigations into the international connections of S.A.R. Geelani have led the intelligence agencies to Delhi University's Jubilee Hall hostel in the north campus.
>
> A team of senior intelligence and Delhi police officials today visited Jubilee Hall and some of the STD phone booths around the hostel.
>
> Intelligence sources said Geelani was 'extremely friendly' with a Jordanian student who had been staying at Jubilee Hall,
>
> The agencies are now trying to trace the Jordanian who, after completing his MSc in Physics from Aligarh University, had enrolled for a PhD at Delhi University a few years ago. 'Geelani used to visit the Jordanian student's room No. 164 regularly where the two used to have long discussions, lasting several hours. Investigations revealed that some of the students at the hostel had become suspicious. They thought that perhaps Geelani and the Jordanian student were hatching some conspiracy,' an investigating official said.[11]

The investigation agencies were now clearly desperate to construct the image of Geelani as a big-time terrorist, and for this they were now trying to find some international links. They had planted stories that he had links in Pakistan but they knew it would not be long before the falsehood was exposed. They therefore tried to invent other international connections, and this time they tried to mystify his friendship with a Jordanian student. In the middle of the *Hindustan Times* story there is a box entitled 'Professor's Proceeds'. This is the first time the 'lecturer' becomes a 'professor'. I reproduce the box:

- Gilani recently purchased a house for Rs 22 lakh in west Delhi.
- Delhi police are investigating how he came upon such a windfall.
- The terrorists who planned the operation were flushed (*sic*) with funds.
- Before carrying out the attack on Parliament, the terrorists had sent back to Srinagar Rs 10 lakh of unspent money and a laptop.[12]

As against all these statements, the actual facts are:

1. Geelani does not have property in Delhi. In fact, many months later, after he was acquitted, journalists in Goa even alleged that he had gone to Goa to look at his 'ancestral property' at Divar Island.
2. The court records show that no money was recovered from him except for Rs 700, which were seized from his wallet at the time of his arrest.

On 18 December 2001, *Rashtriya Sahara* in its Hindi edition carried a story by Sujit Thakur titled *'Aligarh Se England Tak Chhatron Mein Aatankwad Ke Beej Bo Raha Tha Geelani'* (Geelani was sowing the seeds of terrorism among students from Aligarh in England). The sub-title beneath this headline is: *'Jaish-e-Mohammad ne sonpa tha Bharat mein bauddhik aatankwad ki jadein jamane ka jimma'* (Jaish-e-Mohammad had entrusted him with the responsibility of spreading intellectual terrorism in India). The story by Sujit Thakur reads:

Sansad Bhawan parisar par hue aatankwadi hamle ki koshish ki saazish mein shamil Zakir Hussain College ke shikshak Abdul Rahman Geelani Bharat mein bauddhik aatankwad ki jadein jamana chahta tha. Sootron ke anusaar Bharat mein aatankwad ko bauddhik samarthan haasil karwane ke liye Jaish-e-Mohammad ke pas ek vistrut yojana hai, jisko amlijama pehnane ka jimma Geelani ko diya gaya tha. Apne adhyayan adhyapan ke baad Geelani apna wakt collejon, vishwavidyalayon tatha anya shaikshanik sansthanon ke chhatron–shikshakon ke dimaag mein aatankwaad ka beej bone mein lagata tha. Usne Aligarh Muslim Vishwavidyalaya, England sthit London School of Economics tatha kai anya Bharatiya vishwavidyalayon tatha collejon ke chhatron, shikshakon se sampark sadhne ka prayas kiya tha.

Sootron ke anusaar Geelani ne police adhikariyon ke saamne jo bayaan diye hain tatha Geelani ke baare mein jaanch agenciyon ko jo jaankari mili hai us se saaf hota hai ki weh Bharat mein bauddhik aatankwaad ko jamane ke liye Jaish-e-Mohammad ka bada sootradhar tha. Jaish ka aatankwadi masah jo Pakistan mein rehta tha 1997 mein Aligarh Muslim Vishwavidyalaya gaya tha aur kuchh shikshakon se mila tha. In mulakaton ke baad Geelani bhi Aligarh Muslim Vishwavidyalaya ke shikshakon se mila tha.

Geelani ki wakpatuta, karyapaddhati, thos yojana aur samarpan ka hi nateeja tha ki warsh 2000 ke madhya mein Jaish-e-Mohammad ne Bharat mein bauddhik aatankwad phelane ki jimmedari Geelani ko sonp di. Sootron ke anusaar Geelani ne kukhyat aatankwadi Ahmad Umar Saeed Sheikh se bhi baatcheet ki thi aur usne London School of Economics ke aise shikshakon, chaatron ki jankari mangi thi, jinhen baatcheet ke jariye bauddhik aatankwad ka samarthak banaya ja sake. Gaur talab hai ki Ahmad Umar Saeed Sheikh wahi aatankwadi hai jo wimaan sankhya IC–814 apaharan kaand mein Azhar Masood ke saath chhoota tha. Umar Saeed London School of Economics ka chaatra tha aur yahin se woh sakriya aatankwad ki raah par chal pada tha.

(Zakir Hussain College lecturer, Abdul Rahman Geelani, involved in the conspiracy to attack Parliament, wanted to lay the foundation of intellectual terrorism in India. According to sources, Jaish-e-Mohammad had a project to win support for intellectual terrorism, Geelani was given the responsibility to implement this project. After research and teaching, Geelani spent his time in colleges, universities and other educational institutions, sowing seeds of intellectual terrorism among students and teachers. He tried to contact teachers and students of Aligarh Muslim University, London School of Economics and other Indian universities and colleges.

According to sources and information collected by investigation agencies, Geelani has made a statement to the police that he was an agent of Jaish-e-Mohammad for a long time. The leader of Jaish-e-Mohammad visited AMU in 1997 and contacted some students. After this meeting, Geelani went to AMU and met other students.

It was because of Geelani's articulation, style of working and sound planning that in 2000 Jaish-e-Mohammad gave him the responsibility of spreading intellectual terrorism. According to sources, Geelani met terrorist Ahmad Umar Sayed Sheikh and asked him for contacts amongst students of the London

School of Economics who could help him spread
intellectual terrorism. The surprising thing is that
Ahmad Umar Sayed Sheikh is the same terrorist who
was with Azhar Masood during the hijacking of IC-
814. Umar Sayed was a student of the London
School of Economics and it was from there that he
took to the path of terrorism.][13]

I saw this report in *Rashtriya Sahara* on my way back
from the Special Cell. The police had released my
brother's family, including his two children, and we
were returning from the Lodi Road Police Station. We
saw the newspaper on a newsstand in Khan Market. I
was furious when I read the string of lies and phoned
the *Sahara* office and demanded to speak to the editor.

I was told that I was speaking to the editor himself.
So, making a reference to the Sahara motto 'Duty,
Patriotism and Altruism', I asked him which of these
three was involved in this kind of journalism. He asked
me who I was. I introduced myself and demanded an
explanation. I said, 'You haven't bothered to quote any
source but as an interested party I have a right to know
where you got your information from.' There was
silence. Then I gave him a short lecture on journalistic
ethics (which I will not bore you with) and also
threatened to sue him. He then said that the editor was
not there and that he would tell him about my complaint
when he returned. He tried to sound sympathetic by
saying that it was really serious and he would take it up
with the editor and let me know. Then he asked for my
phone number, but by then I was so furious that I just
slammed the receiver down.

Here was a newspaper which was unashamedly
indulging in defamation. Now the media construction

of the mastermind was complete. Geelani had been transformed into an 'intellectual terrorist' with influence from Aligarh to London, and an ideologue of the Jaish-e-Mohammad in India. I wonder why other newspapers did not carry this story as well. Surely *Rashtriya Sahara* did not have exclusive sources on Geelani. Or did the other journalists find these revelations too far-fetched?

On 20 December 2001 the *Times of India* carried a single-column story entitled 'Geelani Was in Bhuj with SIMI Group'.[14] The story was datelined Ahmedabad and quoted the Kutch District Police as its source. This story was meant to link Geelani to the banned Students' Islamic Organization of India (SIMI), and create an image that would shock. There is no way Geelani or any of us could have countered this kind of falsehood. We just read these reports each day with growing concern about Geelani's future.

The next day the newspapers and the electronic media were once again full of stories about the three accused. The journalists had been invited to the Lodi Road Police Station (the office of the Special Cell) for a media conference. Mohammad Afzal was forced to address it and incriminate himself before the entire country. The *Hindustan Times* had a seven-column headline, screaming 'Pak Uses Fanatics to Spread Terror in India'.[15] The story was by Neeta Sharma.

On top of the story was a banner with a one-column bold heading in red, titled 'Confession Time', and then a photo of the three accused along with a quote from their 'confession'. Along with Geelani's photo was this quote: 'I never felt that I belonged to a minority community. I do not know why I did it.'[16]

Neeta Sharma begins her story thus:

The Delhi Police on Thursday allowed four people held in connection with the attack on Parliament to go public with their version of how it was planned and how terrorists operate.

The Jaish-e-Mohammad's chief co-ordinator in India, Mohammad Afzal, was unrepentant, saying that had he not been caught he would have worked to inflict another strike against India.

His accomplices—Shaukat Hussain, Afsan and Syed Abdul Rahman Geelani—were not taking the cue. They claimed that Afzal had drawn them into the dragnet.

If the US and Pakistan want more evidence of the involvement of Pakistan-based groups in terrorism in India, Afzal's disclosures should give them leads.

Among the many disclosures made by the Jaish militant was the claim that the ISI has been funding terrorists from across the border and has set up many bases in the POK to train militants.[17]

Neeta Sharma begins with a lie. Geelani was not allowed to address the press conference—he was not even brought into the room. In addition to this front-page story on 21 December 2001, the *Hindustan Times* carried a story by Swati Chaturvedi, entitled 'Terror Suspect Frequent Visitor to Pak Mission'. This time the journalist quotes 'authoritative sources' who have told her that Geelani visited the Pakistan High Commission. The High Commission itself is quoted as saying: 'As far as we are concerned we do not know him and Pakistan has nothing to do with him.' The report goes on to state (without so much as an 'alleges'):

During interrogation, Gilani has admitted that he had made frequent calls to Pakistan and was in touch with militants belonging to the Jaish-e-Mohammad. He also said he was in touch with relatives in London who were actively involved in funding militancy in Jammu and Kashmir.

Gilani said that he had been provided with funds by some members of the Jaish and told to buy two flats that could be used in militant operations.[18]

The media conference by the Special Cell was designed to help the government in power to prove its case about Pakistan's involvement in the Parliament attack. They needed to do it quickly and could not wait for the trial. In any case when the trial did start it did not go into the actual attack itself.

But that media conference was to serve one other purpose. That was to get Afzal to implicate Geelani. *Aaj Tak* chief reporter Shams Tahir Khan was also present at the media conference. He asked a pointed question of Afzal: '*Aap ka jo sathi hai Geelani uske paas Osama bin Laden ka kucch literature bhi milaa hai. To kya woh Laden ko maanta hai?*'

On what basis did Shams Tahir Khan ask this question? There was nothing to show that any such material had been found on Geelani's person, in his home or at his workplace. It is obvious that the police had told the correspondent to ask this question. Incidentally, the only 'incriminating' document found on Geelani during his personal search was his handwritten copy of his thesis written in Arabic comparing the biographies of the Prophet written in India and in Egypt.

On that occasion Mohammad Afzal made another statement which the *Hindustan Times* did not carry. Afzal told the media that Geelani was innocent (the

Times of India quoted Afzal saying this). Later both Shams Tahir Khan and Manoj Pandey of the *Times of India* testified in court to say that Afzal had exonerated Geelani. Shams Tahir Khan even told the court that ACP Rajbir Singh had shouted at Afzal for making that statement on Geelani and then requested the media not to broadcast that part of his statement. Can there be any clearer evidence of the intention to frame Geelani?

The Delhi High Court observed that the practice of brazenly parading the accused before the public was a misuse of police custody. The Supreme Court also observed that the officer of the Special Cell denied in court that he knew anything about the media conference. In fact, the police had told lies on oath.

On 23 December the *Sunday Times* carried a single-column picture of my brother under the heading 'Person of the Week' with a short paragraph:

> A cellphone call proved his undoing. Delhi University's Syed A.R. Gilani was the first to be arrested in the December 13 case—a shocking reminder that roots of terrorism go far and deep. 'I never felt I belonged to a minority community,' the lecturer was quoted as saying. 'I do not know why I did it.'[19]

By this time Geelani had been sent to judicial custody. He was locked up in the 'high-risk' cell of Tihar Jail in solitary confinement. He was not aware of the media campaign against him. He could do nothing to defend himself. And yet he had withstood the torture and the humiliations and refused to make a false confession, because he wanted to make sure that his university's honour and reputation were not tarnished.

The court records of 21 May 2005 clearly show

that he refused to make any false confession. The records testify to the fact that the police and the media had been deliberately vilifying him on the basis of the so-called confessions he is supposed to have made while in police custody.

The media trial had already condemned Geelani, so it did not come as a surprise that on 18 December 2002 the designated court condemned my brother to death. The scene outside Patiala House Court in Delhi could have been a scene from a Bollywood film. In the courtroom three Kashmiris were being sentenced to death, and lawyers were shouting, 'Death to the lawyers who defend terrorists'. Outside the court, Shiv Sena hooligans were bursting crackers to celebrate.

The 296-page judgement by the trial court was summarized into a poem of twenty-nine lines taken from the judgement in a poster entitled 'Logic of an Anti-Terrorist Court'. The poster was part of an exhibition entitled 'Lies of Our Times', telling the story of Geelani's trial by the All India Defence Committee for S.A.R. Geelani. I am reproducing the poem here:

Terrorism is a scourge of all humanity
Terrorism is sponsored by rogue states
Rogue states are mostly ruled by religious fanatics
Rogue states are despotic and fundamentalist

Terrorists use religious fanatics and modern technology
Fanatics get financial and strategic support from Pakistan
Pakistan is waging war against India
The attack on Parliament was an act of waging war on India
The five men who attacked Parliament were Pakistanis
They were Pakistanis because they looked like Pakistanis
Pakistan is indulging in cross-border terrorism

This cross-border terrorism is in Kashmir
Three accused are Kashmiris from Baramulla
Therefore the three of them are terrorists

Terrorists are enemies of the country
Enemies cannot be given the protection of our Constitution
Constitutional protection need not be given to Geelani
Geelani is a Kashmiri Muslim and a brilliant scholar
Educated people are hired by terrorists
Therefore Geelani must have been hired by terrorists
Terrorists are enemies of the state
Enemies need not be given a fair trial

It is unpatriotic to disbelieve the police or their witnesses
Even if the police are telling lies they do so in the national
    interest
In the national interest the media also suppressed the truth
It is even more anti-national to believe the defence witnesses
Even if defence witnesses are known for their loyalty to the
    Indian Constitution
National interest can be served only if people accused of
    terrorism are hanged
Geelani must be hanged, terrorism must be ended.[20]

These lines read like the plot of a Bollywood film, with Pak-bashing, Kashmiri terrorists and cine-patriotism. I should hasten to add that Indian courts have held that the judicial mind is not susceptible to influence by the media. The question I would naturally want asked is what exactly was the evidence against Geelani. The main piece of evidence was a conversation he had with our youngest brother, Shah Faisal, on 14 December 2001. I reproduce the entire transcript in Kashmiri along with the translations in Hindustani and

English. This was put on record by Sampat Prakash who came from Kashmir at the request of Balraj Puri, convenor of PUCL Jammu, to testify as an expert witness.

Translation of the cassette recorded conversation in Kashmiri. Receiver from Delhi and caller from Kashmir from Kashmir is here by produced in Kashmiri conversation and translated in English language and Hindustani language by me.

		Kashmiri conversation	English Translation	Hindustani Language
1.	Receiver	Hello	Hello	Hello
2.	Caller	Hello, Assalammalaikum Jenab	Hello, Assalammalaikum Sir	Hello, Assalammalaikum Jenab
3.	Receiver	Valaikum Salaam	Valaikum Salaam	Valaikum Salaam
4.	Caller	Vaaray?	Are you well?	Kya aap theek hain?
5.	Receiver	Theek paaeth, khosh, khosh!	Very well, quite happy!	Theek tarah se hoon? Khoush hoon
6.	Caller	....	....	....
7.	Caller	Jaan paaeth	Quite fine	Bahut ache
8.	Receiver	Na apuz kyazi vanay	No, why should I tell lies	Nahin, mein jooth kuon bolun
9.	Caller	Che kati chukh? Gare pathae?	Where are you? Calling from home?	Tum kahan ho? Ghar se bole rahe ho?
10.	Receiver	Na, Na. Ba chhus na gare paethae.	No, No. I am not speaking from home.	Nahin, Nahin. Mein ghar se nahin bole raha hoon.
11.	Caller	Kya?	What?	Kya?
12.	Receiver	....	....	....
13.	Receiver	Ba Chhus gaadi manz.	I am in the bus.	Mein gaadi mein hoon.
14.	Caller	Bassi manz?	In the bus?	Kya bus mein?
15.	Receiver	'I im chhe neran waale. Ba chhus garah pakaan. Ise van che kyah gachhi'?	They are about to leave. I am heading towards home. What do you want?	Woh nikalne waale hein. Mein ghar ja raha hoon. Tumhein kya chahiye?
16.	Caller	Syllabus te prospectus	Syllabus & prospectus.	Syllabus aur prospectus.

Translation of the cassette recorded conversation in Kashmiri. Receiver from Delhi and caller from Kashmir is here by produced in Kashmiri conversation and translated in English language and Hindustani language by me.

	Kashmiri conversation	English Translation	Hindustani Language
17. Receiver	Myani khayala che trav vunkes phone. Vunkes nare na kaaem. Timan chhu yyuni narun. Khan Saa'bas	I deem it advisable for you to drop the phone at this moment. Your job can't be done this time. They have to leave just now. Khan Sahib	Tumhara isi waqt mere khyal mein, phone rakhna theek rahega. Tumhara kaam is waqt nahin ho sakta. Unko abhi jaana hai. Khan Sahib.
18. Caller	Kaman?	Whom?	Kin ko?
19.	....	....	....
20. Receiver	Khan Saa'baas hassa. Ba karay cheer phone. Az ya pagah. Ya doyi teryi dohai. Ya Eed peth. Yunkes Khasan ponsa ziyada.	It is Khan sahib. I will ring you up late at night. Today or tomorrow or on the Eed. Festival. It will cost higher at this time.	Khan sahib hain. Mein der se phone karunga. Aaj ya kal. Ya do ya teen din ke baad. Ya Eed, Per. Is samay paisa zyada lagega.
21. Caller	Accha, Accha, Janeb, Janeb.	Yes, Yes, Sir, Sir.	Haan, Haan, Janab, Janab.
22. Caller	Bae Soruy Theekh?	Rest all well?	Bilkul theek?
23. Receiver	Janeb	Sir	Janab
24. Caller	Ye kyah korva?	What has happened?	Yeh kya hua?
25. Receiver	Kya? Dilli-Ha?	What, in Delhi?	Kya Dilli mein?
26. Caller	Dilli, Kya korva?	What has happened in Delhi?	Dilli mein kya hua?
27. Receiver	Ha! Ha! Ha! (Asaan)	Ha! Ha! Ha! (laughing)	Ha! Ha! Ha! (hansna)
28. Caller	Vuni bihizyava sokha saan.	Relax now.	Ab sakun se rahna.
29. Receiver	Ha! Ha! Ha! (Asaan) Accha che katev chukch? Srinagar ha.	Ha! Ha! Ha! (laughing) O.K. where are you? In Srinagar?	Ha! Ha! Ha! (hansna) Accha tum kahan ho. Tum Srinagar mein ho?
30. Caller	....	....	....
31. Receiver	Che chukha Srinagar?	Are you in Srinagar?	Tum Srinagar mein ho?

Translation of the cassette recorded conversation in Kashmiri. Receiver from Delhi and caller from Kashmir is here by produced in Kashmiri conversation and translated in English language and Hindustani language by me.

	Kashmiri conversation	English Translation	Hindustani Translation
32. Caller	Na, mein kor tate chutee.	No, I am no longer there.	Ab mein wahan nehin hoon.
33. Receiver	Che chukh vanay varmullay?	Are you now at Baramulla?	Kya tum abhi Baramulla mein ho?
34. Caller	Aa.	Yes.	Haan.
35. Receiver	Accha.	O.K.	Accha.
36. Caller	Tate kar mein Chutee.	I have left the place.	Mein ne vahan chod diya hai.
37. Receiver	Accha.	O.K.	Accha.
38. Caller	Accha. Khuda Hafiz	O.K. God bless you.	Accha. Khuda Hafiz
39. Receiver	Khuda Hafiz.	God bless you.	Khuda Hafiz
40. Caller	Accha tharva?	O.K. should I keep the phone?	Kya mein phone rakhun?
41. Receiver	Accha tharva.	O.K. keep the phone.	Haan phone rakh do.

Sampat Prakash
State President.
All Jammu & Kashmir State Govt. Employees Federation,
House No. 240 Sector-IInd, JDA Housing Colony,
Roop Nagar, Jammu, J& K State.
Ph. 0191 - 596817

The prosecution never placed a transcript of the conversation on record, despite repeated requests from Geelani and his lawyers. The sessions court judge, S.N. Dhingra, dismissed the testimony of Sampat Prakash, a veteran trade union leader, and Sanjay Kak, a documentary film-maker, who also testified as an expert witness on behalf of the defence, on the grounds that they were 'interested' witnesses, since they had testified in court on the request of the Defence Committee.

Mr Dhingra decided to treat the uneducated fruit-vendor from Azad Market as the sole expert on the Kashmiri language. At Para 204 of his judgement, the judge surpasses himself in making amazing presumptions:

Defence has criticized Prosecution for calling PW 71 who was only 5th / 6th Standard pass for translating Kashmiri conversation to Hindi. Language is not monopoly of educated and elite class. A child starts learning mother tongue while sucking milk of her mother. A person educated up to 5th or 6th Standard may be knowing his mother tongue much better than a graduate, who after acquiring knowledge of English starts forgetting his mother tongue and can speak only in Hinglish, Chinglish or Kashinglish. Tulsidas, Kabir and several other contemporary personalities had no or little formal education but had command over language and produced great 'works'. Being a fruit seller is no sin. Today we do not understand the dignity of labour and look upon persons earning livelihood by labour as low class. If India is 10th among the most corrupt countries, it is not because of these poor people but because of some other class of people. The witness could not understand English words in the conversation because of lack of knowledge of English language but he understood Kashmiri and Hindi well and translated the conversation to Hindi properly.

Convicted by this judge, my brother spent two years on death row before the Delhi High Court acquitted him on 29 October 2003 and the Supreme Court confirmed the acquittal on 4 August 2005. Both the high court and the Supreme Court held that the 2.16-minute phone conversation intercepted by the police could not possibly link my brother to the conspiracy to attack Parliament.

A version of this essay first appeared in Syed Bismillah Geelani's book *Manufacturing Terrorism: Kashmiri Encounters with Media and the Law*, published by Poles Apart and Promilla & Co. Publishers in association with Bibliophile South Asia.

[4]

THE STRANGE CASE OF
QAYS AL KAREEM

Tripta Wahi

In December 1997, Qays A.M. Abd Al Kareem, a young Jordanian, joined Delhi University as a research student to do his doctoral degree in astrophysics. Five years later, he was back in Jordan, deported from India 'due to his undesirable activities'. He had become yet another victim—though he was lucky to be alive—of the mysterious attack and aftermath of 13 December 2001.

A few months after he enrolled at Delhi University, Qays got accommodation in the Jubilee Hall hostel, a postgraduate hostel for men in the university. He expected to stay there till the completion of his degree, which was likely to take nearly five years. However, as an Arab Muslim, he was to become the target of constant abuse and harassment by some other students resident in Jubilee Hall who were associated with fundamentalist Hindu groups. The harassment was relentless, and the students targeting him eventually succeeded in getting him expelled from Jubilee Hall. During this long period Qays continuously approached the hostel and the university authorities for protection and assistance, but to no avail. He then turned to democratic sections of the university community for help. The person who took him to them was S.A.R. Geelani.[1]

Qays had first met Geelani, lecturer in Arabic at Zakir Hussain College, Delhi, and a civil liberties activist, on the research floor of the Central Reference Library, and later kept in touch because Geelani could speak to him in Arabic and was concerned enough about his situation to help him do something about it. Geelani took him to the People's Union for Civil Liberties (PUCL). The PUCL General Secretary, Gopa Joshi of Ramjas College, Delhi University, intervened to seek alternative accommodation for Qays, so that he could complete his thesis in peace. The university gave him accommodation in the Teachers' Transit Hostel for three months, from October to December 2001, with the understanding that his stay would be extended since the Transit Hostel always remained half-empty. But this was not the end of his troubles.

The communal-minded students who had made Qays's life so difficult in Jubilee Hall made a public issue of him having been given accommodation in the Transit Hostel which is primarily for teachers. Then, the infamous attack on the Parliament happened, and the following day, 14 December 2001, S.A.R. Geelani was arrested in connection with the attack (according to the prosecution, he was arrested on 15 December).

In the days that followed, the media, both print and electronic, abdicated its role of acting as the fourth estate.[2] Geelani was publicly tried by the media on the basis of police statements. Even before his trial began, the media had pronounced him guilty. Within three days, the Jubilee Hall students who had been targeting Qays also came up with 'information' insinuating Geelani's 'international connections' and their 'relevance' to the Parliament attack case. They suggested this by talking of Geelani's friendship with Qays and their long phone calls to destinations in West Asia.[3]

These insinuations—friendship between a Jordanian student and a Kashmiri Muslim (now facing a show trial on a charge of 'terrorism') and therefore the latter's 'connections' in the Arab world—fitted well with the attempts of the investigating agencies and the media to create a 'spin', made potent by the prevailing national and international climate of paranoia related to the 'global war against terror'.

Qays was forced to leave the Teachers' Transit Hostel without notice, without being given time to look for alternative accommodation. In fact, he was locked out of his room with his baggage still inside. All this was happening when he was in the submission stage of his thesis. He was detained by the CID and was called several times by the Special Cell of the Delhi Police, which was handling the Parliament attack case. University officials held back the appointment of examiners for the examination of his thesis. Qays approached a large number of teachers to help him get examiners appointed since his visa had been extended for only six months and time was running out. Meanwhile, fearing for his safety, Qays's family wanted him to return immediately (they had, the previous year, called back his younger brother who was studying mathematics at Delhi University), but Qays, having already invested more than four years in his studies, was resolute that he would return only after getting his degree. Finally, his viva voce was held in October 2002. He did extremely well in his viva and his examiners unambiguously appreciated his thesis for its contribution to its area of study. He earned his degree in the last week of October 2002, which he immediately sent for attestation and authentication to the Embassy of Jordan. He booked his return air ticket to Jordan for 14 November 2002. This ticket was confirmed. But all was not over for Qays; the worst was yet to come.

On 7 November 2002, Qays went to the Foreigners' Registration Regional Office (FRRO) with all his documents to inform the office of his date of departure and to obtain permission for the same. He handed over all his documents, including passport and ticket, for due procedure. He was asked to wait, but his documents were not returned to him, nor was he given any information. After waiting for nearly three hours, Qays rang up N.D. Pancholi, his lawyer and a civil rights activist, to inform him of all that had happened at the FRRO. Pancholi advised him to wait as per official advice. Qays rang Pancholi again at 4 p.m. that day and informed him that he had not been given any information by the office, nor were his papers being returned. Pancholi asked him to call back in an hour. When he hadn't heard from Qays till well after that time, Pancholi went to the FRRO where, with some difficulty, he learnt that Qays had been sent to the Lampur Detention Centre. Pancholi was unable to ascertain the reason for his detention but was informed that there were some instructions 'from above'. Pancholi acted immediately and sent telegrams to the home minister, the police commissioner and the FRRO about Qays's illegal detention.

The following day (8 November 2002), the *Hindustan Times, Indian Express* and the *Times of India* carried reports about Qays's detention. According to these reports, the reason given by the FRRO for his detention was that Qays's air ticket was 'not confirmed'. The reports went on to state that Qays would be deported by the FRRO on the ticket bought by Qays himself, in order to 'ensure his departure'. The reason given by the FRRO was clearly spurious, since Qays's ticket was confirmed, and this could be easily proved. In any event, at no point was any explanation given by the FRRO to Qays himself as to why he was being detained, and why he would be deported.

Fearing for Qays's safety and life, two teachers of Delhi University, Nandita Narain and myself, immediately moved a habeas corpus petition on 8 November 2002 in the Delhi High Court (No. CRLW 1287/2002). The division bench comprising Justice D. Bhandari and Justice H.R. Malhotra asked the Centre and the Delhi Police to produce Qays in court the coming Monday, 11 November 2002, at 10.30 a.m.[4] In view of the anxiety expressed by the petitioners about the safety of Qays, the court asked the Union of India and others to ensure that Qays was brought to the court in good condition.

That Monday, when Qays was brought to the court, the petitioners and N.D. Pancholi were shocked to see his physical state. His spectacles and wristwatch were broken, his shirt was torn and there were scratches all over his forearms. He told the court that the previous evening (i.e., Sunday evening) four policemen had come to the detention centre to take him away. The policemen had told him that they had come to take him to court. Aware that this was not possible on a Sunday evening, Qays had resisted going with them. In this physical resistance his spectacles and wristwatch had been smashed, his shirt torn, and he had received scratches all over his body. He stated that he could finally prevent the policemen from physically dragging him out only when he shouted for help and other inmates of the detention centre came to his rescue. The police flatly denied this, but the physical condition of Qays left no doubt in the minds of all those present in the courtroom. The Hon'ble judges were visibly angry and they reprimanded the Union of India and others, stating that they had given special instructions for Qays's physical well-being and that their instructions had not been obeyed. They were so disturbed by this incident that they asked the Union of India and the Delhi Police to appear in the forenoon. Ms Mukta, Public Prosecutor for the Delhi Government, pleaded with the judges that the Additional Solicitor-General, who was to appear for the Union of India, could only come in the afternoon, but in what was a clear reflection of the judges' anger at Qays's condition, he was ordered to appear no later than noon.

The Additional Solicitor-General of India, when he appeared before the judges, argued that Qays was to be deported on grounds that could not be revealed publicly, that there were 'confidential' reports and documents that warranted his immediate departure. He mentioned Qays's connection with S.A.R. Geelani and stated that Qays had been taken and questioned by CID and the

Special Cell of the Delhi Police several times in
connection with the attack on Parliament. He went on
to state that Qays was to be deported for reasons of
security. On this being contested by Pancholi, the
judges asked for and examined the home ministry's files
with the confidential reports. Their observations about
the contents of the files are very significant. They
commented that although Qays had been taken and
questioned by CID and the special cell several times in
connection with the Parliament attack case, there was
yet no evidence against him, and he had been released
each time. They further added that they saw no apparent
reason for him to be deported when he himself was
leaving the country. During the course of the argument,
the Additional Solicitor-General referred to us petitioners
as 'leftist activists' who were always trying to create
trouble for the State. Finally, he argued that the
government wanted to deport Qays so that he would
not be able to go as a free man and that this should
become a part of his record. He insisted that the
government would deport Qays and send his luggage
later.

It is tragic that the Hon'ble bench finally allowed
the government to deport Qays, although it had found
no evidence in the confidential files to warrant his
deportation. However, when the petitioners passionately
argued that Qays be allowed to sort his own luggage,
since the research material collected over so many years
could easily be lost otherwise, the court permitted him
to collect his luggage at Parmanand Colony in the
presence of a lawyer designated by the court. The court
also sought assurance from the Union of India and the
Delhi Police about Qays's safety till his departure on 14

November 2002, which assurance was given by the State. The petitioners got permission from the court to be present at the time when Qays was to collect his baggage from his residence, and this was done on the evening of the following day, 12 November 2002.

Qays left on the air ticket that he himself had booked and paid for, but with the following observations (made by the FRRO on the day that Qays had gone to that office for permission to leave) inscribed on his passport:

> The holder of this passport is being deported from India due to his undesirable activities by FRRO Delhi vide order No. 1408/ For (I.M. Cell) dated 7/11/02.

The effects of the injustice done to Qays did not disappear with his return to Jordan. He has had to face many problems there arising out of his deportation. He still hasn't had any explanation for what he had to suffer, leave alone an apology.

The case of Qays Al Kareem starkly reveals the subversion of democracy in the name of fighting terrorism, and the extent to which our universities have become communalized. The structures of authority are either in league with communal forces or else they succumb to communal pressures. It is noteworthy that Qays received minimal or no support to his letters of complaint about his harassment. On the contrary, the warden forwarded to the vice chancellor and the Jordanian Embassy a letter of complaint by the students who were harassing Qays, alleging that Qays was hurting their religious sentiments! This letter was forwarded without even a preliminary inquiry. Later, of course, all democratic norms were discarded when Qays was locked out of his TTH room, and officers of the examination branch colluded in his harassment by delaying his thesis evaluation.

While it was quite natural for Qays, an Arab from Jordan, to make friends with the lone teacher of Arabic in the university library, in the wake of S.A.R. Geelani's arrest, this friendship became the cause of his continuous harassment by the CID and the Special Cell in Delhi. Communalism and stereotyped notions of terrorism got intrinsically intertwined and Qays fell victim to this vicious combination.

That Qays was repeatedly taken for questioning by the CID and the Special Police Cell is perhaps understandable, but why he was detained at the Lampur detention centre at the FRRO, when he himself had reported there to inform them of his departure, is intriguing. Even though the court allowed the FRRO to deport Qays, the judges were not convinced of the arguments given by the State. Secondly, the police attempt to drag him out of the detention centre on a Sunday evening in order to produce him in court in connection with the habeas corpus petition on Monday, is highly suspect. Thirdly, why did the police so desperately want to pack Qays' baggage and not allow him to do it himself?

These questions seem to take us to the terrorist attack on Parliament. With the judgement in the Parliament case before us, we know that the Police claimed that the original conspirators of the attack were not educated, and that Geelani, being an educated man, played a crucial role as the conspiracy unfolded. Geelani, thus, was a vital link in the police version of the attack. But—as the high court itself was to later observe in its judgement—there was no evidence to link Geelani with the conspiracy. The police, of course, was aware of this quite basic weakness in its case. Where evidence does not exist, the police fabricates it—this, again, has been noted by the courts. Therefore, the strange case of Qays: it is entirely likely that the police turned to him as a last resort to nail Geelani.

Could it be that Qays was taken to the Lampur detention centre so that the police could secure some 'confession' incriminating Geelani? Could it be that the police was so interested in managing his luggage because it wanted to plant some physical evidence in support of the confession? And could it be that—when everything else had failed—Qays was deported, rather than simply being released and allowed to leave, so that he would never be able to return to India as a witness in a court of law?

Like many other aspects of the '13 December' case, the deportation of Qays Abd Al Kareem, too, leaves many questions unanswered.

This text is edited and excerpted from 'The Qays Deportation Case', published in *Revolutionary Democracy*, Vol. X, No. 2, September 2004.

[5]

'AND HIS LIFE SHOULD BECOME EXTINCT'

THE VERY STRANGE STORY OF THE ATTACK
ON THE INDIAN PARLIAMENT

Arundhati Roy

We know this much: On 13 December 2001 the Indian Parliament was in its Winter Session. (The NDA Government was under attack for yet another corruption scandal.) At 11.30 in the morning, five armed men in a white Ambassador car fitted out with an Improvised Explosive Device drove through the gates of Parliament House. When they were challenged, they jumped out of the car and opened fire. In the gun battle that followed, all the attackers were killed. Eight security personnel and a gardener were killed too. The dead terrorists, the police said, had enough explosives to blow up the Parliament building, and enough ammunition to take on a whole battalion of soldiers. Unlike most terrorists, these five left behind a thick trail of evidence—weapons, mobile phones, phone numbers, ID cards, photographs, packets of dry fruit, and even a love letter.

Not surprisingly, Prime Minister A.B. Vajpayee seized the opportunity to compare the assault to the 9/11 attacks in the US that had happened only three months previously.

On 14 December 2001, the day after the attack on Parliament, the Special Cell of the Delhi Police claimed it had tracked down several people suspected to have been involved in the conspiracy. A day later, on 15 December, it announced that it had 'cracked the case': the attack, the police said, was a joint operation carried out by two Pakistan-based terrorist groups, Lashkar-e-Toiba and Jaish-e-Mohammad. Twelve people were named as being part of the conspiracy. Ghazi Baba of the Jaish-e-Mohammad (Usual Suspect I); Maulana Masood Azhar, also of the Jaish-e-Mohammad (Usual Suspect II); Tariq Ahmed (a 'Pakistani'); five deceased 'Pakistani terrorists' (we still don't know who they are). And three Kashmiri men, S.A.R. Geelani, Shaukat Hussain Guru, and Mohammad Afzal; and Shaukat's wife Afsan (aka Navjot) Guru. These were the only four to be arrested.

In the tense days that followed, Parliament was adjourned. On 21 December 2001 India recalled its High Commissioner from Pakistan, suspended air, rail and bus communications and banned over-flights. It put into motion a massive mobilization of its war machinery, and moved more than half a million troops to the Pakistan border. Foreign embassies evacuated their staff and citizens and tourists travelling to India were issued cautionary Travel Advisories. The world watched with bated breath as the subcontinent was taken to the brink of nuclear war. (All this cost India an estimated Rs 10,000 crores of public money. A few hundred soldiers died just in the panicky process of mobilization.)

Almost three and a half years later, on 5 August 2005, the Supreme Court delivered its final judgement in the case. It endorsed the view that the Parliament Attack be looked upon as an act of war. It said, 'The attempted attack on Parliament is an undoubted invasion of the sovereign attribute of the State including the Government of India which is its *alter ego* . . . the deceased terrorists were roused and impelled to action by a strong anti-Indian feeling as the writing on the fake Home Ministry sticker found on the car (Ex. PW1/8) reveals.' It went on to say, 'the *modus operandi* adopted by the hardcore "fidayeens" are all demonstrative of launching a war against the Government of India.'

The text on the fake Home Ministry sticker read as follows:

> INDIA IS A VERY BAD COUNTRY AND WE HATE INDIA WE WANT TO DESTROY INDIA AND WITH THE GRACE OF GOD WE WILL DO IT GOD IS WITH US AND WE WILL TRY OUR BEST. THIS EDIET WAJPAI AND ADVANI WE WILL KILL THEM. THEY HAVE KILLED MANY INNOCENT PEOPLE AND THEY ARE VERY BAD PERSONS THERE BROTHER BUSH IS ALSO A VERY BAD PERSON HE WILL BE NEXT TARGET HE IS ALSO THE KILLER OF INNOCENT PEOPLE HE HAVE TO DIE AND WE WILL DO IT.

This subtly-worded sticker-manifesto was displayed on the windscreen of the car bomb as it drove into Parliament. (Given the amount of text, it's a wonder the driver could see anything at all. Maybe that's why he collided with the Vice-President's cavalcade?)

The police charge sheet was filed in a special fast-track trial court designated for cases under the Prevention of Terrorism Act (POTA). The trial court sentenced Geelani, Shaukat and Afzal to death. Afsan Guru was sentenced to five years of Rigorous Imprisonment. The High Court subsequently acquitted Geelani and Afsan, but it upheld Shaukat's and Afzal's death sentence. Eventually, the Supreme Court upheld the acquittals, and reduced Shaukat's punishment to 10 years of Rigorous Imprisonment. However, it not just confirmed, but enhanced Mohammed Afzal's sentence. He has been given three life sentences and a double death sentence.

In its 5 August 2005 judgment, the Supreme Court clearly says that there was no evidence that Mohammad Afzal belonged to any terrorist group or organization. But it also says, 'As is the case with most of the conspiracies, there is and could be no direct evidence of the agreement amounting to criminal conspiracy. However, the circumstances cumulatively weighed would unerringly point to the collaboration of the accused Afzal with the slain "fidayeen" terrorists.'

So: No direct evidence, but yes, circumstantial evidence.

A controversial paragraph in the judgement goes on to say: 'The incident, which resulted in heavy casualties, had shaken the entire nation, and the collective conscience of the society will only be satisfied if capital punishment is awarded to the offender. The challenge to the unity, integrity and sovereignty of India by these acts of terrorists and conspirators can only be compensated by giving maximum punishment to the person who is *proved to be* the conspirator in this treacherous act.' [Emphasis mine.]

To invoke the 'collective conscience of society' to validate ritual murder, which is what the death penalty is, skates precariously close to valorizing lynch law. It's chilling to think that this has been laid upon us not by predatory politicians or sensation-seeking journalists (though they too have done that), but as an edict from the highest court in the land.

Spelling out the reasons for awarding Afzal the death penalty, the judgment says, 'The appellant who is a surrendered militant and who was bent upon repeating the acts of treason against the nation, is a menace to the society and his life should become extinct.'

This paragraph combines flawed logic with absolute ignorance of what it means to be a 'surrendered militant' in Kashmir today.

So: Should Mohammad Afzal's life become extinct?

A small, but influential minority of intellectuals, activists, editors, lawyers and public figures have objected to the Death Sentence as a matter of moral principle. They also argue that there is no empirical evidence to suggest that the Death Sentence works as a deterrent to terrorists. (How can it, when in this age of fidayeen and suicide bombers death seems to be the main attraction?)

If opinion polls, letters to the editor and the reactions of live audiences in TV studios are a correct gauge of public opinion in India, then the lynch mob is expanding by the hour. It looks as though an overwhelming majority of Indian citizens would like to see Mohammad Afzal hanged every day, weekends included, for the next few years. L.K. Advani, Leader of the Opposition, displaying an unseemly sense of urgency, wants him to be hanged[1] as soon as possible, without a moment's delay.

Meanwhile in Kashmir, public opinion is equally overwhelming. Huge angry protests make it increasingly obvious that if Afzal is hanged, the consequences will be political. Some protest what they see as a miscarriage of justice, but even as they protest, they do not expect justice from Indian courts. They have lived through too much brutality to believe in courts, affidavits and justice any more. Others would like to see Mohammad Afzal march to the gallows like Maqbool Butt[2], a proud martyr to the cause of Kashmir's freedom struggle. On the whole, most Kashmiris see Mohammad Afzal as a sort of prisoner-of-war being tried in the courts of an occupying power (which India undoubtedly is in Kashmir). Naturally, political parties, in India as well as in Kashmir, have sniffed the breeze and are cynically closing in for the kill.

Sadly, in the midst of the frenzy, Afzal seems to have forfeited the right to be an individual, a real person any more. He's become a vehicle for everybody's fantasies—nationalists, separatists, and anti-capital punishment activists. He has become India's great villain and Kashmir's great hero—proving only that whatever our pundits, policy makers and peace gurus say, all these years later, the war in Kashmir has by no means ended.

In a situation as fraught and politicized as this, it's tempting to believe that the time to intervene has come and gone. After all, the judicial process lasted forty months, and the Supreme Court has examined the evidence before it. It has convicted two of the accused and acquitted the other two. Surely this in itself is proof of judicial objectivity? What more remains to be said?

There's another way of looking at it. Isn't it odd that the prosecution's case, proved to be so egregiously wrong in one half, has been so gloriously vindicated in the other?

The story of Mohammad Afzal is fascinating precisely because he is *not* Maqbool Butt. Yet his story too is inextricably entwined with the story of the Kashmir Valley. It's a story whose coordinates range far beyond the confines of courtrooms and the limited imagination of people who live in the secure heart of a self-declared 'superpower'. Mohammad Afzal's story has its origins in a war zone whose laws are beyond the pale of the fine arguments and delicate sensibilities of normal jurisprudence.

For all these reasons it is critical that we consider carefully the strange, sad, and utterly sinister story of the 13 December Parliament Attack. It tells us a great deal about the way the world's largest 'democracy' really works. It connects the biggest things to the smallest. It traces the pathways that connect what happens in the shadowy grottos of our police stations to what goes on in the cold, snowy streets of Paradise Valley; from there to the impersonal, malign furies that bring nations to the brink of nuclear war. It raises specific questions that deserve specific, and not ideological or rhetorical answers. What hangs in the balance is far more than the fate of one man.

On 4 October 2006, I was one amongst a very small group of people who had gathered at Jantar Mantar in New Delhi to protest against Mohammad Afzal's death sentence. I was there because I believe Mohammad Afzal is only a pawn in a very sinister game. He's not the Dragon he's being made out to be, he's only the Dragon's footprint. And if the footprint is made to 'become extinct', we'll never know who the Dragon was. Is.

Not surprisingly, that afternoon there were more journalists and TV crew than there were protestors. Most of the attention was on Ghalib, Afzal's angelic-looking little son. Kind-hearted people, not sure of what to do with a young boy whose father was going to the gallows, were plying him with ice-creams and cold drinks. As I looked around at the people gathered there, I noted a sad little fact. The convener of the protest, the small, stocky man who was nervously introducing the speakers and making the announcements, was S.A.R. Geelani, a young lecturer in Arabic Literature at Delhi University. Accused Number Three in the Parliament Attack case.

He was arrested on 14 December 2001, a day after the attack, by the Special Cell of the Delhi Police. Though Geelani was brutally tortured in custody, though his family—his wife, young children and brother—were illegally detained, he refused to confess to a crime he hadn't committed. Of course you wouldn't know this if you read newspapers in the days following his arrest. They carried detailed descriptions of an entirely imaginary, non-existent confession. The Delhi Police portrayed Geelani as the evil mastermind of the Indian end of the conspiracy. Its scriptwriters orchestrated a hateful propaganda campaign against him, which was eagerly amplified and embellished by a hyper-nationalistic, thrill-seeking media. The police knew perfectly well that in criminal trials, judges are not supposed to take cognizance of media reports. So they knew that their entirely cold-blooded fabrication of a profile for these 'terrorists' would mould public opinion, and create a climate for the trial. But it would not come in for any legal scrutiny.

Here are some of the malicious, outright lies that appeared in the mainstream press:

'Case cracked: Jaish behind attack'[3]
(*Hindustan Times*)
'In Delhi, the Special Cell Detectives detained a Lecturer in Arabic, who teaches at Zakir Hussain College (Evening) . . . after it was established that he had received a call made by militants on his mobile phone.' Another column in the same paper said: 'Terrorists spoke to him before the attack and the lecturer made a phone call to Pakistan after the strike.'

'DU lecturer was terror plan hub'[4]
(*Times of India*)
'The attack on Parliament on December 13th was a joint operation of the Jaish-e-Mohammad (JeM) and Lashkar-e-Toiba (LeT) terrorist groups in which a Delhi University lecturer, Syed A.R. Gilani, was one of the key facilitators in Delhi, Police Commissioner Ajai Raj Sharma said on Sunday.'

'Varsity don guided "fidayeen"'[5]
(*Hindu*)
'During interrogation Geelani disclosed that he was in the know of the conspiracy since the day the "Fidayeen" attack was planned.'

'Don lectured on terror in free time'[6]
(*Hindustan Times*)
'Investigations have revealed that by evening he was at the college teaching Arabic literature. In his free time, behind closed doors, either at his house or at Shaukat Hussain's, another suspect to be arrested, he took and gave lessons on terrorism . . .'

'Professor's proceeds'[7]
(*Hindustan Times*)
'Geelani recently purchased a house for 22 lakhs in West Delhi. Delhi Police are investigating how he came upon such a windfall . . .'

'*Aligarh se* England *tak chhaatron mein aatankwaad ke beej bo raha tha Geelani*'[8] (Translation: 'From Aligarh to England Geelani was sowing seeds of terrorism amongst students')
(*Rashtriya Sahara*)
(Translated from the original Hindi: '. . . According to sources and information collected by investigation agencies, Geelani has made a statement to the police that he was an agent of Jaish-e-Mohammad for a long time . . . It was because of Geelani's articulation, style of working and sound planning that in 2000 Jaish-e-Mohammad gave him the responsibility of spreading intellectual terrorism.'

'Terror suspect frequent visitor to Pak mission'[9]
(*Hindustan Times*)

'During interrogation, Gilani has admitted that he had made frequent calls to Pakistan and was in touch with militants belonging to Jaish-e-Mohammad . . . Gilani said that he had been provided with funds by some members of the Jaish and told to buy two flats that could be used in militant operations.'

'Person of the Week'[10]
(*Sunday Times of India*)

'A cellphone proved his undoing. Delhi University's Syed A.R. Gilani was the first to be arrested in the December 13th case—a shocking reminder that the roots of terrorism go far and deep.'

Zee TV trumped them all. It produced a film called *December 13th*, a 'docudrama' that claimed to be the 'truth based on the police charge sheet'. (A contradiction in terms, wouldn't you say?) It showed actors playing the part of the 'terrorists', including Geelani. It showed them meeting and planning the attack. The film was privately screened for Prime Minster A.B. Vajpayee and Home Minister L.K. Advani. Both men applauded the film. Their approbation was widely reported by the media. The Supreme Court dismissed an appeal to stay the broadcast of the film on the grounds that judges are not influenced by the media. (Would the Supreme Court concede that even if judges are beyond being influenced by media reports, the 'collective conscience of the society' might not be?) *December 13th* was broadcast on Zee TV's national network a few days before the fast-track trial court sentenced Geelani, Afzal and Shaukat to Death. Geelani eventually spent eighteen months in jail, many of them in solitary confinement, on death row.

He was released when the Delhi High Court acquitted him and Afsan Guru. (Afsan, who was pregnant when she was arrested, had her baby in prison. Her experience broke her. She now suffers from a serious psychotic condition.) The Supreme Court upheld the acquittal. It found absolutely no evidence to link Geelani with the Parliament Attack or with any terrorist organization. *Not a single newspaper or journalist or TV channel has seen fit to apologize to him (or any of the others) for their lies.*

But S.A.R. Geelani's troubles didn't end there. His acquittal left the Special Cell with a plot, but no 'mastermind'. This, as we shall see, becomes something of a problem. More importantly, Geelani was a free man now—free to meet the press, talk to lawyers, clear his name. On the evening of 8 February 2005, during the course of the final hearings at the Supreme Court, Geelani was making his way to his lawyer's house. A mysterious gunman appeared from the shadows and fired five bullets into his body. Miraculously, he survived. It was an unbelievable new twist to the story. Clearly, somebody was worried about what he knew, what he would say . . . One would imagine that the police would give this investigation top priority, hoping it would throw up some vital new leads into the Parliament Attack case. Instead, the Special Cell treated Geelani as though *he* was the prime suspect in his own assassination. They confiscated his computer and took away his car. Hundreds of activists gathered outside the

hospital and called for an inquiry into the assassination
attempt, which would include an investigation into the
Special Cell itself. (Of course, that never happened.
More than a year has passed, nobody shows any
interest in pursuing the matter. Odd.)

So here he was now, S.A.R. Geelani, having survived
this terrible ordeal, standing up in public at Jantar
Mantar, saying that Mohammad Afzal didn't deserve a
death sentence. How much easier it would be for him
to keep his head down, stay at home. I was profoundly
moved, humbled, by this quiet display of courage.

Across the line from S.A.R. Geelani, in the jostling
crowd of journalists and photographers, trying his best
to look inconspicuous in a lemon T-shirt and gaberdine
pants, holding a little tape-recorder, was another Gilani.
Iftikhar Gilani. He had been in prison too. He was
arrested and taken into police custody on 9 June 2002.
At the time he was a reporter for the Jammu-based
Kashmir Times. He was charged under the Official
Secrets Act. His 'crime' was that he supposedly possessed
information on Indian troop deployment in 'Indian
held Kashmir'. (This 'information', it turns out, was a
published monograph by a Pakistani research institute,
and was freely available on the Internet for anybody
who wished to download it.) Iftikhar Gilani's computer
was seized. IB officials tampered with his hard drive,
meddled with the downloaded file, changed the words
'Indian-held Kashmir' to 'Jammu and Kashmir' to make
it sound like an Indian document, and added the words
'Only for Reference. Strictly Not for Circulation', to
make it seem like a secret document smuggled out of
the Home Ministry. The Directorate General of Military

Intelligence—though it had been given a photocopy of the monograph—ignored repeated appeals from Iftikhar Gilani's counsel, kept quiet, and refused to clarify the matter for a whole six months.

Once again the malicious lies put out by the Special Cell were obediently reproduced in the newspapers. Here are a few of the lies they told:

'Iftikhar Gilani, 35-year-old son-in-law of Hurriyat hardliner Syed Ali Shah Gilani is believed to have admitted in a city court that he was an agent of Pakistan's spy agency.' (*Hindustan Times*)[11]

'Iftikhar Gilani was the pin-point man of Syed Salahuddin of Hizbul Mujahideen. Investigations have revealed that Iftikhar used to pass information to Salahuddin about the moves of Indian security agencies. He had camouflaged his real motives behind his journalist's façade so well that it took years to unmask him, well-placed sources said.' (*Pioneer*)[12]

'*Gilani ke daamaad ke ghar aaykar chhaapon mein behisaab sampati wa samwaidansheil dastaweiz baraamad.*' (Translation: 'Enormous wealth and sensitive documents recovered from the house of Gilani's son-in-law during Income-tax raids.') (*Hindustan*)[13]

Never mind that the police charge sheet recorded a recovery of only Rs 3,450 from his house. Meanwhile, other media reports said that he had a three-bedroom flat, an undisclosed income of Rs 22 lakhs, had evaded income-tax of Rs 79 lakhs, that he and his wife were absconding to evade arrest.

But arrested he was. In jail, Iftikhar Gilani was beaten, abjectly humiliated. In his book *My Days In Prison*[14] he tells of how, among other things, he was made to clean the toilet with his shirt and then wear the same shirt for days. After six months of court arguments and lobbying by his colleagues, when it became obvious that if the case against him continued it would lead to serious embarrassment, he was released.

Here he was now. A free man, a reporter come to Jantar Mantar to cover a story. It occurred to me that S.A.R. Geelani, Iftikhar Gilani and Mohammad Afzal would have been in Tihar jail at the same time. (Along with scores of other less well-known Kashmiris whose stories we may never learn.)

It can, and will be argued that the cases of both S.A.R. Geelani and Iftikhar Gilani serve only to demonstrate the objectivity of the Indian judicial system and its capacity for self-correction, they do not discredit it. That's only partly true. Both Iftikhar Gilani and S.A.R. Geelani are fortunate to be Delhi-based Kashmiris with a community of articulate, middle-class peers, journalists and university teachers, who knew them well and rallied around them in their time of need. S.A.R. Geelani's lawyer Nandita Haksar put together an All India Defence Committee for S.A.R. Geelani (of which I was a member). There was a coordinated campaign by activists, lawyers and journalists to rally behind Geelani. Well-known lawyers represented him. They showed up the case for what it was—a pack of absurd assumptions, suppositions and outright lies, bolstered by fabricated evidence. So *of course* judicial objectivity exists. But it's a shy beast that lives somewhere deep in the labyrinth of our legal system. It shows itself rarely. It takes whole teams of top lawyers to coax it out of its lair and make it come out and play. It's what in newspaper-speak would be called a Herculean Task. Mohammad Afzal did not have Hercules on his side.

For five months, from the time he was arrested to the day the police charge sheet was filed, Mohammad Afzal, lodged in a high-security prison, had no legal defence, no legal advice. No top lawyers, no defence committee (in India or Kashmir), and no campaign. Of all the four accused, he was the most vulnerable. His case was far more complicated than Geelani's. Significantly, during much of this time, Afzal's younger brother Hilal was illegally detained by the Special Operations Group (SOG) in Kashmir. He was released after the charge sheet was filed. (This is a piece of the puzzle that will only fall into place as the story unfolds.)

In a serious lapse of procedure, on 20 December 2001, the Investigating Officer, Assistant Commissioner of Police (ACP) Rajbir Singh (affectionately known as Delhi's 'encounter specialist' for the number of 'terrorists' he has killed in 'encounters'), called a press conference at the Special Cell. Mohammad Afzal was made to 'confess' before the media. Deputy Commissioner of Police (DCP) Ashok Chand told the press that Afzal had already confessed to the police. This turned out to be untrue. Afzal's formal confession to the police took place only the next day (after which he continued to remain in police custody and vulnerable to torture, another serious procedural lapse). In his media 'confession' Afzal incriminated himself in the Parliament Attack completely.[15]

During the course of this 'media confession' a curious thing happened. In an answer to a direct question, Afzal clearly said that Geelani had nothing to do with the Attack and was completely innocent. At this point, ACP Rajbir Singh shouted at him and forced him to shut up, and requested the media not to carry this part of Afzal's 'confession'. *And they obeyed*! The story came out only three months later when the television channel *Aaj Tak* re-broadcast the 'confession' in a programme called '*Hamle Ke Sau Din*' ('Hundred Days of the Attack') and somehow kept this part in. Meanwhile, in the eyes of the general public, including people like myself—who know little about the law and criminal procedure—Afzal's public 'confession' only confirmed his guilt. The verdict of the 'collective conscience of society' would not have been hard to second guess.

The day after this 'media' confession, Afzal's 'official' confession was extracted from him. The flawlessly structured, perfectly fluent narrative dictated in articulate English to DCP Ashok Chand, (in the DCP's words, 'he kept on narrating and I kept on writing') was delivered in a sealed envelope to a judicial magistrate. In this confession, Afzal, now the sheet-anchor of the prosecution's case, weaves a masterful tale that connected Ghazi Baba, Maulana Masood Azhar, a man called Tariq, and the five dead terrorists; their equipment, arms and ammunition, Home Ministry passes, a laptop, and fake ID cards; detailed lists of exactly how many kilos of what chemical he bought from where, the exact ratio in which they were mixed to make explosives; and the exact times at which he made and received calls on which mobile number. (For some reason, by then Afzal had also changed his mind about Geelani and implicated him completely in the conspiracy.)

Each point of the 'confession' corresponded perfectly with the evidence that the police had already gathered.

In other words, Afzal's confessional statement slipped perfectly into the version that the police had already offered the press days ago, like Cinderella's foot into the glass slipper. (If it were a film, you could say it was a screenplay, which came with its own box of props. Actually, as we know now, it *was* made into a film. Zee TV owes Afzal some royalty payments.)

Eventually, the Supreme Court set aside Afzal's confession citing 'lapses and violations of procedural safeguards'. But Afzal's confession somehow survives as the phantom keystone in the prosecution's case. And before it was technically and legally set aside, the confessional document had already served a major extra-legal purpose: On 21 December 2001, when the Government of India launched its war effort against Pakistan, it said it had 'incontrovertible evidence' of Pakistan's involvement. Afzal's confession was the only 'proof' of Pakistan's involvement that the government had! Afzal's confession. And the sticker-manifesto. Think about it. On the basis of this illegal confession extracted under torture, hundreds of thousands of soldiers were moved to the Pakistan border at huge cost to the public exchequer, and the subcontinent devolved into a game of nuclear brinkmanship in which the whole world was held hostage.

Big Whispered Question: Could it have been the other way around? Did the confession precipitate the war, or did the need for a war precipitate the need for the confession?

Later, when Afzal's confession was set aside by the Supreme Court, all talk of Jaish-e-Mohammad and Lashkar-e-Toiba ceased. The only other link to Pakistan was the identity of the five dead fidayeen. Mohammad

Afzal, still in police custody, identified them as
Mohammed, Rana, Raja, Hamza and Haider. The
Home Minister said they 'looked like Pakistanis', the
police said they were Pakistanis, the trial court judge
said they were Pakistanis. And there the matter rests.
Had we been told that their names were Happy,
Bouncy, Lucky, Jolly and Kidingamani from Scandinavia,
we would have had to accept that too. We still don't
know who they really were, or where they were from.
Is anyone curious? Doesn't look like it. The high court
said, '. . . identity of the five deceased thus stands
established. Even otherwise it makes no difference.
What is relevant is the association of the accused with
the said five persons and not their names.'

In his Statement of the Accused (which, unlike the
confession, is made in court and not police custody)
Afzal says: 'I had not identified any terrorist. Police
told me the names of terrorists and forced me to
identify them.'[16] But by then it was too late for him. On
the first day of the trial, the lawyer appointed by the
trial court judge agreed to accept Afzal's identification
of the bodies (and the postmortem reports) as *undisputed
evidence,* without *formal proof*!. This baffling move was
to have serious consequences for Afzal. To quote from
the Supreme Court judgement, 'The first circumstance
against the accused Afzal is that Afzal knew who the
deceased terrorists were. He identified the dead bodies
of the deceased terrorists. On this aspect the evidence
remains unshattered.'

Of course, it's possible that the dead terrorists were
foreign militants. But it is just as possible that they

were not. Killing people and falsely identifying them as 'foreign terrorists', or falsely identifying dead people as 'foreign terrorists', or falsely identifying living people as terrorists, is not uncommon among the police or security forces in Kashmir, or even on the streets of Delhi.

The best known among the many well-documented cases in Kashmir, one that went on to become an international scandal, is the killing that took place outside a village called Pathribal, after the Chhittisingpora massacre. On the night of 20 April 2000, just before the US President Bill Clinton arrived in New Delhi, thirty-five Sikhs were killed in the village of Chhittisingpora, by 'unidentified gunmen' wearing Indian Army uniforms. (In Kashmir many people suspect that Indian security forces were behind the massacre.) Five days later, the SOG and the 7th Rashtriya Rifles, a Counter Insurgency unit of the Army, killed five people in a joint operation in Pathribal. The next morning they announced that the men were the Pakistan-based foreign militants who had killed the Sikhs in Chhittisingpora. The bodies were found burned and disfigured. Under their (unburned) Army uniforms, they were in ordinary civilian clothes. It turned out that they were all local people, rounded up from Anantnag district and brutally killed in cold blood.

There are others:

On 20 October 2003 the Srinagar newspaper *Al-safa* printed a picture of a Pakistani 'militant' who the 18th Rashtriya Rifles claimed they had killed while he was trying to storm an army camp. A baker in Kupwara, Wali Khan, saw the picture and recognized it as his son, Farooq Ahmed Khan, who had been picked up by soldiers in a Gypsy two months earlier. His body was finally exhumed more than a year later.

On 20 April 2004, the 18th Rashtriya Rifles posted in the Lolab valley claimed they had killed four foreign militants in a fierce encounter. It later turned out that all four were ordinary labourers from Jammu, hired by the Army and taken to Kupwara. An anonymous letter tipped off the labourers' families who travelled to Kupwara and eventually had the bodies exhumed.

On 9 November 2004 the Army showcased forty-seven surrendered 'militants' to the press at Nagrota, Jammu in the presence of the General Officer Commanding XVI Corps and the Director General of Police, J&K. The J&K police later found that twenty-seven of them were just unemployed men who had been given fake names and fake aliases and promised government jobs in return for playing their part in the charade.

These are just a few quick examples to illustrate the fact that in the absence of any other evidence the police's word is *just not good enough*.

The hearings in the fast-track trial court began in 2002. May Let's not forget the climate in which the trial took place. The frenzy over the 9/11 attacks was still in the air. The US was gloating over its victory in Afghanistan. Gujarat was convulsed by communal frenzy. A few months previously, Coach S-6 of the Sabarmati Express had been set on fire and fifty-eight Hindu pilgrims had been burned alive inside. As 'revenge', in an orchestrated pogrom, more than 2000 Muslims were publicly butchered and more than 1,50,000 driven from their homes.

For Afzal, everything that could go wrong went wrong. He was incarcerated in a high-security prison, with no access to the outside world, and no money to hire a professional lawyer. Three weeks into the trial the lawyer appointed by the Court asked to be discharged from the case because she had now been professionally hired to be on the team of lawyers for S.A.R. Geelani's defence. The Court appointed her junior, a lawyer with very little experience, to represent Afzal. He did not once visit his client in jail to take instructions. He did not summon a single witness for Afzal's defence and barely cross-questioned any of the prosecution witnesses. Five days after he was appointed, on 8 July, Afzal asked the court for another lawyer and gave the court a list of lawyers whom he hoped the court might hire for him. Each of them refused. (Given the frenzy of propaganda in the media, it was hardly surprising. At a later stage of the trial, when Senior Advocate Ram Jethmalani agreed to represent Geelani, Shiv Sena mobs ransacked his Bombay office.) The judge expressed his inability to do anything about this, and gave Afzal the right to cross-examine witnesses. It's astonishing for the judge to expect a layperson to be able to cross-examine witnesses in a criminal trial. It's a virtually impossible task for someone who does not have a sophisticated understanding of criminal law, including new laws that had just been passed, like POTA, and the amendments to the Evidence Act and the Telegraph Act. Even experienced lawyers were having to work overtime to bring themselves up to date.

The case against Afzal was built up in the trial court on the strength of the testimonies of almost eighty prosecution witnesses: landlords, shopkeepers, technicians from cell-phone companies, the police themselves. This was a crucial period of the trial, when the legal foundation of the case was being laid. It required meticulous back-breaking legal work in which evidence needed to be amassed and put on record, witnesses for the defence summoned, and testimonies from prosecution witnesses cross-questioned. Even if the verdict of the trial court went against the accused (trial courts are notoriously conservative) the evidence could then be worked upon by lawyers in the higher courts. Through this absolutely critical period, Afzal went virtually undefended. It was at this stage that the bottom fell out of his case, and the noose tightened around his neck.

Still, during the trial, the skeletons began to clatter out of the Special Cell's cupboard in an embarrassing heap. It became clear that the accumulation of lies, fabrications, forged documents and serious lapses in procedure began from the very first day of the investigation. The high court and Supreme Court judgements have pointed these things out, but they have just wagged an admonitory finger at the police, or occasionally called it a 'disturbing feature', which is a disturbing feature in itself. At no point in the trial has the police been seriously reprimanded, leave alone penalized. In fact, almost every step of the way, the Special Cell displayed an egregious disregard for procedural norms. The shoddy callousness with which the investigations were carried out demonstrates a worrying confidence that they wouldn't be 'found out,' and if they were, it wouldn't matter very much. They seem to have been dead right.

There is fudging in almost every part of the investigation.

Consider the **Time and Place of the Arrests and Seizures:** The Delhi Police said that Afzal and Shaukat were arrested in Srinagar based on information given to them by Geelani following his arrest. The court records show that the message to look out for Afzal and Shaukat was flashed to the police in Srinagar on 15 December at 5.45 a.m. But according to the Delhi Police's records, Geelani was arrested in Delhi on 15 December at 10 a.m.—four hours *after* they had started looking for Afzal and Shaukat in Srinagar. They haven't been able to explain this discrepancy. The high court judgement puts it on record that the police version contains a 'material contradiction' and cannot be true. It goes down as a 'disturbing feature'. Why the Delhi police needed to lie is a question that remains unasked, and unanswered.

When the police arrest somebody, procedure requires them to have public witnesses for the arrest, who sign an Arrest Memo and a Seizure Memo for what they may have 'seized' from those who have been arrested—goods, cash, documents, whatever. The police claim they arrested Afzal and Shaukat together on 15 December at 11 a.m. in Srinagar. They say they 'seized' the truck the two men were fleeing in (it was registered in the name of Shaukat's wife). They also say they seized a Nokia mobile phone, a laptop and Rs 10 lakh from Afzal. In his Statement of the Accused, Afzal says he was arrested at a bus stop in Srinagar and that no laptop, mobile phone or money was 'seized' from him.

Scandalously, the Arrest Memos for both Afzal and Shaukat have been signed in *Delhi*, by Bismillah, Geelani's younger brother, who was at the time being held in illegal confinement at the Lodhi Road Police

Station. Meanwhile, the two witnesses who signed the seizure memo for the phone, the laptop and the Rs 10 lakh are both from the J&K Police. One of them is Head Constable Mohammad Akbar (PW—Prosecution Witness—62) who, as we shall see later, is no stranger to Mohammad Afzal, and is not just any old policeman who happened to be passing by. Even by the J&K Police's own admission, they first located Afzal and Shaukat in Parimpura Fruit Mandi. For reasons they don't state, the police didn't arrest them there. They say they followed them to a less public place—where there were no public witnesses.

So here's another serious inconsistency in the prosecution's case. Of this the High Court judgement says, 'The time of arrest of accused persons has been seriously dented.' Shockingly, it is *at this contested time and place of arrest that the police claim to have recovered the most vital evidence that implicates Afzal in the conspiracy*: the mobile phone and the laptop. Once again, in the matter of the date and time of the arrests, and in the alleged seizure of the incriminating laptop and the Rs 10 lakh, we have only the word of the police, against the word of a 'terrorist'.

The **Seizures continued:** The seized laptop, the police said, contained the files that created the fake Home Ministry pass and the fake identity cards. It contained no other useful information. They claimed that Afzal was carrying it to Srinagar in order to return it to Ghazi Baba. The Investigating Officer ACP Rajbir Singh said that the hard disk of the computer had been sealed on 16 January 2002 (a whole month after the seizure). But the computer shows that it was accessed even after that date. The courts have considered this, but taken no cognizance of it. (On a speculative note, isn't it strange that the only incriminating information found on the computer were the files used to make the fake passes and ID cards? And a Zee TV film clip showing the Parliament Building? If other incriminating information had been deleted, why wasn't this? And why did Ghazi Baba, Chief of Operations of an international terrorist organization, need a laptop— with bad artwork on it—so urgently? To do a spell-check perhaps?)

Consider the **Mobile Cell-phone Call Records:** Stared at for long enough, a lot of the 'hard evidence' produced by the Special Cell begins to look dubious. The backbone of the prosecution's case has to do with the recovery of mobile phones, SIM cards, computerized call records, and the testimonies of officials from cell-phone companies and shopkeepers who sold the phones and SIM cards to Afzal and his accomplices. The call records that were produced to show that Shaukat, Afzal, Geelani and Mohammad (one of the dead militants) had all been in touch with each other very close to the time of the Attack, were uncertified computer printouts, not even copies of primary documents. They were outputs of the billing system, stored as text files that could have been easily doctored at any time. For example, the call records that were produced show that two calls had been made at exactly the same time from the same SIM card, but from *separate* handsets with *separate* IMEI numbers. This means that either the SIM card had been cloned or the call records were doctored.

Consider the **SIM Card:** To prop up its version of the story, the prosecution relies heavily on one particular mobile phone number—9811489429. The police say it was Afzal's number—the number that connected Afzal to Mohammad (one of the dead terrorists), Afzal to Shaukat, and Shaukat to Geelani. The police also say that this number was written on the back of the identity tags found on the dead terrorists. Pretty convenient. *Lost Kitten*! *Call Mom at 9811489429.* (It's worth mentioning that normal procedure requires evidence gathered at the scene of a crime to be sealed. The ID cards were never sealed and remained in the custody of the police and could have been tampered with at any time.)

The only evidence the police have that 9811489429 was indeed Afzal's number, is Afzal's confession, which as we have seen is *no* evidence at all. The SIM card has never been found. The Police produced a prosecution witness, Kamal Kishore, who identified Afzal and said that he had sold him a Motorola phone and a SIM card on 4 December 2001. However, the call records that the prosecution relied on show that that particular SIM card was already in use on 6 November, *a whole month before Afzal* is *supposed to have bought it!* So either the witness is lying, or the call records are false. The high court glosses over this discrepancy by saying that Kamal Kishore had only said that he sold Afzal a SIM card, not *this* particular SIM card. The Supreme Court judgment loftily says, 'The SIM card should necessarily have been sold to Afzal prior to 4.12.2001.' And that, my friends, is that.

Consider the **Identification of the Accused:** A series of prosecution witnesses, most of them shopkeepers, identified Afzal as the man to whom they had sold various things: ammonium nitrate, aluminium powder, sulphur, a Sujata mixy-grinder, packets of dry fruit and so on. Normal procedure would require these shopkeepers to pick Afzal out from a number of people in a Test Identification Parade. This didn't happen. Instead, Afzal was identified by them when he 'led' the police to these shops while he was in police custody, and introduced to the witnesses as an Accused in the Parliament Attack. (Are we allowed to speculate about whether *he* led the police or the police led *him* to the shops? After all, he was still in their custody, still vulnerable to torture. If his confession under these circumstances is legally suspect, then why not all of this?)

The judges have pondered the violation of these procedural norms but have not taken them very seriously. They said that they did not see why ordinary members of the public would have reason to falsely implicate an innocent person. But does this hold true, given the orgy of media propaganda that ordinary members of the public were subjected to, particularly in this case? Does this hold true, if you take into account the fact that ordinary shopkeepers, particularly those who sell electronic goods without receipts in the 'grey market', are completely beholden to the Delhi Police?

None of the inconsistencies that I have written about so far are the result of spectacular detective work on my part. A lot of them are documented in an excellent book called *December 13: Terror Over Democracy* by Nirmalangshu Mukherjee;[17] in two reports—*Trial of Errors* and *Balancing Act*—published by the Peoples' Union for Democratic Rights, Delhi; and, most important of all, in the three thick volumes of judgements of the trial court, the high court and the Supreme Court.

All these are public documents, lying on my desk. Why is it that when there is this whole murky universe begging to be revealed, our TV channels are busy staging hollow debates between un-informed people and grasping politicians? Why is it that apart from a few independent commentators, our newspapers carry front-page stories about who the Hangman is going to be, and macabre details about the length (60 metres) and weight (3.75kg) of the rope that will be used to hang Mohammad Afzal (*Indian Express,* 16 October 2006)? Shall we pause for a moment to say a few hosannas for the Free Press?

It's not an easy thing for most people to do, but if you can, unmoor yourself conceptually, if only for a moment, from the 'Police is Good/Terrorists are Evil' ideology. The evidence on offer *minus its ideological trappings* opens up a chasm of terrifying possibilities. It points in directions which most of us would prefer not to look.

The prize for the Most Ignored Legal Document in the entire case goes to the Statement of the Accused Mohammad Afzal under Section 313 of the Criminal Procedure Code. In this document, the evidence against him is put to him by the court in the form of questions. He can either accept the evidence or dispute it, and has the opportunity to put down his version of his story in his own words. In Afzal's case, given that he has never had any real opportunity to be heard, this document tells his story in his voice.

In this document, Afzal accepts certain charges made against him by the prosecution. He accepts that he met a man called Tariq. He accepts that Tariq introduced him to a man called Mohammad. He accepts that he helped Mohammad come to Delhi and helped him to buy a second-hand white Ambassador car. He accepts that Mohammad was one of the five fidayeen who was killed in the Attack. The important thing about Afzal's Statement of the Accused is that he makes no effort to completely absolve himself or claim innocence. But he puts his actions in a context that is devastating. Afzal's statement explains the inadvertent, peripheral part he played in the Parliament Attack. But it also ushers us towards an understanding of some possible reasons why the investigation was so shoddy, why it pulls up short at the most crucial junctures and why it is vital that we do not dismiss this as just incompetence and shoddiness. Even if we don't believe Afzal, given what we *do* know about the trial and the role of the Special Cell, it is inexcusable not to look in the direction he's pointing. He gives specific information—names, places, dates. (This could not have been easy, given that his family, his brothers, his wife and young son live in Kashmir and are easy meat for the people he mentions in his deposition.)

In Afzal's words:

> I live in Sopre J&K and in the year 2000 when I was there Army used to harass me almost daily, then said once a week. One Raja Mohan Rai used to tell me that I should give information to him about militants. I was a surrendered militant and all militants have to mark Attendance at Army Camp every Sunday. I was not being physically torture by me. He used to only just threatened me. I used to give him small information which I used to gather from newspaper, in order to save myself. In June/July 2000 I migrated from my village and went to town Baramullah. I was

having a shop of distribution of surgical instruments which I was running on commission basis. One day when I was going on my scooter S.T.F (State Task Force) people came and picked me up and they continuously tortured me for five days. Somebody had given information to S.T.F that I was again indulging in militant activities. That person was confronted with me and released in my presence. Then I was kept by them in custody for about 25 days and I got myself released by paying Rs 1 lakh. Special Cell People had confirmed this incident. Thereafter I was given a certificate by the S.T.F and they made me a Special Police Officer for six months. They were knowing I will not work for them. Tariq met me in Palhalan S.T.F camp where I was in custody of S.T.F. Tariq met me later on in Sri Nagar and told me he was basically working for S.T.F. I told him I was also working for S.T.F. Mohammad who was killed in Attack on Parliament was along with Tariq. Tariq told me he was from Reran sector of Kashmir and he told me that I should take Mohammad to Delhi as Mohammed has to go out of country from Delhi after some time. I don't know why I was caught by the police of Sri Nagar on 15.12.2001. I was boarding bus at Sri Nagar bus stop, for going home when police caught me. Witness Akbar who had deposed in the court that he had apprehended Shaukat and me in Sri Nagar had conducted a raid at my shop about a year prior to December 2001 and told me that I was selling fake surgical instruments and he took Rs 5000/- from me. I was tortured at Special Cell and one Bhoop Singh even compelled me to take urine and I saw family of S.A.R. Geelani also there, Geelani was in miserable condition. He was not in a position to stand. We were taken to Doctor for examination but instructions used to be issued that we have to tell Doctor that everything was alright with a threat that if we do not do so we be again tortured.

Afzal then asks the court's permission to add some more information:

Mohammad the slain terrorist of Parliament attack had come along with me from Kashmir. The person who handed him over to me is Tariq. Tariq is working with Security Force and S.T.F JK Police, Tariq told me that if I face any problem due to Mohammed he will help me as he knew the security forces and S.T.F very well . . . Tariq had told me that I just have to drop Mohammed at Delhi and do nothing else. And if I would not take Mohammad with me to Delhi I would be implicated in some other case. I under these circumstances brought Mohammed to Delhi under a compulsion without knowing he was a terrorist.

So now we have a picture emerging of someone who could be a key player: 'Witness Akbar' (PW 62), Mohammad Akbar, Head Constable, Parimpora Police Station, the J&K policeman who signed the Seizure Memo at the time of Afzal's arrest. In a letter to Sushil Kumar, his Supreme Court lawyer, Afzal describes a chilling moment at one point in the trial. In the Court, Witness Akbar, who had come from Srinagar to testify about the Seizure Memo, reassured Afzal in Kashmiri that 'his family was alright'. Afzal immediately recognized that this was a veiled threat. Afzal also says that after he was arrested in Srinagar he was taken to the Parimpora police station and beaten, and plainly told that his wife and family would suffer dire consequences if he did not cooperate. (We already know that Afzal's brother Hilal had been held in illegal detention by the SOG during some crucial months.)

In this letter Afzal describes how he was tortured in the STF camp—with electrodes on his genitals and chillies and petrol in his anus. He mentions the name of Deputy Superintendent of Police Davinder Singh who said he needed him to do a 'small job' for him in Delhi. He also says that some of the phone numbers mentioned in the charge sheet can be traced to an STF camp in Kashmir.

It is Afzal's story that gives us a glimpse into what life is really like in the Kashmir Valley. It's only in the Noddy Book version we read about in our newspapers that Security Forces battle Militants and innocent Kashmiris are caught in the cross-fire. In the adult version, Kashmir is a valley awash with militants, renegades, security forces, double-crossers, informers, spooks, blackmailers, blackmailees, extortionists, spies, both Indian and Pakistani Intelligence agencies, human rights activists, NGOs and unimaginable amounts of unaccounted-for money and weapons. There are not always clear lines that demarcate the boundaries between all these things and people, it's not easy to tell who is working for whom.

Truth, in Kashmir, is probably more dangerous than anything else. The deeper you dig, the worse it gets. At the bottom of the pit are the SOG and STF that Afzal talks about. These are the most ruthless, undisciplined and dreaded elements of the Indian security apparatus in Kashmir. Unlike the more formal forces, they operate in a twilight zone where policemen, surrendered militants, renegades and common criminals do business. They prey upon the local population, particularly in rural Kashmir. Their primary victims are the thousands of young Kashmiri men who rose up in revolt in the anarchic uprising of the early nineties and have since surrendered and are trying to live normal lives.

In 1989, when Afzal crossed the border to be trained as a militant, he was only twenty. He returned with no training, disillusioned with his experience. He put down his gun and enrolled himself in Delhi University. In 1993, without ever having been a practicing militant, he *voluntarily* surrendered to the Border Security Force (BSF). Illogically enough, it was at this point that his nightmares began. His surrender was treated as a crime and his life became hell. Can young Kashmiri men be blamed if the lesson they draw from Afzal's story is that it would be not just stupid, but *insane* to surrender their weapons and submit to the vast range of myriad cruelties the Indian State has on offer for them?

The story of Mohammed Afzal has enraged Kashmiris because his story is their story too. What has happened to him could have happened, is happening and has happened to thousands of young Kashmiri men and their families. The only difference is that their stories are played out in the dingy bowels of Joint Interrogation Centres, Army Camps and Police Stations, where they have been burned, beaten, electrocuted, blackmailed and killed, their bodies thrown out of the backs of trucks for passers by to find. Whereas Afzal's story is being performed like a piece of medieval theatre on the national stage, in the clear light of day, with the legal sanction of a 'fair trial', the hollow benefits of a 'free press' and all the pomp and ceremony of a so-called democracy.

If Mohammad Afzal is hanged, we will never know the answer to the real question: Who attacked the Indian Parliament? Was it the Lashkar-e-Toiba? The Jaish-e-Mohammad? Or does the answer lie somewhere deep in the secret heart of this country that we all live in and love and hate in our own beautiful, intricate, various, and thorny ways?

There ought to be a Parliamentary Inquiry into the 13 December Attack on Parliament. While the inquiry is pending, Afzal's family in Sopore must be protected because they are vulnerable hostages in this bizarre story.

To hang Mohammad Afzal without knowing what really happened is a misdeed that will not easily be forgotten. Or forgiven. Nor should it be.

Notwithstanding the 10% Growth Rate.

This essay was first published in *Outlook*, 31 October 2006.

[6]

SHOULD MOHAMMAD AFZAL DIE?

Nirmalangshu Mukherji

On 4 August 2005, the Supreme Court delivered its judgement on the case relating to the 13 December 2001 attack on the Indian Parliament. It acquitted S.A.R. Geelani and Afsan Guru, and reduced the sentence for Shaukat Hussain Guru, absolving him of all charges of conspiracy. However, it upheld the judgement of the high court in sentencing Mohammad Afzal to death for actively participating in the conspiracy to attack the Parliament and waging war against the Indian State. It also described Afzal as a 'menace to the society', a man whose 'life should become extinct' to satisfy 'the collective conscience of the society'.[1]

Within a day, the *Hindu,* a respected newspaper known for its coverage of issues of human rights and justice, commented on this judgement in its editorial. It took a characteristically human view of the verdicts on Geelani, Afsan and Shaukat. For Afzal, however, the paper joined the judges in speaking on behalf of the 'collective conscience of the society': 'There is no warrant for any special sympathy for Mohammad Afzal whose role as a conspirator in the Parliament attack case— which has been detailed by the prosecution and confirmed by three courts of law—has been established beyond a shadow of doubt.'[2]

With three of the 'estates of democracy' surrounding him, Mohammad Afzal has little chance of escaping the hangman. More significantly, as the noose tightens, Afzal will die in silence. There is yet the legislature— the first estate. Is there a case for Mohammad Afzal before the forum of the people?

Confession for the State

The judicial proceedings recorded two occasions on which Mohammad Afzal spoke before the law: his confessional statement before the police and his statement under Section 313 of the Criminal Procedure Code. There was also the 'disclosure statement' recorded by the police soon after his arrest. But disclosure statements by themselves are not admissible as evidence.

In his confessional statement, Afzal narrated the entire conspiracy and the operational details of the attack on Parliament.[3] The conspiracy story goes like this: Maulana Masood Azhar, the leader of Jaish-e-Mohammad, based in Pakistan, instructed, at the instance of the Inter-Services Intelligence (ISI), one Ghazi Baba, the supreme commander of the outfit in Kashmir, to carry out actions on important institutions in India. Ghazi Baba directed one Tariq Ahmed to arrange for an operation. Tariq got in touch with Mohammad Afzal and motivated him to join the jehad for the liberation of Kashmir. Afzal met Ghazi Baba and the plan was worked out. It was going to be a joint operation of Jaish-e-Mohammad and Lashkar-e-Toiba. Beginning with one Mohammad, Afzal arranged for several militants—Haider, Hamza, Raja and Rana—to bring huge quantities of arms, explosives and a laptop computer to Delhi, into pre-arranged hide-outs. In Delhi, the team got in touch with Afzal's cousin, Shaukat Hussain Guru, Shaukat's wife Afsan Guru and S.A.R. Geelani, a lecturer of Arabic in Delhi University.

In the beginning, the terrorists kept their options open between the Delhi assembly, UK and US embassies, the Parliament and the airport. Reconnaissance was conducted accordingly. However, Ghazi Baba instructed them over satellite telephone to attack the Parliament. In a final meeting on the night of 12 December 2001, the militants handed over Rs 10 lakh to Afzal, Shaukat and Geelani for their part in the conspiracy; they also handed over the laptop, to be returned to Ghazi Baba.

This story was presented by the police, argued for by the prosecution, propagated repeatedly in full colour by the print and visual media over three and a half years, and ratified by two courts of law. The prosecution's story was transformed into a telefilm by Zee TV. 'The film was shown to the then Prime Minister and the then home minister, and the media recorded their approval of the film,' Nandita Haksar wrote in her report 'Tried by the Media: The S.A.R. Geelani Trial'. The film was telecast repeatedly before the first judgement on the case was delivered.

Apart from Afzal's confessional statement, there was never an iota of independent evidence corroborating this story. Citing 'incontrovertible evidence' on the floor of the Parliament and holding Pakistan responsible for the attack, the government mounted a massive military offensive that brought India and Pakistan to the brink of war, with fingers on the nuclear trigger. Nearly 10,000 crore rupees were spent and 800 soldiers died in the war effort. Reportedly, over 100 children died and many farmers lost their livelihood due to heavy mining in the border areas. 'After the unfortunate incident,' the high court observed, 'the clouds of war with our neighbour loomed large for a long period of time . . . the nation suffered not only an economic strain, but even the trauma of an imminent war.'[4]

The Supreme Court has now set aside Mohammad Afzal's confessional statement with the following words: 'All these lapses and violations of procedural safeguards guaranteed in the statute itself impel us to hold that it is not safe to act on the alleged confessional statement of Afzal and place reliance on this item of evidence on which the prosecution places heavy reliance.'[5]

With the confession set aside, the story of a conspiracy linking the ISI, Masood Azhar, Jaish-e-Mohammad, Lashkar-e-Toiba, Ghazi Baba, Tariq and the rest disappears from the judgement of the court. All we've gathered—all that the court judgement tells us—is that five heavily armed men with rather commonplace names attacked our Parliament—and were all killed—and that Mohammad Afzal participated in the conspiracy. This, after five years, is all that we know about the 13 December attack. The entire media has failed to mention this single, enormous fact.

The Supreme Court's rejection of the confession had two parts. In the first, it mentioned a series of objections raised by the defence which the court found 'plausible and persuasive'.[6] However, the court held that 'it is not necessary to rest our conclusion on these probabilities'[7], since, in the second part, the court found some direct reasons to set aside the confession. The investigating agency, namely, the Special Cell of the Delhi police, violated even the minimal safeguards sanctioned under the otherwise draconian POTA. These included the denial of legal assistance to the accused after POTA was introduced in the case, failure to inform any relative, taking the accused back into police custody after the confession, and failure to give the confessor sufficient time to reflect before the confession. (The high court had observed earlier that Afzal's arrest memo was signed by Geelani's brother Bismillah while the latter was himself in 'illegal confinement'[8], and was forced to 'sign papers'.) According to the court, these violations themselves have a 'bearing on the voluntariness of confession'.

Why were these basic safeguards systematically violated? For an answer, it is worth discussing the 'probabilities' which the court found 'plausible and persuasive'; they lead us far beyond the restricted legal window through which the court looked at the Parliament attack case. For brevity, we will discuss just the issue of the timing of the confession.[9]

The confessions were recorded on 21 December 2001, after POTO was introduced in the case on 19 December. As noted, Afzal and Shaukat allegedly made disclosure statements immediately after their arrest on 15 December 2001. Displaying incredible loquacity, both Afzal and Shaukat had apparently poured out everything they knew about the conspiracy. Following these alleged disclosures, the police had already gathered most of the so-called facts of the case before 19

December. The confessions themselves did not contain anything that was not already available to the police on independent investigation based on the earlier disclosures. Why then were the confessions, allowed by POTO, needed?

More importantly, the judgement states, 'There was no perceptible reason why the accused should not have been produced before a judicial magistrate for recording a confession under the provision of CrPC.'[10] According to the court, the defence held that the accused were 'not prepared to make the confession in a court and, therefore, the investigating authorities found the ingenuity of adding POTA offences at that stage so as to get the confession recorded by a police officer according to the wishes of the investigators'. As noted, the court found this argument 'plausible and persuasive'.

Until alternative explanations are offered, the following picture emerges: The government wanted to use the 'window of opportunity' offered by the attack on the Parliament to go to war against Pakistan. After the investigations were virtually over within days after the attack, there was no evidence to link the attack with Pakistan-sponsored terrorism. Hence, POTO was belatedly introduced on 19 December; soon after, the government mobilized its troops. Afzal was made to confess before the media on the 20 December so as to lend credibility to the official confession to follow on 21 December. The eminent lawyer Shanti Bhusan suggested that 'the police failed to crack the case' as 'all the five militants died in the attack'. So, as an article in *Tehelka* (16 October 2004)[11] stated, the police 'framed people' in order 'to create a conspiracy case' for the government to take the country 'to the brink of a nuclear war'.

Once POTO was introduced, Rajbir Singh, an assistant commissioner of police in the special cell, and an 'encounter specialist', was made the investigating officer (IO) of the case. In his article 'Victims of December 13' (*Guardian* Weekly, 5 July 2005), Basharat Peer writes, 'Singh was already under a cloud when the home ministry, then under L.K. Advani, appointed him to head the investigation into the attack on the Indian Parliament.'[12]

The appointment was technically correct, yet one wonders if it was proper to appoint such a junior officer as IO in this immensely complex and sensitive case. The modus operandi of securing the confession throws light on the issue. With ACP Rajbir Singh as IO, the confession was obtained by DCP Ashok Chand in the special cell itself. It is not surprising that legal assistance was not offered, that no relatives were informed and that Afzal was taken back into police custody on some pretext. Things stayed within the special cell, no chances were taken. Mohammad Afzal was a pawn in the designs of the State.

Trial by Design

The introduction of POTO also allowed the trial to be held in the designated special court for POTA. The Indian law ministry appointed Shiv Narayan Dhingra as a special judge. Basharat Peer's comment on the appointment is telling: 'By the 1990s, he [Dhingra] was handling cases of terrorism and had earned the name "the hanging judge"[13].' The trial began in June 2002 in an atmosphere in which the trauma of an imminent war and the smoke from the pogroms in Gujarat hung over the nation, the country was baying for the blood of the accused after a massive propaganda by the police and the media, and POTA had become the law of the land.

Very few lawyers were willing to oblige: most 'did not want to be associated with the Parliament attack case'.[14] Moreover, the special judge ordered a 'fast track' trial in this immensely complex case. The trial lasted just over five months, in which time the prosecution presented eighty witnesses. It is hard to see how a fair trial could be accomplished under these conditions.

The defence of Mohammad Afzal, the key figure in the State-sponsored story of conspiracy, suffered the most. With great difficulty, Geelani's defence managed to produce some witnesses; Afzal had none. He had no legal defence in the period between his arrest on 15 December 2001 and the filing of the chargesheet on 14 May 2005; in other words, no counsel had studied the complex case. According to the Supreme Court judgement, when he 'declined to engage a counsel on his own'[15], the special judge appointed the noted criminal lawyer Seema Gulati, who took charge on 17 May along with her junior Neeraj Bansal.

On 5 June, all the defence lawyers agreed not to dispute postmortem reports, MLCs and documents related to the recovery of guns and explosive substances at the spot resulting in 'the drop of a considerable number of witnesses for the prosecution'. The court did not dispute the contention of the defence counsel at the Supreme Court that Gulati 'took no instructions from Afzal or discussed the case with him'[16]. Taking a strictly legalistic view, the court merely held that the 'counsel had exercised her discretion reasonably. The appellant accused did not object to this course adopted by the amicus throughout the trial'. It also states that on 1 July, Gulati 'filed an application praying for her discharge from the case citing a curious reason that she had been engaged by another accused, Geelani'[17].

On 2 July, Gulati's junior Neeraj Bansal was appointed amicus. Afzal protested against this nomination on 8 July and submitted a list of four senior advocates. Since none was willing to take up the case, Bansal continued as amicus for the rest of the trial. 'In capital cases,' Ram Jethmalani observed, 'particularly those that arouse public prejudice and anger against the accused making it difficult for them to arrange for their own defence, it is the duty of the court to provide adequate defence at state expense.' In response, taking a strictly legalistic view, the Supreme Court held that 'taking an overall view of the assistance given by the court and the performance of the counsel, it cannot be said that the accused was denied the facility of effective defence'[18].

The amicus, Neeraj Bansal, did not even pay a visit to his client. 'His presence and participation have caused confusion and prejudice vitiating the trial,' Jethmalani observed in a written submission on behalf of Geelani.[19] Afzal's wife Tabassum says in 'A Wife's Appeal for Justice' (*Kashmir Times,* 21 October 2004), 'The court appointed a lawyer who never took instructions from Afzal, or cross-examined the prosecution witnesses. That lawyer was communal and showed his hatred for my husband.'[20] The Supreme Court held that the 'criticism against the counsel seems to be an afterthought raised at the appellate stage'.[21] But where else could it be raised, and who could have raised it at the trial stage?

These concerns assume immense significance now that the Supreme Court has sentenced Mohammad Afzal to death on the sole basis of circumstantial evidence admitted in the trial. We must also note that this body of evidence was presented by an investigating agency widely known for false arrests and fake encounters. In the Parliament case itself it is now clear that the special cell tried to frame at least three innocent persons. Earlier, the high court had mentioned the production of false arrest memos, doctoring of telephone conversations and illegal confinement of people to force them to sign blank papers. As we saw, it is evident that false confessions were extracted by force.

This is not the place to study in detail the Supreme Court's handling of the circumstantial evidence against Mohammad Afzal. We will cite just two pieces of evidence to illustrate the general problem.

(1) The court held that Afzal knew the deceased terrorists since he identified them. Afzal also admitted the same in his confession. With the confession set aside, the sole evidence against Afzal is that he identified them in the morgue. The evidence has two parts: the identification memo prepared by the police (PW76), and Afzal's signature against the column 'identified by' in the postmortem report. As for the identification memo, the court relied on it because 'there was not even a suggestion put to PW76 touching on the genuineness of the documents relating to identification memo'[22]; in other words, Neeraj Bansal did not object. As for the signatures, the defence counsels decided

not to dispute the postmortem reports, as noted. It did not materially affect the other accused, but Afzal is likely to pay with his life for this decision taken without his consent. In his statement under Section 313 of the Criminal Procedure Code, Afzal said: 'I had not identified any terrorist. Police told me the names of terrorists and forced me to identify.'[23]

(2) It is a crucial part of the prosecution's story that the police explain how they reached Mohammad Afzal beginning with the site of attack; otherwise, the arrests would seem to be pre-planned rather than based on a chain of leading evidence. The prosecution claimed that the police finally reached Afzal through a sequence of arrests beginning with Geelani, whom the police could trace first because he held a mobile phone registered with the telecom company Airtel. But the letter from Airtel furnishing the call records and Geelani's residential address was dated 17 December 2001; all the accused had been arrested by 15 December. How could the police arrest Geelani two days before it got the phone records that 'led' them to him? This letter poses other serious problems for the prosecution's case regarding the actual date on which POTO was introduced in the case. However, the court did not 'consider it necessary to delve further' into this letter since 'no question was put to PW35—the security manager of Airtel'.[24] It further noted, 'none of the witnesses pertaining to the FIR were cross-examined'. Whatever be the legal merit of the court's judgement on

Afzal, the question arises as to whether there is a moral warrant for capital punishment on the basis of a trial like this.

A Surrendered Militant

The question of moral warrant arises from another more insidious direction. Given the involuntary nature of the confession, it is pertinent to reflect on the fact that Afzal agreed to sign the document at all. Was Afzal a free agent during those early turbulent days right after the attack when he was in police custody before and after making the confession? Could he afford to refuse the recording of his confession at that stage when he had already done the rounds with the police, allegedly incriminating himself in everything that the police wanted?

These queries are compounded by the fact, as repeatedly noted in all the judgements, that Afzal is a surrendered militant. Afzal was not only supposed to report regularly to the security forces, but was also under their surveillance. How could such a person mastermind and execute such a complex conspiracy? And how could a terrorist organization rely upon such a person as the principal link for their operation? Did he enter into some arrangement with the security forces to buy his survival? Some dark answers to these questions begin to form when we look at Afzal's statement 313.

The statement 313, unlike a confession under POTA, is made by an accused before the court rather than before a police officer; also, this statement is made when an accused is in judicial custody, not in police custody. The special judge of the POTA court recorded the fact that 'a surrendered terrorist has to mark his attendance with regular intervals at the STF, J&K'[25] (para 222). 'STF, J&K' stands for State Task Force, Jammu and Kashmir, a shadowy counter-insurgency outfit of the state. To our knowledge, this fact is stated only in Afzal's statement under Section 313 Criminal Procedure Code. With this citation, therefore, the special court judgement lends credibility to the statement. Furthermore, there are manifest instances of honesty and truthfulness in Afzal's statement 313. For example, Afzal did not shy away from admitting the possibly incriminating fact that he brought Mohammad from Kashmir and that he accompanied Mohammad when the latter purchased a second-hand Ambassador. The Supreme Court judgement recorded that when his lawyer attempted to deny this fact during the trial, Afzal intervened to insist that he had indeed accompanied Mohammad.

Pursuing the relevant paragraph of this statement then, we learn about the circumstances of Afzal's surrender to the BSF in 1993 in detail. Afzal states that he was frequently asked by the STF to work for them; he often paid large sums of money to the STF to escape detention; yet, he was detained as late as in 2000; he was asked to become a special police officer, which is an euphemism for 'police informer'; he met one Tariq in the STF camp; this Tariq was already working for the STF and he wanted Afzal to join the force as well; Afzal was introduced to one Mohammad by Tariq also in the STF camp; Tariq persuaded him to take Mohammad to Delhi from where Mohammad was planning to go abroad.

A number of disturbing consequences follow. First, Afzal was in close touch with the security agencies throughout 1993 to at least 2000. Second, three of the persons allegedly involved in the attack—Tariq, Afzal, Mohammad—the mastermind, the link and the leader of the attack—originated from the STF camp itself. In addition, we now know of a press report from Thane that four terrorists including one 'Hamza'—the same name as one of the terrorists killed in the Parliament attack—had been arrested by the Thane police in November 2000 and handed over to the J & K police for further investigation.[26]

Grave, unanswered questions surround the Parliament attack case even after three judicial pronouncements. Who attacked the Parliament and what was the conspiracy? On what basis did the NDA government take the country close to a nuclear war? What was the role of the State Task Force (J&K) on surrendered militants? What was the role of the special cell of the Delhi police in conducting the case?

It will be a travesty of justice to hang Mohammad Afzal without ascertaining answers to these questions. Given the momentous nature of these questions, for the future of Indian democracy, nothing less than a Parliamentary inquiry is needed to address them.

This essay was first published in the *Economic and Political Weekly*, 17 September 2005.

[7]

AFZAL MUST NOT HANG

Praful Bidwai

Our higher judiciary has come to play an ultra-conservative role that increasingly resembles its status in the 1950s and 1960s as a defender of privilege. Then, the Supreme Court and most high courts acted as bulwarks of opposition to egalitarianism and ruled against progressive measures, including land reforms abolition of privy purses and bank nationalization. They saw themselves as guardians of private property and interpreted freedoms and rights in largely individualistic terms.

It took a systemic upheaval—including changes in judicial appointment procedures, major shifts in the political balance of forces and the public mood, and a change of guard in the ruling party—before the higher judiciary stopped obstructing laws that promoted popular interest. Then followed a brief spring of judicial creativity with a liberal reinterpretation of fundamental rights and a flowering of public interest litigations.

Over the past decade or more, the process has been

reversed. The courts have handed down conservative judgements on numerous issues—from environmental protection to slum-dwellers' rights, from education to secularism, and from entrepreneurs' privileges to Bhopal. Recent verdicts show a consistent conservative inclination, whether on the Narmada dam issue (which failed to uphold the imperative of rehabilitation), labour rights (subordinated to employers' profit), social policy (reservations, tribal rights, and so on), and urban issues (on which it is totally elitist), not to speak of the Hindutva-is-secularism judgement (1995).

The courts' failures to deliver a modicum of justice to the victims of the Gujarat carnage in four-and-a-half years (barring retrial in the Zaheera Sheikh case), and to intervene to stop one of the greatest corporate frauds in India's history (Enron), contrast sharply with their zealous micro-management of urban issues, including large-scale demolitions in Delhi, which have destroyed thousands of livelihoods. All this has weakened the public's faith in the higher judiciary.

In one respect, today's justice system is even worse than its earlier conservative avatar. Earlier, judges usually took a lenient view of personal liberties, including the physical person's rights, and did not put an overly stringent interpretation on crime and punishment, with harsh sentences. For instance, the perpetrator of a crime was not equated with someone who conspires to commit it or is accessory to it.

Thus, Gopal Godse was not hanged for Gandhi's assassination, although he was fully complicit in that conspiracy. In 1983, the Supreme Court spelt out death penalty guidelines in the Machhi Singh case: as a rule, a murderer must be sentenced to life; capital punishment must be awarded in 'the rarest of rare' cases—where murder is committed in an extremely brutal, grotesque, diabolical or revolting manner, or to punish a particular caste or community, and so on.[1]

But in recent years, in response to terrorism, the judiciary's stance has considerably hardened. A decisive break was the Kehar Singh case (1989),[2] when a conspirator was sentenced to death, although he did not assassinate Indira Gandhi. This represents a definite erosion of liberal values, at a time when the abolition of the death penalty has emerged the world over as a precondition for a country being considered civilized.

Today, we are witnessing yet another, perhaps even more distressing, retrogression: in Mohammad Afzal's case pertaining to the Parliament House attack of 2001. Afzal's appeal against his death sentence was rejected by the Delhi High Court and the Supreme Court. Served with the infamous 'black warrant',[3] he was sentenced to be executed on 20 October 2006.

Afzal's hanging will be a grave miscarriage of justice and an offence to civilized conscience. It will have a profoundly negative impact on opinion in Kashmir at this extremely delicate juncture in the peace process. The widespread, spirited protests in the Kashmir valley are only the first sign of this.

The demand of all parties in Kashmir, barring the Bharatiya Janata Party (BJP), for clemency for Afzal represents the pervasive view that he was not directly responsible for the attack; nor is he beyond the pale of reform. The Indian state will commit a huge blunder if it does not prevent Afzal's hanging.

Lest it be contended that this is only a 'political' argument, considering the jurisprudential issues, it is nobody's case that Afzal personally committed murder or participated in the attack. Yet, he has been sentenced to death for murder (Section 302 of the Indian Penal Code), waging war against the state (Sections 121 and 121A) and criminal conspiracy (Sections 120A & B). On the face of it, the punishment is excessive and wholly disproportionate to the crime.

Afzal was tried under the Prevention of Terrorism Act (POTA), but sentenced under the Indian Penal Code. POTA clearly distinguishes between committing a terrorist act resulting in death (punishable by death), and conspiracy in the act (penalty, life imprisonment). It makes no sense to invoke a harsher law selectively when a specific anti-terrorist law exists.

The courts relied both on Afzal's own testimony—which showed that he, a surrendered militant, brought one of the five attackers (Mohammad alias Burger) from Kashmir to Delhi and helped him purchase a second-hand car—and on circumstantial evidence, which crucially hinges on the recovery of explosives from his house and records of cellphone calls with the five militants.

Both are open to doubt. The police say that they found explosives in Afzal's house when he was in custody, but cannot satisfactorily explain why they broke into it when the landlord had the key. This puts a question mark over the evidence. The cellphone records were all traced to a Delhi number used on an instrument allegedly found on Afzal when he was arrested in Srinagar. The instrument did not contain a SIM (Subscriber Identity Module) card; it was identified through the IMEI (International Mobile Equipment Identity) number (which is unique to each instrument).

But how did the police discover the IMEI number? This can only be done in two ways: you either open the instrument and read the number; or you dial a code and it is displayed. But the policeman who made the recovery said on oath that he neither opened the instrument nor operated it. (Remarkably, Jammu and Kashmir did not have a cellular network in 2001.)

It is open to doubt whether Afzal actually had the cellphone that was so crucial to establishing that he was in contact with all five terrorists. In the absence of conclusive evidence that the number belonged to and was used by Afzal, a deep, substantive conspiracy cannot be established.

There is another grey area. The police produced a dealer who deposed that Afzal had bought the cellphone on 14 December, with a new SIM card. But the police's own records show that the number was in use since 6 November.

All this casts doubt on the circumstantial evidence, and warrants circumspection and caution in concluding that Afzal was involved in a deep conspiracy.

Equally significant is Afzal's personal deposition of how he was drawn into secessionist militancy and crossed over to Azad Kashmir, but got disillusioned. As a surrendered militant, he was constantly harassed and subjected to extortion by the Special Task Force (STF). He claims that he was ordered by one Tariq, connected with the STF, to escort Mohammad to Delhi, and did so. This was never controverted.

The picture that emerges from the testimony is that of a person who does not readily lie and can be forthright to the point of incriminating himself. Minimally, this suggests that he is capable of acting in good faith, and not beyond reform.

Because Afzal did not commit murder, the death sentence verdict turns pivotally on the 'waging war against the state' charge. But such treason is marked by great ambiguity. The idea derives from the early medieval doctrine of *lese majeste*, which holds that any affront to the sovereign (the king, with his divine sanction), is always grave enough to deserve death.

A secondary premise is that Parliament House is an embodiment of sovereignty—not just metaphorically or symbolically. Therefore, attacking it is tantamount to waging war on India. This is surely a literalist over-reading. By this criterion, the members of the radical Dalit Panthers, who burned the Constitution in the 1970s, should have been hanged. Yet, the higher judiciary itself warned against such excess in 1951 vis-a-vis the Bihar police mutiny, during which the rebels fired on the army.

The inference that Afzal is guilty of waging war, murder and conspiracy is based on doubtful surmises. The element of doubt is so large that it would be unconscionable to extinguish a human life. President Kalam must act to prevent such miscarriage of justice. He should unhesitatingly commute Afzal's sentence. He has every power to review and reappraise the case. It is his moral and constitutional duty to apply humane criteria and ensure that misinterpretation of the law and anti-terrorist zeal do not result in death.

This essay first appeared in *Frontline*, 20 October 2006.

[8]

A DEATH SENTENCE AND
A TEA PARTY

Jawed Naqvi

If the Indian State doesn't yield to reason, Mohammed Afzal Guru will die. Much is being made of the day the Kashmiri man will be hanged. It is Jummatul Wida, the last solemn Friday of the holy month of Ramazan. Some politicians, playing to the galleries, have argued that the hanging should be postponed as it could otherwise send a wrong signal to Kashmir's alienated Muslims. The suggestion of course is meaningless, if also insensitive. There is no auspicious day to execute someone, legally or otherwise.

In the absence of any other remedy, Afzal and his family will no doubt seek a presidential pardon even if this means grudging admission of guilt. The long-drawn mechanism involved in the President's decision could allow him to live for a few more weeks, perhaps months, if he is lucky. But he will live on death row in Tihar Jail anxious to hear a verdict which can go any way. If Afzal has political sense he will know that in the prevailing atmosphere of hard-line measures to combat terrorism, anyone who takes a decision to spare his life would be mocked for the rest of their lives by India's right-wing Hindutva hordes.

The one material defence that could save Afzal had come not from his state-sponsored defence counsel at the trial court but from an account of the tragedy given by his wife Tabassum. It was published in the *Kashmir Times* on 21 October 2004.[1] The forceful argument of that appeal went unheeded at the trial court. Thus the most compelling reason to free Afzal was never produced before the trial judge. Tabassum was not summoned as a witness even once. We'll come to the crux of her harrowing tale in a moment.

However, at the heart of Afzal's woes is the Indian strategy to combat terrorism. The signal to adopt a hard-line position has come from the very top. It is thus that we find former police chief K.P.S. Gill, of Punjab notoriety, heading to the Indian heartland to exterminate Naxalites across this vast country.[2] Extermination is the word used by Mr Gill. The authority for the militarist enterprise came from elsewhere.

At the international level 'the war on terrorism' is led by two main dramatis personae: Messrs Blair and Bush. Blair is seen as the European face of the war, who claims to be as much a victim of terror as the United States itself, if not more. However, Britain's Constitution, like those of the rest of Europe, does not permit the death penalty, which is just the opposite of the way Bush would like it. The United States itself is vertically and horizontally divided over the issue of capital punishment, with a dozen states banning it. That federal law endorses the death penalty must be a source of strength for the right-wing administration.

And yet the only person so far convicted in the United States of involvement in the 9/11 attack—Zacarias Moussaoui—was spared capital punishment by the federal jury. We can take this as a rebuke to the face of the Bush administration, which tried every trick in the trade to send at least one surviving suspect of 9/11 to the gallows.

But Moussaoui would not be so lucky in India. Going by the experience of Afzal, he would have long ago made a detailed confession before a gaggle of specially invited TV journalists, who would have scooped their story in the lock-up where crime branch sleuths would serve them tea and biscuits.[3] If the cameras focussed on his hands they would see the handcuffs tightly secure around the wrists as the confession flowed. Moussaoui's testimony before Indian television cameras would be a repetition of what the police would have coerced from him, valid evidence under the anti-terror laws of the time. That the Supreme Court threw out Afzal's confession is a small victory for justice. The high court too castigated Afzal's trial by the media but that was too little and too late.

This is not to suggest that Mohammed Afzal Guru was blameless in the making of his own tragedy. The argument here is to hear him out fairly—which clearly didn't happen in the trial court—and then decide. Also, death by hanging is an abhorrent punishment laid down by India's colonial rulers. As we know, one of the charges against Afzal was that he had conspired to attack the Indian Parliament on 13 December 2001. In legal parlance he had sought to wage war against the

State. The same law was used against Gandhi and still continues to invite capital punishment.

It is odd that India's legendary democracy has refused to unlearn the lessons of colonialism whereas the erstwhile conquerors have cleansed themselves of the opprobrium by abolishing an inhuman law they had preached and practiced. There are disturbing indications that European nations are themselves becoming impatient with their vastly more civilized laws. This is to be expected in the face of provocations like the Madrid bombings and last year's July disaster that struck London's subway trains. But isn't that what the terrorists want—to subvert the core of Western democracies?

India has reasons to draw lessons from its own experience with terrorism rather than lean on someone else's methods of handing down retribution. For example, it should ask, how did the state benefit from the hanging of Maqbool Butt in Tihar Jail twenty-two years ago? Butt's appeal against his death sentence was pending since 1976. He was then hanged, suddenly, on a February morning in 1984 and buried within the prison premises. Did the death of this erstwhile leader of JKLF and conspirator in the hijacking of an Indian Airlines plane to Pakistan in 1971 deter eventual violence in Jammu and Kashmir? Did the death of countless others in encounters and in torture chambers help the Indian cause? And what does death mean to the new genre of rebels—the fedayeen? They are there to embrace death anyway, so what can the poor Indian hangman do to deter them?

Deprived of the spirit of Nehru or Gandhi, there is a bloody-mindedness in India today as never before.

Television anchors are baying for blood and quick retribution. Right-wing Hindutva hordes are not alone in seeking short-cut methods that override constitutional safeguards promised to an accused. Even after the courts berated the media for carrying Afzal's illegally acquired 'confession', the TV channels are still using the footage to beef up their TRP ratings. The '*desi*' versions leave the avowedly rabid Fox TV way behind in their one-track obsession with consumable terror stories.

Where does all this leave someone like Afzal's wife? All over India, Tabassum wrote in the *Kashmir Times*, people have condemned the attack on Parliament. 'And I agree that it was a terrorist attack and must be condemned. However, it is also important that the people accused of such a serious crime be given a fair trial and their story be fully heard before they are punished. I believe that no one has heard my husband's story and he has so far never been represented in the court properly,' Tabassum's protest note said.

"I appeal to you to hear our story and then decide for yourselves whether justice has been done. Afzal's and my story is the story of many young Kashmiri couples. Our story represents the tragedy facing our people.'[4] Anyone who cares for Indian democracy should read Tabassum's appeal. They would see that she has a point or two that can mark the difference between life and death for hundreds of thousands of Afzals facing state terror in Kashmir, and elsewhere in India.

A version of this essay first appeared in *Dawn*, 2 October 2006.

HOUR OF THE HANGMAN

THE AFTERMATH OF AFZAL'S HANGING
MAY BE LONG AND COSTLY

Ashok Mitra

Bloodthirstiness, thou art afoot, and not just in Iraq. Shrieking followers of the second largest party in our country, led by no less a person than a former Prime Minister, are out on the streets demanding the immediate hanging of Mohammad Afzal, with no intervention on the part of the President. A recent Supreme Court judgement, annulling the decision of the Andhra Pradesh governor to reduce from ten years to five the prison term passed on a Congress party worker, has added to their zeal.[1] The power, under Article 161 of the Constitution, of a state governor to grant pardon or to suspend, remit or commute sentences is not, according to this judgement, absolute, but subject to judicial review. What applies in the case of a state governor, the Bharatiya Janata Party maintains, should equally apply to similar discretionary powers enjoyed under Article 72 by the President.

Even those who hold an ideological position altogether contrary to the BJP's might be tempted to take a cynical view of the proceedings: where scores of young people are being systematically gunned down in Kashmir without let or hindrance by the security forces, the state-organized ceremonial killing of another person, who happens to bear the name Mohammad Afzal, would not make much of a difference. Cynics are honourable members of society; their wry comments often put to shame unthinking, righteous-minded people in authority. In the present instance, though, there is genuine ground for doubting the relevance of banter. For Afzal's case involves several complex issues all jumbled together: moral, legal, constitutional and, most importantly, political.

The moral or humanitarian issue may, for the present, be kept aside. Thanks to the likes of George W. Bush and Tony Blair, morality has, at this moment, lost its value as currency; we would therefore do no worse by concentrating initially on the legal and constitutional aspects of the case. Afzal's conviction is largely based on a confession extracted from him. Under what circumstances or on the basis of what assurances this confession was obtained is yet to be ascertained. In many countries, including the United States of America, self-incrimination is barred, either by law or by the nation's Constitution. As far as India is concerned, this is still a grey area.

It would nonetheless be both awkward and irrational to refuse to face a number of facts. Afzal was not a direct participant in the attack on Parliament; he was nowhere in the vicinity of New Delhi on that particular day. The Supreme Court has also disbelieved the claim that he belonged to any organized terrorist group. All he has been found guilty of is conspiracy for murder. However, under the Prevention of Terrorism Act, the penalty of death does not apply in the case of conspiracy, and it was under the provisions of POTA that he was arrested and sent for trial. The authorities chose to tag an additional charge against him—abetment of murder—under the Indian Penal Code, a procedure not adopted for others prosecuted along with him. It is a puzzle why this seeming invidiousness was not taken notice of by the nation's highest judiciary.

Should the legal doubts fail to cut much ice with the ultimate arbiters of Afzal's destiny, the constitutional issue would still remain much in the fore. The ruling in the Andhra Pradesh case notwithstanding, the power of the President to remit the death penalty, it can be argued, continues to hold good, for Article 72 has to be read along with Article 74. The latter article makes it obligatory for the President to go by the decision of the Council of Ministers in all matters under the sun. Whether to commute the death sentence on Afzal is a matter on which the President, too, is obliged to go by the views of his council of ministers. Moreover, Clause 2 of the Article writes in an exclusive directive: 'The question whether any, and if so what, advice was tendered by ministers to the President shall not be inquired into in any court.' No such admonition is attached to the provisions under Article 161 defining a state governor's power to offer pardon or commute a sentence; the goose-gander analogy therefore does not apply. The final decision whether to hang Afzal or allow him to live rests squarely on the Union council of ministers. And this is where the political factors involved come into overwhelming consideration.

All political parties that have a relevance in Jammu and Kashmir—with the exception, of course, of the Bharatiya Janata Party—are agreed that Afzal must be allowed a reprieve from the death sentence; they are worried no end over the fearsome repercussions in the valley if Afzal, who hails from there, is put to death. The state unit of the Congress had obviously gone along with this view, and an impression was created to the effect that the Congress chief minister of the coalition regime in the state had spoken to the Union government requesting commutation of the death sentence.[2] The leaders of the Congress party in the state of Delhi have their own calculations to make; it is a Hindu-majority territory, and there is the danger of the BJP, with its jingoist stance in the matter, running away with the Hindu vote in the not-so-distant state Assembly polls. The Congress chief minister of Delhi has therefore lost little time to inform the Centre that she and her colleagues want Afzal to hang. Presumably because of party pressure at the national level, the Jammu and Kashmir chief minister has now backtracked somewhat: what he had earlier conveyed to the Centre, he has laboriously explained, was his personal opinion; he is in principle against the death penalty.[3] The Jammu and Kashmir chief minister hems and haws because Afzal hails from his state; the Delhi chief minister feels equally qualified to go on record on the issue since the crime was perpetrated in her state. But while the murders were committed within the Parliament complex, the conspiracy was supposedly hatched elsewhere. That apart, does not the Parliament of India belong to the entire country and was not the attack targeted against MPs coming from all over the country? Along with the government of Delhi, that of every other state too, it follows, ought to be asked to submit their views in the matter; the Union Cabinet, before rendering its advice to the President, must take into account this collective judgement.

In any event, should not the larger long-range interests of the nation be of prime consideration here? According to New Delhi's own admission, incidents of violence are on the wane in the Valley; infiltrations across the border have also shrunk significantly in recent months. Cross-border travel has resumed, even though on a partial scale. The heads of government of the two countries met recently at Havana and pledged to set up a joint consultative machinery to resolve outstanding bilateral issues. By far the major such issue is that of Kashmir. One has only to recollect the upheaval that took place in the Valley when, more than a decade ago, another person accused of terrorist activities, Maqbool Butt, was hanged. Does the Government of India want a repeat of that gory season? What the fallout of such a turn of events would be on India's defence and security expenditure and, therefore, on funds that can be spared for economic development and social welfare, is not hard to imagine.

Hanging a person is a process which does not take beyond ten minutes. The aftermath of such a hanging might be devastatingly long and enormously costly. The crowd thirsty for Afzal's blood is, thus viewed, the biggest enemy of the country.

This essay first appeared in the *Telegraph*, 10 November 2006.

[10]

HANG THE TRUTH

Sonia Jabbar

Those arguing that Mohammad Afzal's death sentence should not be commuted to life imprisonment are doing so on the grounds that a) the Indian courts pronounced the sentence after a fair trial and appealing to the President for intervention would be undermining the judiciary and b) it would send out a wrong message—that India is a weak State, soft on terrorism. Both arguments are flawed.

First, the Presidential review is hardly illegal or controversial, enshrined as it is in the Indian Constitution under Article 72, precisely to check cases where the death penalty is deemed as too harsh a sentence or in cases where there has been a miscarriage of justice. Second, the Supreme Court had a choice of sentencing Afzal under two laws for conspiracy and chose the harsher (Sec 120B read with Sec 302 IPC), not because it was the only law that would serve the purpose but because *it believed that only the death sentence could satisfy the Indian public:* '. . . the collective conscience of the society (sic) will only be satisfied if capital punishment is awarded to the offender.'[1]

So the court projecting the imagined desires of an imagined society tosses the ball into the court of the citizens of India, and the citizens of India, citing the judgement, toss the ball right back into the courts in an absurd game of circular logic.

The second argument of 'sending out a wrong message' is intimately tied up with assumptions of Afzal's guilt. Television shows are full of people indignantly proclaiming Afzal to be a terrorist and the mastermind of the Parliament attack.

Both are patently false.

The investigation agencies and the prosecution named three masterminds: Maulana Masood Azhar, chief of Jaish-e-Mohammad, and the prisoner exchanged for the IC 814 hostages; Ghazi Baba, alleged chief of Jaish operations in J&K; and Tariq Ahmed, a Kashmiri. The Supreme Court acknowledged that Afzal was neither the mastermind nor the executor of the Parliament attack, and that it had no direct evidence but only circumstantial evidence to prove Afzal's guilt as a conspirator. The Parliament attack was a serious and unprecedented crime and Afzal's sensational arrest two days after the attack, his trial and subsequent debates on the death sentence all serve to divert attention away from the crime itself.

On 13 December 2001, an Ambassador with five armed men entered the Parliament premises while it was in session. The security personnel apprehended the car and in the exchange of gunfire that lasted for thirty minutes, all five terrorists were killed. Seven policemen on duty at the time also lost their lives. Considering the enormity of the attack and the fact that we nearly went to war with Pakistan, the Home Ministry, in a departure from all norms (where the CBI would investigate such

a case), named ACP Rajbir Singh of Delhi Police as
Investigating Officer. And who was this man? A self-
proclaimed encounter specialist, who later conducted
the dubious Ansal Plaza encounter and was finally
disgraced with charges of corruption when he attempted
to blackmail a couple of west Delhi businessmen.

Not surprisingly, the Parliament attack investigation
was completed in a record seventeen days. But with the
Supreme Court setting aside Afzal's confessional
statement as unreliable, there is nothing else that
confirms the sequence of events or the conspiracy
theory linking the masterminds with Afzal. Who were
the attackers? Who were the masterminds? What was
the conspiracy? Five years after the Parliament attack
the Indian public still doesn't know the truth and seems
to be content to hang a man, close the case and sweep
the rest under the carpet.

Afzal's own statement recorded by the courts blows
holes in the police version, and yet the honourable
judges have selectively ignored the startling revelations.
According to Afzal he joined the JKLF in 1990 but was
disillusioned and surrendered before the BSF in 1993.
As the courts noted, Afzal had to regularly report to the
Special Task Force (STF) as per laws governing
surrendered militants. Regarding Tariq Ahmad, named
by the prosecution as one of the masterminds, Afzal
says that it was at an STF camp that he was introduced
to Ahmad. As for Mohammad, the terrorist killed in
the attack, Afzal says that Tariq took him to meet the
DSP of Humhuma Chowk, Davinder Singh, who then
introduced him to Mohammad. Singh allegedly
instructed Afzal to take Mohammad to Delhi, find him
accommodation and help him out generally.

Afzal admits doing this and accompanying

Mohammad to purchase the Ambassador, which was later used in the attack. According to Afzal, his role began and ended with these specific acts done at the behest of Tariq Ahmad and Davinder Singh, and yet no one—the investigating team, the prosecution, the learned judges or the phalanx of eager reporters—have bothered with investigating this further. Where is Tariq Ahmad? Is there any truth to the Davinder Singh link? Does none of this merit investigation?

For those who may be tempted to dismiss this story, Afzal begs us to investigate the call records to his cellphone and to Mohammad's from Srinagar. He claims that there were many calls to both these numbers from DSP Davinder Singh. This is easily verifiable and yet has not been investigated. Curiously, although the apex court alludes[2] to the terrorist Mohammad making and receiving other phone calls from Dubai and Mumbai, no one has thought it fit to scrutinize these telephone numbers. Why has the focus of the investigation been limited to Afzal, Shaukat, Geelani and Afsan Guru and the ambit of investigations not enlarged?

The role of the police is also suspect because of their claims and counter-claims. The Jammu and Kashmir and Delhi Police both announced that Mohammad was Sunny Ahmad Qazi, the very same 'Burger', the hijacker of IC 814. On investigation the CBI found this to be untrue. If this were so, why has the CBI not probed into the other claims made by the same agencies? On 19 December, the Thane Police Commissioner, S.M. Shangari, made a startling announcement. He said the Mohammad killed in the Parliament attack was the same Mohammad Yasin Fateh Mohammad of the Lashkar-e-Toiba whom he had arrested in Mumbra (a Mumbai suburb) on 23

November 2000 and handed over to the J&K Police on 8 December 2000.

The Commissioner was well acquainted with the terrorist and described Mohammad in detail, giving his address in Pakistan, and even narrating how he fought the police in hand-to-hand combat after he was grievously injured. And yet, the following day, IGP Rajendran of Kashmir Range rubbished the claim as 'totally false'. He was backed by DCP Ashok Chand of Delhi Police who issued a completely misleading press statement, 'The terrorist named Hamza killed in Delhi on Dec. 13th was definitely different from the one Thane police claim to have arrested last year.'[3] Thereafter we hear nothing further on this. Who was lying and why? If the Parliament attack Mohammad was different from the one captured in Thane, what happened to the Thane Mohammad, why was he not produced? Why wasn't anyone even remotely interested in cross-checking this claim?

And how hard did the investigators try to catch the alleged masterminds, Masood Azhar, Ghazi Baba and Tariq Ahmad? The Delhi Police claims that the Srinagar Police arrested Afzal and Shaukat when they were going to meet Ghazi Baba with Mohammad's laptop and Rs 10 lakh in cash. In which case why were they nabbed before, and not followed to the rendezvous with Ghazi Baba? Why did the Srinagar Police not want to catch the suspected mastermind when they had specific information, allegedly from Afsan Guru, Shaukat's wife, about this meeting?

On 3 April 2002, Judge S.N. Dhingra asked the Delhi Police whether the Interpol had been alerted for the arrest of the three masterminds, to which a senior police officer replied that the 'matter was being looked into'. Thereafter, we hear nothing more about Interpol or any further activity to apprehend the masterminds. And apart from a few members of civil society no one—not the judges, the many security experts, the investigating agencies, the Indian intelligence agencies, Members of Parliament, journalists—thought it fit to demand a probe. In 2003, nearly two years after the Parliament attack, Ghazi Baba was killed by the BSF in a routine operation in Srinagar. One can only assume that this was done without the knowledge and coordination of the team investigating the Parliament attack, or more care would have been taken, perhaps, to capture him alive, bring him to trial and get to the truth of the conspiracy.

If I were the mastermind, would hanging Afzal deter me from planning further attacks, or would it only confirm my suspicions that India is content to leave me untouched as long as they get *somebody* to hang? The Supreme Court observed, 'The challenge to the unity, integrity and sovereignty of India by these acts of terrorists can only be compensated by giving the maximum punishment to the person who is proved to be the conspirator in this act . . .'[4] I beg to differ. Afzal is the reddest herring that has appeared before the Indian republic in a long time, and the challenge to this country's 'unity, integrity and sovereignty' would be far better met by conducting a thorough and professional probe into the Parliament attack instead of hanging a man who is so clearly the scapegoat in the whole sordid affair.

This essay was first published in a slightly different form, in the *Hindustan Times*, 17 October 2006.

[11]

GUILTY OF AN UNSOLVED CRIME?

Mihir Srivastava

'Five heavily armed persons stormed the Parliament House complex and inflicted heavy casualties on the security men on duty. This unprecedented event bewildered the entire nation and sent shockwaves across the globe. In the gun battle that lasted thirty minutes, these five terrorists who tried to gain entry into the Parliament when it was in session, were killed. Nine persons including eight security personnel and one gardener succumbed to the bullets of the terrorists and sixteen persons including thirteen security men received injuries. The five terrorists were ultimately killed . . .'

—From the Supreme Court judgement
on the attack on the Indian Parliament

Six years and three judgements later, we still do not 'reliably' know who attacked Parliament on 13 December 2001. What we do know is that Mohammad

Afzal Guru, the alleged conspirator, was awarded the death penalty, but is he being made a scapegoat? Is Afzal being held guilty for a crime that is still unsolved?

Consider this: the 'comprehensive investigation' of the attack on Parliament was completed in seventeen days flat by the investigators, the Special Cell of the Delhi Police. The prosecution story of who attacked Parliament, which is popularly believed to be the real story, is based on the confession of the main accused under the Prevention of Terrorism Act (POTA), Afzal Guru, to the police, but the Supreme Court itself has dubbed this confession, and thus, in effect, the conspiracy theory behind the attack floated by the police, as 'unreliable'.[1]

There are twelve accused in the Parliament attack case. Five of them—Mohammad, Tariq, Hamza, Rana and Raja—were killed when they tried to lay siege on Parliament. Three—Ghazi Baba, Masood Azhar and Tariq, allegedly the masterminds behind the attack and Lashkar-e-Toiba (LeT) and Jaish-e-Mohammad (JeM) operatives—were never arrested; Ghazi Baba was shot in an encounter with security forces in 2004 (his body was recognized by Afzal's brother). Only four of the twelve accused were arrested: Afzal Guru, his cousin Shaukat Hussain Guru, Shaukat's wife Afsan Guru and S.A.R. Geelani, a teacher of Arabic in Delhi University. Not one of them was convicted under POTA charges. Geelani and Afsan were acquitted.

Shaukat was sentenced to ten years' rigorous imprisonment because he knew about the conspiracy. Afzal was given the death sentence on the charges of murder and waging war against the State.

The thoroughness with which the investigations of

such an important case were carried out can be judged by the remarks made by the Delhi High Court. The court has pulled up the investigators for the production of false arrest memos, doctoring of telephone conversations and the illegal confining of people to force them to sign blank papers.[2] Though, as Nandita Haksar, Geelani's lawyer, points out, despite these observations, 'the courts did not pass any strictures against the officers for their shoddy and illegal investigations.'

There is no direct evidence against Afzal. None of the eighty prosecution witnesses ever even alleged that Afzal belonged to or was in any way associated with any terrorist organization. He has been awarded the death sentence entirely on the basis of circumstantial evidence. Afzal did not shy away from admitting the possibly incriminating fact that he brought Mohammad from Kashmir and that he accompanied him when the latter purchased a second-hand Ambassador, two days before the attack. The Supreme Court, too, in its judgement, observes that even when his lawyer attempted to deny this fact during the trial, Afzal insisted that he indeed had accompanied Mohammad.[3]

But Afzal maintains that he did this at the behest of the Special Task Force (STF) of the Jammu and Kashmir police. Afzal alleged in a letter to his lawyer Sushil Kumar in the Supreme Court that Davinder Singh, Deputy SP of Humhama in Jammu and Kashmir, asked him to take Mohammad to Delhi and arrange for his stay there. 'Since I was not knowing the man . . . but I suspected this man is not Kashmiri, as he did not speak Kashmiri,' wrote Afzal.[4] Nandita Haksar charges that the facts of this letter were never put on record before the courts.

It is clear from the case records that Afzal is a surrendered militant who gave himself up to the BSF in 1993. Further, Afzal told the court that he was frequently asked by the STF to work for them (a senior police official has confirmed this to *Tehelka*). He said the STF extorted large sums of money from him for not arresting him. But he was detained as late as 2000 and was offered the job of a special police officer. He met Tariq (a co-accused, who is absconding) in the STF camp, where the latter was working. It was Tariq who introduced Mohammad to him in the STF camp. The alleged role of the STF in the Parliament attack, as per the court record, has not been investigated at all. Davinder Singh confirmed that no investigator ever got back to him and sought clarification on his alleged role in sending Mohammad to Delhi with Afzal's help. 'Why will they ask me this? He [Afzal] is saying this to save his own skin,' said Singh.

Denying the allegations, Singh asked, 'Do you want to say that we are behind the Parliament attack?' He also acknowledged that he had once detained Afzal for interrogation. 'We had reliable information that he knew the whereabouts of Ghazi Baba, one of the most dreaded terrorists in Kashmir [and an accused in the case]. But we couldn't get anything out of him and let him go.'

Later, the Delhi Police Special Cell had only Afzal to identify the bodies of the five assassins gunned down in Parliament. There is no other corroborative evidence that sheds light on the identities of these five terrorists. However, in court, Afzal denied identifying them. 'I had not identified any terrorists. Police told me the names of the terrorists and forced me to identify them,'

Afzal told the court in his statement made under Section 313 of the Criminal Procedure Code.[5]

In the absence of any direct evidence against Afzal, the Supreme Court said in its judgement: 'The incident, which resulted in heavy casualty, has shaken the entire nation and the collective conscience of the society will only be satisfied if capital punishment will be awarded to the offender.'[6] Haksar does not agree with the court's view. 'The Supreme Court,' she says, 'has not passed any strictures against the corrupt officers for their shoddy and illegal investigations and has held that there is no direct evidence against Afzal. However they have confirmed the death sentence because they believe that this death is necessary to assuage Indian citizens.'

Another controversy that was brushed aside in the investigations was one that again pointed to a possible Jammu and Kashmir police connection with the Parliament attack. The Thane Police swung into action after the identity of the five terrorists killed in the Parliament attack was made public. S.M. Shangari, the then Thane Police commissioner, claimed that his force had arrested four LeT operatives and one of them had the same name as a militant killed in Parliament: Hamza.[7] These four terrorists were handed over to the Jammu and Kashmir Police on 8 December 2000. In addition there was a stark similarity in the blueprints, arms and ammunition seized from these four arrested in Thane and what was recovered from the slain terrorists in Parliament.

K. Rajendra, the then inspector-general of J&K Police, rebuffed Shangari's enquiries. He was reportedly quoted by a Thane daily that no such person was ever handed over by the Thane police and that Hamza is a common Muslim name.[8] He dismissed it all as a case of mistaken identity. To this, Shangari responded by saying that he had only mentioned that it could possibly be the same person because the name was common; he had not said they were the same person. Just to make sure, Shangari then sent an official to Delhi with a photograph of Hamza.

Tehelka contacted Shangari, who retired a few years ago as the director-general of Maharashtra Police. 'They were sent to Jammu and Kashmir on the orders of the Thane district court,' he said. 'I do not know what happened after that. This issue was not new. The intelligence agencies were aware of it. We send them periodic reports on these issues.' The crucial question of whether Hamza's photograph—sent from Thane—was matched with that of the slain Hamza in the Parliament attack remains unanswered.

'Mistaken identity can only be proved once we are sure of the identities. It cannot be a matter of speculation,' says Nirmalangshu Mukherji, human rights activist and author of the book *December 13*. For instance, there is no clarity till date on who Mohammad—the man whom Afzal admits having accompanied to Delhi at the behest of the STF—was. After the attack, the police claimed that Mohammad was the leader of the suicide squad, and was also involved in the IC-814 hijack in which he was codenamed 'Burger'. The police had said at that time that it would show pictures of Mohammad to the wife of Ripan Katyal who was killed by the hijackers of IC-814. 'Burger' is believed to have stabbed Katyal on that flight. However, as per court records, after being

mentioned in the charge sheet and in Afzal's confession,
this move to corroborate Mohammad's identification
was not followed up. So, as Haksar points out, 'In fact,
we do not know the identities of the five men who
attacked Parliament and were all killed.'

As per the charge sheet, the JeM supreme commander
in India, Ghazi Baba, was in touch with Afzal and
Shaukat through satellite phone number 8821651150059
and Swiss telephone number 491722290100. Here,
again, the police didn't investigate the matter any
further. The charge sheet records, 'A request for
obtaining the call details of the international telephone
numbers and satellite phone numbers, which figured
during the investigation of the case, has been made to
Interpol, but the report is still awaited.' This was in
May 2002. After this mention, it was never again
registered in the court record or pursued by the
investigating agencies. This was confirmed by Sushil
Kumar, Afzal's lawyer in the Supreme Court. There is
no mention of the Interpol report in the case records.'
What happened to the Interpol report? Where was this
international call coming from? This omission assumes
significance if it is considered in the light of what Afzal
had to say on these phone calls, 'If phone number
records will be seen carefully the court would have
come to know the phone number of STF. I was not
given chance in the designated court to tell the real
story,' Afzal wrote to his lawyer Kumar.

Afzal says he was under duress to make a particular
kind of statement in the media and then in the
confession. In a letter to Kumar, he clarifies: 'In Srinagar
at Parompora police station [after he was arrested]

everything of my belongings was seized and then they beat me and threatened me of dire consequences regarding my wife and family. Even my younger brother was taken in the police custody.'

The fact that he was under threat and duress, and was instructed to utter only a select few things that suited the prosecution story, to the media is clearly shown when the investigating officer of this case, Rajbir Singh, then ACP in the Special Cell, shouted at Afzal in front of the rolling cameras, when the latter said 'Geelani is innocent.' Shams Tahir Khan of *Aaj Tak* did the interview. He told the court in his submission that Singh shouted at Afzal, directing him not to say a word about Geelani. 'Rajbeer had requested us not to telecast that line spoken by accused [Afzal] about Geelani. So when the programme was telecast on 20 December this line was removed.'

Afzal made a confession on similar lines a day later on 21 December. While Geelani refused to confess, Afzal explained, 'This was first told to me by Rajbir Singh . . . if I will speak according to their wishes they will not harm my family members and also gave me false assurances that they will make my case [the case against him] weak so that after some time I will be released.'

The same confession was cited as 'incontrovertible evidence' on the floor of Parliament. And it was the basis on which Pakistan was held responsible for the attack. As a reaction, the Central government mounted a massive military offensive that brought the neighbours to the brink of nuclear war. The Delhi High Court observed: 'The nation suffered not only an economic strain, but even the trauma of an imminent war.'

Further, Afzal was denied proper legal assistance. He had no defence lawyer in the period between his arrest on 15 December 2001, and the filing of the charge sheet on 14 May 2005; in other words, no counsel had studied the complex case. The court appointed Neeraj Bansal as amicus curiae.

Afzal's wife Tabassum had this to say on Bansal's efforts in the court: 'The court-appointed lawyer never took instructions from Afzal, or cross-examined the prosecution witnesses. That lawyer was communal and showed his hatred for my husband.'[9] Afzal's lawyer in the high court, Colin Gonsalves, says, 'Amicus curiae is an aid to the court and not a defence lawyer.' In an application dated 8 July 2002, to the trial court, Afzal expressed his helplessness. 'I am not satisfied by the state counsel appointed by the court. I need a competent senior advocate. The way the court is treating with me I could not get justice.'

The holes in the prosecution story are too big to be missed. And the problems start at the very beginning, with the question of S.A.R. Geelani's arrest. The prosecution claimed that the police reached Afzal through a sequence of arrests beginning with Geelani, whom the police could trace first because he held a mobile phone registered with the telecom company Airtel. But the letter from Airtel furnishing the call records and Geelani's residential address was dated 17 December 2001; all the accused had been arrested by 15 December.

How did the Delhi Police get to Geelani, the first person arrested in the case, in the early hours of 15 December, just two days after the attack? There was no evidence in the case records to link Geelani to the site of crime till the details of call records from Airtel arrived on 17 December, which was cited by the police in their charge sheet as the clue that enabled them to trace Geelani (and through him, Afzal). So how and why did they pick him up two days earlier?

The police allegedly recovered slips of paper from the pockets of the slain terrorists, each containing five mobile numbers. None of these numbers belonged to Afzal or Geelani. Further, the police recovered six SIM cards and three mobiles from the deceased terrorists. Apart from this, it is alleged that Afzal's number 9811489429 was written on all the fake I-cards of 'Xansa Web City', recovered from the militants. This fact emboldened the police to zero in on Afzal but the SIM card for this number has not been recovered. Further, the fake I-cards that carried Afzal's number were not sealed. They were just pasted on paper and remained in the investigators' custody. Prosecution Witness 8, Head Constable Ashwini Kumar posted at the Parliament Street police station, was among the first to arrive at the site of the crime and prepared the seizure memos listing the articles recovered from the site and the bodies. He told the court that as far as he could remember, 'the telephone number was not written on the seizure.'

When it was pointed out in court that there was no known way to reach Geelani before the receipt of the Airtel letter, the Delhi High Court gave the benefit of doubt to the prosecution, saying that this could be a 'typographical error'. The court did not 'consider it necessary to delve further' into the controversy emanating from this letter since 'no question was put to the security manager of Airtel,' the Supreme Court observed. Further, 'none of the witnesses pertaining to the FIR were cross-examined.'[10]

But if there was a 'typographical error' and the Airtel note was written before 17 December, it creates another problem. The note said, 'responding to the police request for call records refer to section 3/4/5/21/ 22 POTO . . .' The Prevention of Terrorist Activities Ordinance (POTO) was promulgated only on 19 December that year. How could the police apply POTO provisions before the ordinance came into force?

Call records placed before the court were uncertified computer printouts. These records show that two calls were made between Shaukat and Afzal, the called and calling numbers were identical, the time and location were identical, but the IMEI number—the handset's number apart from the phone number—was different. According to the records, on 13 December 2001, at 11:19:14 a.m., two calls were made simultaneously from Afzal to Shaukat but from different handsets. The same thing occurred again at 11:32:40 a.m.

As per the charge sheet, Inspector Mohan Chand had already mounted surveillance on Geelani's mobile on 13 December 2001. The next day, a call from Srinagar was intercepted on this cell. The sequence of arrests began on the morning of 15 December, with Geelani's arrest at 10, Afsan's at 10.45, and Afzal's and Shaukat's in Srinagar at 11.30 a.m. Allegedly, Geelani disclosed information leading to the arrest of the others. But in his disclosure statement, Geelani doesn't mention any mobile phone, and he denied in court that he told the police about any mobile number that belonged to Afzal or Shaukat.

Coming back to the crucial question, then: How did the police first reach Geelani? At best, this remains an unsolved riddle.

There also remain a lot of unanswered questions as far as the investigation into the Parliament attack is concerned. Who masterminded the attack on Parliament and what was the conspiracy? What was the STF doing with surrendered militants? What was the role of the Special Cell of the Delhi Police in conducting the case? Till these questions are satisfactorily answered, a shadow will continue to be cast over Afzal's death sentence.

This essay is a composite of two related reports that first appeared in *Tehelka*, 28 October 2006.

POPULAR FEELING IN KASHMIR IS VALID GROUND TO GRANT AFZAL PARDON

A. G. Noorani

'Constitutional law is not at all a science, but applied politics, using the word in its noble sense.' It was in the spirit of Justice Felix Frankfurthen's aphorism that, on 8 September 1974, US President Gerald Ford granted pardon to his predecessor, Richard Nixon.[1] He acted against public opinion and in the knowledge that it would cost him the election in 1976, which it did. History has, however, vindicated him.

A nation torn apart by race riots, protests on Vietnam and partisanship could ill-afford the trauma. The US's prestige in the world would have sunk low. The Special Watergate Prosecutor, Leon Jaworski, was flooded with appeals to challenge the pardon. His memoirs, *The Right and the Power,* record agonizingly why he refused to do so.[2]

Never before has Kashmir witnessed such intense unanimity—from Chief Minister Ghulam Nabi Azad to the separatists—as on pardon for Mohammad Afzal.

What we need to ask ourselves is why do Kashmiris react as they do? The answer we shirk is that they feel oppressed and humiliated. Afzal is no popular hero, unlike Maqbool Butt. But it is their own tragic condition they lament each time. They protest thus. We must address earnestly the roots of Kashmiri alienation, not dismiss the popular clamour as some do.

'It looks to me to be narrow and pedantic, to apply the ordinary ideas of criminal justice to this great public contest. I do not know the method of drawing up an indictment against a whole people. I cannot insult and ridicule the feelings of millions of my countrymen.'[3] What Edmund Burke said in his immortal speech in Britain's House of Commons on 22 March 1775, on conciliation with the US, is true of Kashmiris as well.

Has anyone ever heard of a death sentence on a man who was undefended at his trial? This monstrous miscarriage of justice warrants retrial. The Supreme Court has used emotional language. No PM has accused militants of 'treason' as it has. Medieval rulers ordered humans to 'become extinct'. Judges do not. The court rightly calls the crime a 'terrorist act' but ends up holding that it 'might very well be an act of waging war'.[4] The two judges on the bench claim 'to view the expression with the eyes of the people of free India' and 'dissociate ourselves from the old English and Indian authorities', create new law and send a man to the gallows, along with some basics of criminal jurisprudence.

Both must be saved. All Constitutional tests would justify pardon on one ground alone—popular feeling in a state charged with alienation, where a peace process is underway.

B.R. Ambedkar told the Constituent Assembly on 29 December 1948: 'The home minister who would be advising the governor on a mercy petition . . . would be in a better position to advise the governor having regard to his intimate knowledge of the circumstances of the case and the situation prevailing in that area.' There, then, are relevant factors. They are all the more true of the Union home minister when advising the President apropos Kashmir. It is germane to the power of pardon.

Clamour for Afzal's scalp comes ill from men who have, like accused persons of the lesser breed, avoided trial for over a decade in the Babri Masjid demolition case. The chief among them, L.K. Advani, shamelessly said that it was 'a political case' and did not involve 'moral turpitude' (20 December 1999).[5] What a message by the then Union home minister to militants all over the country.

Commenting on judicial independence, De Smith, an eminent authority on constitutional law, asked whether this implied 'that judges should be entirely aloof from public sentiment and always disregard the strength of local feeling on an issue before them? If not, to what extent should judges take into account consideration of public policy, and how far can the government or its unruly supporters or opponents be permitted to determine what is the public interest? Judges not infrequently have to determine what is in the public interest, or whether a transaction is contrary to public policy, or whether it is necessary to impose a deterrent sentence because of the prevalence of a social evil; and in coming to such decisions, they are expected to have some regard to the general sense of the community and not to rely merely on idiosyncratic opinions. Moreover, in some political contexts, the courts allow the executive or the House of Commons the first and last word.'

It is preposterous to cry 'violation of the rule of law'. The power of pardon is an integral part of the legal process that begins with arrest and investigation and proceeds to trial and sentence. Public policy is as valid a consideration in the grant of pardon as it is in the decision to launch or withdraw a prosecution.

English texts speak of 'political' in two different senses: 'a party political', which is motivated by expediency or party loyalty. The Supreme Court rightly struck down pardon in a case of this kind on October 2006.[6] But 'political' is used in another sense also, which is synonymous with considerations of the State or the public interest.

In Britain, the Attorney General (AG) exercised for long the power to launch prosecutions for certain offences and to withdraw all prosecutions in his sole discretion. He consults ministers, if at all, if he so wishes. The Franks Committee on the Official Secrets Act, 1911, noted that he 'may consult ministerial colleagues before taking his decision to prosecute. He will do this in cases where he thinks there may be important considerations of public policy or of a political or international character to be taken into account'. Thus, even if there is a clear offence of breach of official secrecy, the AG will not bring a case if these considerations apply.

Two distinguished AGs have expounded the law in terms which bear directly on Afzal's case. Delivering the Sir George Bean Memorial Lecture in Manchester on 29 October 1978, Samuel Silkin said that the need to enforce the law should sometimes be balanced by political considerations. 'What if their enforcement will lead inevitably to law-breaking on a scale out of all proportion to that which is penalized or to consequences so unfair or so harmful as heavily to outweigh the harm done by the breach itself?'[7]

One consideration that had to be borne in mind, Silkin said, was the fear that minority groups, believing themselves to be unprotected and under attack, might react. 'If I make my decision on a party political basis, I deserve all the criticism which I am likely to receive. But if I ignore political considerations in the widest sense of that term, then I am failing in my responsibilities and courting disaster.'

Lord Shawcross's letter to *The Times* (London) of 29 July 1989, is a locus classicus on the subject. It concerned the proposal to prosecute Nazi war criminals. The AG's discretion was 'not to be settled by Parliament'. He repeated Lord Simon's dictum that there is no greater nonsense talked about the AG's duties in this context than the suggestion that he should prosecute because there is what the lawyers call 'a case'. He should consider 'all the relevant facts'. That would include 'public morale and order' and 'public policy and interest in the widest sense'.

If Advani's officials had succeeded in the parleys with the Hizbul Mujahideen in 2000, is there the slightest doubt that its chief, Syed Salahuddin, and his men would have received pardon? So, undoubtedly, would the Naga militants if the talks with them succeeded. Conditions for pardon are common in peace accords. In the Federalist Papers, Hamilton supported giving this power to the executive, rather than the legislature, so that 'in seasons of insurrection or rebellion' an offer of pardon is made in time instead of 'letting slip the golden opportunity'[8] for peace. That is certain to happen in Kashmir if Afzal is executed.

This essay first appeared in the *Hindustan Times*, 24 October 2006.

[13]

SATYAMEVA JAYATE?

WITH REGARD TO THE IMPENDING EXECUTION
OF MOHAMMAD AFZAL GURU IN TIHAR JAIL

Shuddhabrata Sengupta

A few days from now, a man called Mohammad Afzal Guru, son of Habibullah Guru, currently resident in Ward Number 6 of Jail Number 1 in Tihar Central Prison in Delhi, will probably hang to satisfy the bloodlust of the Indian republic, unless the President of India thinks otherwise. A few weeks ago, I recall reading the NDTV newscaster Barkha Dutt's breathless three cheers (in NDTV Columns, 20 September 2006)[1] for the fact that India retains the death penalty (so that the indignant tears in the eyes of television presenters like herself, and the loved ones of murder victims, can be wiped away with each rope that tightens around the neck of condemned prisoners).*

---

* Subsequently, on 11 November, Barkha Dutt wrote another column in the *Hindustan Times* titled 'Warning, Handle With Care', where she does a volte face, arguing for sparing Afzal's life (so as to ensure

At times like this, when hangmen are asked to practise their moves, nothing comes more handy than the Teflon-coated enthusiasm for capital punishment of television crusaders. Great democracies, like the United States of America, the Islamic republics of Iran and Pakistan, the People's Republic of China, the Democratic People's Republic of Korea and enlightened States like the Kingdom of Saudi Arabia are

---

Kashmir does not go up in flames—a variant of the position that Ghulam Nabi Azad allowed to be ascribed to him). She does this while simultaneously criticizing a host of other arguments that have been made in favour of a commutation of the death sentence on the grounds that they amount to an assertion of Afzal's innocence. No substantive critiques of the death sentence on Afzal, mine included, have ever tried to comment on Afzal's purported innocence or guilt. All that some of us have been trying to say is that Afzal's statements indicate that he was acting under compulsion and that they point to the possibility of a wider nexus, one that includes elements of the state apparatus, in the entire 13 December episode. Our demand is that this needs further investigation before any decision can be made. First, it would be a gross miscarriage of justice were we to condemn a man to death by holding him responsible for the things he may have been forced to do, especially while those who compelled him to do what he did remain untouched because of the positions they hold or held. Secondly, a thorough investigation of the matter in its entirety, which is necessary before we can apportion responsibility, culpability or blame with any justice and precision, requires Afzal to live, and to testify. Barkha Dutt is unwilling now to let Afzal hang, on strictly 'pragmatic' grounds. However, she has not recanted her principled support for the death penalty as an instrument of justice, nor does she bring up the matter of the implications of Afzal's statement. She merely parrots the charge that Afzal is a terrorist and that 'he needs to be punished, and punished hard'. In doing so, Barkha Dutt wants Afzal to live, but not to be able to have his say. She does not want to listen to what he is saying, or to think about its implications. She condemns him, essentially, to death by silence.

known for their zeal in retaining the death penalty as
a necessary part of State ritual. The Republic of India
is in eminent company, and I am grateful to Barkha
Dutt for making me remember that. I need not advance
moral and ethical arguments against the death penalty
here, because they have been so well countered by Ms
Dutt. Never mind the fact that States that have done
away with the death penalty have lower rates of violent
crime, never mind the fact that the innocence of people
condemned to die has often been established after they
have been executed. Ms Dutt has demonstrated that the
death penalty is the balm that comforts her agonized
soul. And many of those who argue that the President
should not in fact assent to the petition filed by Afzal's
family are also arguing that Afzal must hang so that
Indian democracy and the loved ones of those who died
defending the Indian Parliament may rest in peace. The
dignity of the Indian republic hinges on the lever that
will catapult Afzal into the empty space under the
gallows in Tihar Jail. As the noose tightens, our polity
will blossom with renewed vigour.

In championing capital punishment, Barkha Dutt
also joins the illustrious pantheon of the good and the
great in India, such as Shri L.K. Advani, Shri
Maninderjeet Singh Bitta (of the All India Anti-Terrorist
Front) and Shri Buddhadev Bhattacharya who have all,
from time to time, publicly expressed their desire to see
different people hanged to death. Politicians such as
Ghulam Nabi Azad who have apparently pleaded for a
'postponement' of Afzal's execution in view of 'prevailing
circumstances' are as cynical as those (especially in the
BJP) who demand that Afzal be hanged as soon as
possible while simultaneously demanding that the

unfortunate man called Sarabjit Singh who is held in death row in a Pakistani prison be released.

Broadly echoing the Ghulam Nabi Azad line (with some nuanced differences) is the gerontocracy of the Communist Party of India, which has not found fault with the verdict, only expressed an apprehension about the consequences of its execution. The central leadership of the Communist Part of India (Marxist) has maintained an undignified and convenient silence, even though its prominent legislator in Kashmir, Yusuf Tarigami, has publicly opposed the death penalty for Afzal. Farooq Abdullah of the National Conference in Jammu and Kashmir has suddenly discovered what he calls 'innocence' in Mohammad Afzal Guru in an interview given to Karan Thapar, and this is somewhat belated, because he never said a word about the 13 December case while he was a coalition partner of the then ruling NDA. Presumably, the National Conference's sensitivity to the issue of human rights violations in Jammu and Kashmir has an inverse relationship to the fact of its being in office in that state.

Even Rahul Mahajan, the illustrious son of the late BJP leader Pramod Mahajan, has attempted to pave his entry into the bosom of nationalist politics (somewhat derailed by the embarrassing episode pertaining to the circumstances that led to the public disclosure of his flirtation with cocaine) by participating in a BJP Yuva Morcha (Youth Front) meeting in Mumbai. His indignation at the prospect of Afzal continuing to live was evident when he said, 'The way the nation is being held at ransom by certain people [asking for clemency for Afzal] is disgusting. How can we pardon a terrorist mastermind? My blood was boiling when I saw the news and when they [BJP] asked me to participate in the morcha, I immediately agreed.' He indicated that his willingness to join the campaign against any deferral or clemency in the matter of Afzal Guru was evidence of his commitment to the BJP: 'I have been brought up in the BJP and the party is in my blood. I will definitely participate in such events in future, especially if the issue is close to my heart.' Clearly, patriotism, commitment to the BJP, 'anti-terrorist' activism and an implacable hatred for Afzal Guru run furiously alongside traces of other and equally powerful narcotic substances in Rahul Mahajan's bloodstream.

The only Indian politician of any stature who has publicly expressed a principled opposition to the death penalty, and to capital punishment as such, is the DMK patriarch K. Karunanidhi. The Indian political class's romance with the death penalty is not anything new, and we must remember that even Mohandas Karamchand Gandhi could see nothing wrong in Bhagat Singh being hanged. Capital punishment and the core values of Indian nationalism seem to have a close relationship. Perhaps they are both predicated on the idea that the nation-state and the rule of law demands sacrificial victims from time to time to re-invigorate the tired vitality of its foundations. The Indian State hanged Kehar Singh when it could not find anyone else to hang in order to restore it's vitality in the Indira Gandhi assassination case, and this time, Mohammad Afzal Guru must serve that necessary function. Perhaps Giorgio Agamben—whose rediscovery of the concept of the pariah-turned-sacrificial victim of the foundational violence of the State through the term *Homo Sacer*— has found such contemporary resonance in the light of

Abu Ghraib and Guantanamo Bay—needs to turn his attention to the precincts of the maximum security ward in Tihar Jail. Mohammad Afzal Guru is as likely a candidate today as any for the status of Homo Sacer.

Recently, Vir Sanghvi, another eminent media mandarin, wrestled with his conscience about whether or not Afzal should hang in a large op-ed piece in the *Hindustan Times* (15 October 2006),[2] next to a smaller piece from Karan Thapar[3] that hesitantly takes a different view. And like all good Indian liberals who won debating prizes in high school, Sanghvi too does this by dispassionately examining the pros (good strong signal to 'terrorists') and cons (this damn inconvenience of the fact that he did not really have a legal defence) of execution before saying something like 'Um, yes, maybe, there will be some good that can come out of hanging him, because you know, it might, you know, stop a hijacking, because, you know, you can't really hijack a plane to ask for a dead man to be brought alive, can you.' Impeccable reasoning, and so much more reassuring for Vir Sanghvi the next time he checks in to fly. Dead Afzal, no hijackers. It's as simple as that. In fact we should logically follow through with the Sanghvi logic to propose that all the prisoners in Tihar Jail be summarily executed tomorrow. It would solve the burgeoning Indian aviation industry's security concerns for the next ten years. Conscientious citizens like Barkha Dutt and Vir Sanghvi should be invited to conduct executions, preferably live, on television (there is always such a shortage of hangmen, and it would make for such good reality TV, and people could phone in saying how much more tranquil they feel when they watch an execution) in order to redeem frequent-flyer points against swift and successful hangings. The more they hang, the higher they will fly. Fasten seat belts and hang a Kashmiri.

I wish I were in Delhi, where I could get more of a sense of what is going on, talk to people, get a grip on the fact that there are faces that I would see and voices that I would hear of many people I know who would not be as hysterically celebratory about hanging people in prisons as the firm of Dutt, Sanghvi & Co. But all I can do is read what I can where I am from the Internet. So my day begins (when I get online) by typing the words 'Afzal', 'Guru' and 'hanging' on Google, and hoping that I can soon add 'clemency' or 'commutation' to my search string to yield some hopeful result. When I did add the word 'clemency' or 'pardon' recently, I got a result that confirmed my long-held views on the wisdom inherent in our republic's judicial apparatus. The Lords Justices of the Supreme Court of India, in another recent judgement, have sent out a thinly veiled warning addressed to the President and to state governors, instructing them to act with caution, or else provoke a judicial review of the executive authority of the presidential and gubernatorial powers. Their words suggest that the President must exercise the utmost restraint and consideration, and not be carried away by passion, in arriving at any decision regarding the death penalty awarded to Mohammad Afzal Guru.

It seems remarkable to me to think that the State's decision to kill a man in cold blood should be prefaced in terms of reason, caution, consideration and restraint, and that the mere consideration of reasons to save that life should be qualified by terms that suggest that even the entertainment of such a thought could be unreasonable, excessive, rash and impudent.

I have remarked on the sagacity of the Supreme Court of India on other occasions, especially when the Lords Justices have passed innovative verdicts that suggest that illegal squatters on urban land should think more carefully about inclement weather, but I am once again amazed at the wisdom and sophistication that some Lord Justices of the Supreme Court, and other distinguished legal professionals like Soli Sorabjee, our erstwhile Attorney General, have displayed in suggesting that even the banal human quality of compassion, or the ordinary, commonplace tendency to doubt that justice has been done when an accused person has gone unheard, or apprehensions about the unleashing of a new spiral of violence, can on occasion be wild, unreasonable, excessive and ever so intemperate. It is evident from the tenor of their pronouncements that cheap sentiments like sympathy, or ordinary doubts about the due processes of trial, or worries about more loss of life, when seen through the exalted filter of national security, are but irritating excesses that need to be held in check. It is as if truth alone must not triumph over what the Supreme Court, the Ministry of Home Affairs and the Intelligence Bureau deem acceptable for the health of the republic.

In view of this, we might as well propose an amendment to the Constitution such that the national motto be expanded to read 'Sravoccha Nyayalaya-cha-Guptachara Vibhaga-cha-Griha Mantralayasya Satyameva Jayate'. Such a move would yield a national motto that would render a resonant and precise statement about the present status of the concept known as 'Truth' in the Indian republic, especially in the wake of the events of 13 December 2001. To have all manner

of truths, especially crassly inconvenient and common
ones—such as the fact that the Indian State is a brutal
colonial power that holds Kashmir and parts of the
North-East with the aid of 'shoot at whim' laws such
as the Armed Forces Special Powers Act—emerge
triumphant will simply not do. We need refined and
processed truths—such as those that condemn
Mohammad Afzal Guru to hang.

Still, it is possible that A.P.J. Abdul Kalam (the
man, not necessarily the President, or the erstwhile
weapons designer) may have some residual human
qualities that may make him look askance at the fact
that Mohammad Afzal Guru is sentenced to be hanged
in a few days on the basis of statements that actually
clearly implicate agencies of the Indian government
such as the Special Task Force (STF) that operate in the
territory of Jammu and Kashmir in the affair of the
attack on the Indian parliament. That is why the
Supreme Court must rush to protect A.P.J. Abdul
Kalam the President from being swayed by A.P.J.
Abdul Kalam the human being. No untoward
considerations, such as the possibility of the outbreak
of rage in the wake of a blatantly unfair execution, or
the simple injustice of a man being killed for being
trapped in circumstances that were totally beyond his
control, must be allowed to stay the President's or the
hangman's hand. He has listened to Afzal's son and
wife. He has given them his time, and that shows how
magnanimous the Indian State can be, and now, he
must say no. Afzal must die.

We do not need a reminder of the fact that Afzal's
alleged involvement in the planning of this attack is the
only reason why he is being sentenced to die. Unlike

other instances of the award of capital punishment, where the accused are likely to be people who have actually killed other people in particularly heinous ways, Afzal is accused only of being an actor in a conspiracy, a cog in the wheel of terror. His was not a hand that held a gun on that day. He fired no shots, killed no one. He was caught because his phone number was in the phone directory in one of the mobile phones found on the person of one of the dead terrorists. In a letter written to his Supreme Court defence lawyer, Afzal points out that his mobile phone also has numbers of STF personnel, and the same logic by which he is implicated in the conspiracy of 13 December should logically lead to an investigation of the STF personnel's role in the event.

If that is so, then it would be natural for us to expect that all leads as to who else may be implicated in this conspiracy would have to be exhausted before any one of the conspirators or actors (in this case Afzal) is given the ultimate punishment. We know that Afzal did not have adequate legal representation in the course of his trial, but we also know that he made statements that the court took note of, in the sense that they are in the court records, which include statements that implicate officers of the STF in Jammu and Kashmir. These are public documents, and they have been meticulously collated in Nirmalangshu Mukherjee's courageous and disturbing book on the 13 December case (*December 13: Terror over Democracy*).[4] This book is available at any good bookshop in Delhi, and I am amazed that the media has not in fact made more of this story than it has.

Perhaps, once again, phone calls from the Intelligence

Bureau and the Home Ministry to editorial offices of newspapers and television channels have done their job. That is the charitable explanation, that the majority of the media has acted out of fear. The uncharitable explanation is that the media is silent about Afzal's relationship with the STF for the same reason that it was so vocal in loud mouthing S.A.R. Geelani's presumed culpability in the same case. The mainstream media, to a very large extent, is not an organ that takes orders from the intelligence apparatus. It is, in fact, a *part* of the intelligence apparatus. The 13 December case will go down in the history of modern India as an instance that revealed the extent of embedding of the intelligence apparatus of the Indian State within the so-called 'free' media in India.

In this delicate game of silence and overstatement, the courts have based their indictment of Afzal partly on the statements made by him and partly on confessions extracted under brutal physical and mental torture in police custody, and the majority of the reporting in the media has conveniently overlooked the fact that the names that have been named by Afzal in these very statements point in the direction of the Indian government's security, intelligence and counter-insurgency apparatus in Jammu and Kashmir. The 'needle of suspicion', to use another favourite Supreme Court phrase, is pointing all over the place, but no one seems to be looking. There is a pattern here that we need to recognize—when things are obvious, look away, and when truths need to be manufactured, use every tool in the book to manufacture them.

We need only to remember that, barring Shams Tahir Khan of *Aaj Tak,* no other journalist present during Afzal's infamous press conference stage-managed by Rajbir Singh—the sometime decorated special cell police officer, encounter expert and part-time extortionist—had the gumption to report that Afzal had in fact stated that S.A.R. Geelani was in no way involved with the events of 13 December. All other journalists and the news channels that they represented, who had been present at that 'encounter' with the truth according to the Delhi Police's Special Cell, had fallen in line with Rajbir Singh's 'request' to edit out that part of Afzal's testimony. The only English language national level newspapers or publications that more or less consistently maintained an independent tone were the *Hindu* and, to some extent, *Frontline*. The only news website that toed a slightly different line was rediff.com, and the only detailed unbiased reports that were published could actually only be found in regional newspapers and publications, mainly in Kashmir, and one, oddly, in Kerala.

What this suggests is that the intensity in the court's and the national mainstream media's desire to execute Afzal and to focus on him alone actually constitutes a move to consign aspects of the truth of what lay behind the events of 13 December, and the possible part played in them by the 'deep state' in India, into a kind of oblivion—a black hole of judicially mandated and media-packaged silence from which nothing can be recovered for posterity. With Afzal's death, the possibility of concrete evidence for alternative explanations behind the events of that day will die. We will never know who or what entity actually masterminded the shootout in the Parliament that almost provoked a nuclear war and ensured the legislation of the infamous and now repealed Prevention of Terrorism Act (POTA) by the then BJP-led NDA ruling alliance. If the sentence is carried out, we will never know how much the shadowy senior echelons of the intelligence community in India, or the then Home Minister and Deputy Prime Minister L.K. Advani, or the then Defence Minister George Fernandes, or the then Prime Minister A.B. Vajpayee knew about the fact that a medical and surgical equipment salesman and surrendered JKLF militant called Mohammad Afzal Guru was being 'cultivated' through torture, threats and extortion by STF personnel and serving military and para-military officers. We will never know as to whether or not this 'cultivation' led up to the processes that included his being instructed to take a man called Mohammad to Delhi, who eventually turned up as the body of a slain terrorist outside the Indian Parliament in Delhi on 13 December. If Afzal dies, the deep state in India will just get a few fathoms deeper, and many uncomfortable secrets will die in its depths.

As I write this, I am sitting in faraway London, looking at pictures of Andamanese skulls, composite photographs of prisoners in British prisons and fingerprint impressions of convicts, taken in unnamed colonial prisons in nineteenth-century India. Sometimes I do this in two rooms scattered on the campus of the University College of London that houses the remains of what was once founded as the National Eugenics Laboratory by Francis Galton. Galton championed the idea that all social problems could be solved by lessons learnt through indexing, recording and measuring bodies and minds. The truths he sought to legislate, about innate criminality and intrinsic genius, about racial characteristics and inherited traits, were to be made concrete by measuring heads and deducing patterns from accumulated fingerprint impressions. In a series of haunting photographs, Galton produces what he calls 'photo-composites'—anthropometric images obtained by layering portraits on to each other so that the features blend in to create a composite face. A face that takes something from all the faces that go into it. So you have the average criminal, the average lunatic, the average East End Jew, the average of eight Andamanese crania. When I think of the events that unfolded on 13 December 2001, I cannot but help think of Galton's photo-composites, and his attempts at deducing the extent of criminality in a given population by producing an average image based on the statistical relationships of the distance of their noses from their chins. Remember how Mr Advani, the then home minister, said on 13 December that the slain 'terrorists' 'looked like Pakistanis'. Perhaps he had an image of the 'average' Pakistani stored in the database in his cranium, with which he could compare the features of the dead men and come to this remarkable conclusion. Afzal's indictment, too, is an instance of the photo-compositing method of jurisprudence. He is a Kashmiri Muslim man of a certain age, he once was a JKLF activist, he moved often between Srinagar and Delhi for reasons to do with his business. It goes like this—you take any Kashmiri Muslim man of a certain age, and they should look and sound adequately Kashmiri, you identify the fact that they may sympathize or may once have sympathized with the movement to rid Kashmir of brutal military occupation (which is not hard to do, because most human beings would want an end to the

particular oppressions that beset them), you zero in on
the fact that he moved between Delhi and Srinagar with
some frequency, and you mix these facts together to
produce the face of a terrorist. There are thousands of
such faces, and what matters is not individual culpability
in a given act, or even whether a person was coerced or
bludgeoned or cajoled into participating in a chain of
events, but that he should 'look' the part. His face
should be an echo of the 'composite' of the visage of
the terrorist that we have learnt to see in our heads.

So much so that when the judges see Afzal, they
also see Maqbool Butt, the Kashmiri man whose hanging
on 11 February 1984, precipitated by a crime (the
assassination of the Indian diplomat Ravindra Mhatre in
Birmingham) that he did not commit, was one of the
sparks that stoked the ongoing Kashmir uprising.
Maqbool Butt, who spent long years in Indian and
Pakistani prisons, was like Afzal dogged by the persistent
shadow of his entanglement in Indian (and Pakistani)
intelligence manoeuvres. Butt had been sentenced to
death many years previously for the alleged murder of
an Indian military officer during the prehistory of the
insurgency in Kashmir in the 1960s, when he had first
started a ragtag band of partisans called the National
Liberation Front. Subsequently, he may well have come
under the shadow once again of Indian intelligence
outfits, who used him, it is alleged, to mastermind the
hijack of the Indian Airlines plane Ganga in 1971 (a
remarkably non-violent hijack in which no passengers
or crew were harmed, but an ageing plane that had
been out of commission and was surprisingly brought
back into use days before the hijack was conveniently
blown up while stationary in a Pakistani airfield).

The shadowy truths of the RAW's involvement (through the Border Security Force) in the hijacking of the Indian Airlines Fokker Friendship plane Ganga (one of the precipitating factors of the 1971 war) with which Butt had something to do, is one of those episodes in the history of modern India which has never quite seen the light of day. And Butt, too, like Afzal, may have eventually been a pawn in a game far more complex then he could have comprehended at the time. It is possible that Butt, too, like Afzal, was acting at least part of the time under orders that emanated from quarters deep within the Indian deep state. Eventually, Butt, the secular idealist, the sometime double agent, the victim of Indian as well as Pakistani justice, returned to India, was arrested and put away to be forgotten in Tihar Jail, and in the wake of Mhatre's kidnap and murder, made to walk to the gallows. While alive, he had been an obscure, little-known agitator, in death he became 'Shaheed-e-Kashmir'. He proved to be far more dangerous in his death to the Indian State then he was when he had been alive, so much so that the Indian army routinely swoops down on his village on 11 February each year to prevent his family from holding a private memorial function in his honour. His brother too was killed in an encounter, his family was prevented from coming to Delhi on the day of his execution, and all pictures or portraits of him have been taken away from the private homes of his immediate family. The cynical short-sightedness and the awkward combination of memory and forgetfulness that characterizes Indian State policy in Kashmir may once again produce another martyr, who will join Maqbool Butt in the pantheon of shahadat.

I abhor martyrdom, and following Bertolt Brecht, can only 'pity the people who need heroes'. Yet, it is the tragic destiny of Kashmir that the history of the subcontinent will offer them a harvest of martyrs every season. In death, their biographies become abstracted to conform to a monotonous pattern of resistance, imprisonment and violent death. Each of these individuals would have been valuable human beings if they were alive. Often they are, like Mohammad Afzal, sensitive and intelligent persons, someone who wanted to be a doctor, or someone who liked literature and was considered by his peers to be one of the ablest of his generation.

These lives have been twisted out of shape by the history of our times, so much so that they become shadows of their former selves, trapped, manipulated, always on the run, always with too many secrets crowded into their fragile minds. Death, preferably the death of a martyr, then becomes an apotheosis. In death they can become an abstraction, a dull average standard of ideal machismo for some and the remorseless death mask of the 'terrorist' for others. There is nothing to look forward to in this death, it is to me far less attractive than the promise of the people they still would have been if they had remained alive. Afzal's impending death will diminish us all, because in his dying, our times will have cheated us of a life that could have made a difference to very many people. All we gain is a composite image, a face made up of the features of Maqbool Butt and Mohammad Afzal and the countless others whose lives have ended brutally, whose lives have been annexed to the closely interwoven annals of martyrdom and terror. In the end, they become only numbers, so many hundreds of 'terrorists' neutralized for the sake of defending the Indian republic, or so many martyrs sacrificed for freedom in Kashmir. These numbers replace moments, memories, conversations, and the million uncountable things that make up the complexity of a single life. Even the life of a man sitting in a condemned cell in Tihar Jail. Counting days, counting hours, reading what may be his last novel, perhaps writing what might be his last few letters.

Francis Galton's racially motivated pseudo-science died a quiet death, and persists mainly as an object lesson in the dangers of the attempt to harvest truths about the human condition on the basis of numbers alone. But it is making a quiet back-door entry through the new sciences of biometrics that are at the core of the information technology of the war against terrorism—which itself is the key operation of the setting up of a new kind of State machinery predicated on the hyperintensive surveillance of those it rules. This includes the impossible holy grail of machine-assisted facial recognition as a preventive forensic measure designed to identify and neutralize potential terrorists. This would mean giving a scientific edge to, say, the act of hanging Mohammad Afzal Guru, were it to take place, before, not after 13 December.

In some crude ways this pre-cognitive neutralization of the terrorist-to-be is already a refined science in Indian statecraft. It includes the provisions of the Armed Forces Special Powers Act (AFSPA) which enable armed forces personnel to shoot to kill on the basis of suspicion. It is the theory of the practice known as the 'encounter'. Last week [early October 2006], even as the attempts

to protest against the impending execution of
Mohammad Afzal Guru were gaining momentum, two
other events occurred in Delhi which merit our attention.
The first was a demonstration against the arrest and
forced feeding of Irom Sharmila, a young Manipuri
woman who has been on a continuous hunger strike
against the AFSPA, and the suspected 'encounter' death
of Irshad Ahmed Lone, a young Kashmiri man in Delhi.
While the first may have got some attention, the second
is once again wrapped in silence. Protests rocked the
Channapora neighbourhood of Srinagar at the manner
in which his naked body showed visible marks of
torture. But the Delhi Police, and its Special Cell,
thought it wise not to display him as yet another trophy
in their war against terror. Perhaps, they thought, it
would be too much to exhibit another 'encounter' in
the days leading up to Afzal's execution.

In the light of this silence, it may be instructive to
read a report that appeared on the website of the
Kashmir Times newspaper on 11 October. It merits a
lengthy quotation.

Kashmiri youth tortured, killed in Delhi
Protests rock Srinagar, custodial killing alleged

SRINAGAR, OCT 11: People took to streets and
held strong demonstrations at Channapora here today
in protest against the murder of a local youth, Irshad
Ahmad Lone, an automobile engineer, in New Delhi.
Police burst smoke shells and resorted to lathi charge
to disperse the demonstrators, who retaliated by
pelting stones on cops . . .

The bereaved family accused Delhi police of
arresting Irshad and later killing him in custody.

According to them the youth had gone to New Delhi for a job in an automobile company on September 21. He was arrested by police there and brutally tortured. Later they were informed by a cop from the union capital on telephone that Irshad is in an unconscious condition in a hospital. The youth later succumbed to his injuries.

Ali Mohammad father of Irshad said that in the morning of October 8 he received a telephone call at his residence from New Delhi. The caller identified himself as assistant sub inspector Ram Ji Lal of Inter-State Bus Terminus (ISBT) police chowki Kashmiri Gate. The cop asked him whether he knew Irshad. Ali Mohammad informed that he was his son. The subinspector told Ali Mohammad that his son was in an unconscious condition at Sushrutra Trauma Centre.

Irshad's brother, Tariq Ahmad, rushed to Delhi. According to him, his brother was in an unconscious condition with visible torture marks on his body. Irshad's arms, throat and head had torture marks. He later succumbed to his injuries. Tariq asked Ram Ji Lal as to what had happened to Irshad. The cop claimed that they found Irshad in a naked condition on a highway at ISBT Kashmiri Gate and that he was unconscious. Asked as to how he got the telephone number of their residence in Srinagar, Ram Ji Lal claimed that Irshad gave the number before he lost his consciousness.

The bereaved family members said if police got their phone number from Irshad why it did not ask him as to who had tortured him. They said Irshad was arrested, tortured and then killed by Delhi police. Since this morning large number of people visited the affected family and were waiting for the body till late this evening. The body is likely to reach here during night hours . . .

Senior separatist leaders Mohammad Yasin Malik, chairman JKLF, and Shabir Ahmad Shah, president of Democratic Freedom Party (DFP) visited the bereaved family to offer their condolences. Addressing the people there, Shah said the way Irshad was murdered it clearly indicated that Kashmiri youth cannot go to any Indian state. 'Their only fault is that they are Kashmiri,' he said.

Shah alleged that on one side government of India is talking about peace and on the other side leaving no stone unturned to murder Kashmiri youth. The DFP president was placed under house arrest. JKLF chairman Mohammad Yasin Malik visited the residence of Irshad immediately after his return from New Delhi. Accompanied by other party leaders, he took part in protest demonstrations. Addressing the people, Malik strongly condemned the killing. He asked as to what crime Irshad had committed.' Is being a Kashmiri the biggest crime', the JKLF chairman asked. He said the slain engineer had qualified the interview for a job in Delhi on merit. 'But he was denied the job for being a Kashmiri. When he was about to return his home, he was killed by unidentified men', Malik said.

It appears from this report, and from the arrest of Irom Sharmila and the police action in Delhi against those demonstrating in solidarity with her and against the AFSPA, that being a certain kind of Kashmiri or having Manipuri or identifiably 'North-Eastern' features is in fact a crime in the capital of the Indian republic. The pre-cognitive faculties of the State know that 'people like that' are potential subversives, and that no effort should be spared in neutralizing them. If this does result in the occasional execution of a Mohammad Afzal Guru or the death on the streets of Delhi of an

Irshad Ahmad Lone, then it is way too small a price to pay for the integrity and security of the Indian State.

It is said that it took the massacres of Algerians in Paris in 1961 for a generation of French Intellectuals to begin to understand the actual nature of French colonialism in Algeria. How many Kashmiris will need to die in Delhi's streets and in Tihar (since the number of dead in Kashmir does not seem to have much of an effect) for the Indian intelligentsia to wake up to the fact that the Indian State is a colonial State, and it acts like those of any occupying power in Kashmir and significant parts of the North-East?

In his written statement to his lawyer Sushil Kumar, Afzal points out how Indian security officers routinely extorted money from him because he was a 'surrendered militant' who had not become a special police officer (SPO). In this sordid tale of greed, where different police officers demand varying sums of money after torturing Afzal, lies one of the secrets of Indian 'occupation' in Kashmir. Our army is in Kashmir, Indian soldiers and countless Kashmiris are dying in Kashmir, also because there is money to be made in this business. 'Terrorists' are just as necessary a part of this equation. Because 'terrorists' become 'surrendered terrorists', and 'surrendered terrorists' are excellent sources of cash, because if they do not pay up, they can be made to become 'terrorists' again. Here is the time-honoured police and gangster tradition of the 'hafta' and 'vasuli' ratcheted up through the brute force of a military occupation. This in fact is one of the sad truths of the Indian State's presence in Kashmir, and for the sake of the triumph of this truth, Mohammad Afzal Guru is sentenced to die.

I can only hope that A.P.J. Abdul Kalam looks carefully at the motto inscribed on his website, his stationery, his cutlery and his towels before he goes to sleep each night in the next few days as he weighs the decision about whether to assent to the clemency petition filed by Afzal's family: Satyameva Jayate.

This essay has been adapted from a posting made on the Sarai Reader List on 16 October 2006 and www.kafila.org.

[14]

MEETING AFZAL

Indira Jaising

The more I read about Afzal's case, the more I am convinced that he did not have adequate and effective legal representation at the trial which led to his conviction and the imposition of a death sentence. As a practising lawyer in the evening of my career, I am appalled that any human being could be sent to death without being given an opportunity to be heard. This was meant to be a civilized nation, with the guaranteed fundamental right to state legal aid for the indigent and those otherwise unable to access legal service.

The right to legal aid commences with the arrest and continues through the trial and all appeals. Afzal was denied this right. Until he made the 'confession'— in full media glare and surrounded by police—he had no lawyer.[1] The confession was later discarded by the Supreme Court as being contrary to law, but by that time the damage was already done, a damage that has not been undone till today. The NDA government was in power when the attack on Parliament took place and the arrest was made. They managed to whip up near mass hysteria about the nation being in danger due to the attack on Parliament. Afzal had no one to turn to. He did not even see his family until six months into the trial. When he did see them, it was for a few minutes in court. There was no one to mobilize a lawyer for him.

At the trial, Afzal named four lawyers whom he wished to have defending him. The judge, S.N. Dhingra, records that all four refused, but there is no evidence to show that they did. Indeed, the evidence actually suggests that they were never approached by the judge and asked if they would represent Afzal. This is again the most blatant denial of the right to representation, a denial which ultimately led to a death sentence being imposed.

At one hearing in court, the judge said that, as Afzal had no lawyer, Ms Seema Gulati would be assigned to him as his lawyer, a woman he knew nothing about. He never met her, except during the trial in court. On being appointed, Ms Gulati admitted some of the most crucial documents relating to the case which ultimately led to Afzal's conviction—the identification document of the men who attacked Parliament (all of whom were killed) and the post-mortem reports.

Soon thereafter, Ms Gulati withdrew her appearance in favour of another accused. At that point, the judge appointed her junior Niraj Bansal as Afzal's lawyer. Afzal had no hand in making the choices. During the trial, he noticed that he was not being properly represented. Facts that he had admitted were being denied by Niraj Bansal. At that point, Afzal rejected

Niraj Bansal and said he did not want the man to represent him. Notwithstanding the rejection, the Judge Dhingra insisted that Bansal continue, this time, as *amicus curiae*—a friend of the court! What this means is that Afzal was unrepresented, while the court had a 'friend' to assist it!

This shocks my conscience, as it should anyone else's, but apparently, the sessions court, the high court and the Supreme Court were all convinced that Afzal was adequately represented. The truth is exactly, and emphatically, the opposite.

Records show that Afzal was cross-examining witnesses himself. This he had to do without being provided with copies of the depositions that would have enabled him to point out the inconsistencies. Besides, cross-examination by an accused facing a death penalty is no substitute for cross-examination by a legally trained mind. What emerges is not only that Afzal did not have a lawyer, but that he actually rejected the lawyer thrust upon him, for what he perceived to be the man's incompetence! A greater mockery of the due process of law cannot be imagined. Afzal was denied the most basic right to legal aid.

The clinching evidence of this denial and its most devastating consequence came at the stage of sentencing. There was hardly any argument made at that stage to indicate the mitigating circumstances which could have led to a lesser sentence.

Disturbed by the turn of events and by the spectacle of people thirsting for his execution, I decided to examine the record. I was convinced that Afzal was unrepresented at the trial, leading to a massive miscarriage of justice. There was no question in my mind that the Supreme Court should be asked to revisit the issue in a 'curative' petition, a petition that can be filed if there has been a grave miscarriage of justice.

The more I read, the more I was convinced that a man was being sent to his death without a hearing, without him having had his day in court, despite three courts having heard his case.

I looked closely at the right to state legal aid. What I discovered shocked me even further. By law, the court is meant to maintain a list of lawyers who can be appointed for an accused. There is indeed a long list. Why was someone not chosen from this list to represent Afzal? A failure to do this naturally led to a 'friendly' lawyer, friendly to the prosecution, being foisted on the accused.

And here is the final injustice: A lawyer appointed at state expense is paid Rs 3000 for conducting a capital sentence case! What quality of legal representation can one expect in these circumstances? While senior lawyers today can charge unlimited amounts to represent the accused, how can Rs 3000 for the entire case be said to meet with any standard of reasonableness? The constitutional obligation is to provide *adequate* and *effective* representation, not just any representation, especially in death sentence cases. It is futile to argue that lawyers providing legal aid are meant to do so free of charge or for a pittance. This kind of volunteerism is not what the law requires. It is the obligation of the state to provide the legal aid and to fulfil that obligation appropriate fees must be paid, to ensure that competent lawyers appear for indigent accused. The National Legal Services Authority is well endowed with funds, much of which are used for conferences. It would be interesting to make an analysis of what proportion of the budget is used for legal aid and what proportion for air fares and conferences.

These are the considerations that compelled me to give a certificate that there had been a gross miscarriage of justice in Afzal's case and that a curative petition be filed to establish the primacy of the right to legal representation at state expense.

I met Afzal in Tihar Jail in my capacity as a lawyer. He was amazingly aware of what was happening to him. He confirmed every fact about the denial of legal aid. He knew the names of the four lawyers he had requested for, and who had allegedly declined to represent him (as mentioned earlier, there is no evidence to indicate that they were actually asked). He confirmed that Niraj Bansal was denying facts that he (Afzal) was admitting to and that, when he decided to get rid of him, the judge insisted on his continuance as a friend of the court. He confirmed that he cross-examined some of the prosecution witnesses himself, without access to the depositions against him. Throughout our conversation, he was consistent in his version of events.

I had been apprehensive about meeting Afzal. How would a man on death row feel, and what could I say to someone who would be executed any day? In fact, the black warrant had already been issued. Thankfully, the law provides that if any petition is filed with any authority, the warrant cannot be executed. Afzal had filed a clemency petition; hence, the warrant had been kept in abeyance.

Afzal was calm. I marvelled at his composure. We were meeting as we would have met in any normal circumstances, except that this was inside Tihar Jail, in the office of the deputy superintendent, not even in private. Afzal was telling me the story of his life. He talked about his ordinary life, his employment with several well-known business houses. How could the press say that he was doing 'odd jobs', as if there was no dignity in his work? He talked about the fact that he gave tuitions to several well-placed students, whose names he did not wish to disclose to me. He said the press would get hold of the information and he did not want these students, now married and well settled, to live with the stigma that they had been students of Afzal. I tried to persuade him that this information was relevant to sentencing, to show that he was a valuable and trusted member of society. But he refused to give me the names.

He told me that he was kept in solitary confinement and wished to be moved and kept with other prisoners. I asked if he had been reading the newspapers. He said the newspapers were given to him after cutting out all information relating to his case. I was meeting him the day after his elder brother, in a sting operation shown on a TV 'news' channel, had said that he (Afzal) was indeed a terrorist and should be hanged.[2] Afzal laughed and said, 'There is no mystery about that, he is in the care and custody of the STF [Special Task Force].' His brother had told him that he was in any case condemned to death, why take the rest of the family with him? There was not a trace of bitterness on Afzal's face as he told me this. He was too strangely cheerful, in a manner I could not understand, for a man facing an unjust death sentence. I asked him about this. His answer was that when the sentence was first pronounced he was nervous and afraid. Now he felt whatever would be would be. It was not with resignation that he was saying this, but with full awareness of the limitations of the system, with knowledge of the role of the dreaded and shadowy STF in his life, the lives of ordinary people in Kashmir, where his family lives. All we want, he said, is peace.

I had given him the petition drafted by me to read. I asked him if there was anything he wanted to say in addition to what I had mentioned. He only asked a question: 'Why is it that when the same role was attributed to me and Shoukat, he has been given ten years and I have been given the death penalty?' The answer, he said, was self-evident—Shoukat had top-class lawyers; he had none.

December 2006

Postscript, February 2007

On 12 January 2007, roughly a month after this article was written, and this book published, the Supreme Court of India dismissed Afzal's curative petition. This will have far-reaching consequences for thousands of people in this country. To send a man to his death without legal representation is not only unconstitutional but also barbaric. Why go through an elaborate trial if the accused is not represented by a lawyer? One might as well be judge, prosecutor, and counsel for the accused and pronounce judgment.

The law laid down by the Supreme Court visualizes the filing of a curative petition to cure a miscarriage of justice. That was done by Afzal—to no avail. Now, only the President of India can have the last word. We can only give opinions that there has been a gross miscarriage of justice.

[15]

LAST CHANCE TO KNOW

Nirmalangshu Mukherji

The Supreme Court of India has sentenced Mohammad Afzal to death. We wait now for the President to accept or reject his clemency petition. But as we wait to be told if a man will or will not hang for his alleged role in the December 2001 Parliament attack case, have we at all understood this major event of contemporary Indian history? More importantly, will the completion of the judicial process, whether it ends in Afzal being hanged to death or imprisoned for life, in fact scuttle our efforts at understanding the event?

Limits of the Judiciary

The questions just asked presuppose that the judgement of the Supreme Court failed to provide the required understanding. Why? As a court of law, it is bound by a structure of responsibilities. In the present case, the court was faced with four appeals, two by the Delhi Police and one each by Afzal and Shaukat (two of the four originally accused in the Parliament attack case). To that end, it examined the evidence produced before the trial court and the subsequent judgements by the trial court and the high court.

The evidence was produced by an authorized investigating agency, namely, the Special Cell of the Delhi Police, with ACP Rajbir Singh as the investigating officer. The evidence was presented in the trial court with supporting materials and witnesses. Most of the evidence, especially in Afzal's case, went unchallenged. The trial court provided Afzal with an accredited lawyer who chose to remain largely inactive.

In fairness, we must note that whenever the defence—especially Gilani's and Shaukat's eminent team of lawyers—was able to question some evidence successfully, the high court and the Supreme Court did take notice of that and set the evidence aside. This is particularly true of the confessions obtained from Afzal and Shaukat; setting them aside created a huge dent in the case, as the Supreme Court noted. The high court in fact reprimanded the police in fairly strong terms for fabricating the arrest memos and for keeping people under illegal confinement.[1] In each case, Gilani's defence team successfully produced counter-evidence. As for the overwhelming evidence produced against Afzal, almost nothing was challenged at the trial court, making the task virtually insurmountable for his defence in the appeal courts. Looking at this evidence, therefore, the Supreme Court was obliged to conclude that Afzal was guilty of aiding and abetting the men who attacked Parliament.

To emphasize, although this has been fully documented (in, among other documents, the book

December 13: Terror over Democracy[2] and reports by the People's Union for Democratic Rights[3]), the Supreme Court was not seized of the notorious character of the investigating agency, the mindset of the trial judge, the role of Afzal's trial lawyer and, of course, the role of the media in fanning pre-trial hysteria. These factors clearly contaminated the evidence against Afzal and its judicial examination. By design, the limited legal window through which the court examined the case did not allow any other light to enter. In particular, the court was not endowed with the task of explaining the attack. Nonetheless, as noted, when presented with credible arguments by the defence, the court did take the bold step to set aside the confessions. Since the confessions carried the only story of the conspiracy to attack Parliament, the court's story of the attack was swift and short.

What we learn from the judgement is that five persons with sundry names attacked the Parliament, killed some people, and died. And Mohammad Afzal aided these attackers. Period.

Voices

The wider issues that surround the case—including the role, if any, of Mohammad Afzal—can and must, then, be addressed in forums other than a court of law. A large number of writers, academicians and lawyers have raised many grave issues concerning the Parliament attack case to which the judgement of the court provides no answers. Importantly, as we will see below, many of these concerns were raised while the court deliberated on the case, and the concerns continue even after the judgement has been delivered.

What are these issues? While the hearing in the court was nearing its end, lawyer Usha Ramanathan wrote (*Frontline*, 6 May 2005): 'The court will not, and is not expected to, concern itself with aspects that are not directly relevant to the case of the accused before it. So, many questions will inevitably, and predictably, remain uninvestigated in the court's docket.'[4] One of the questions Ramanathan asked was, 'Was it an act of war? Or was it a terrorist act? Or perhaps a protest employing extremist methods? We don't know. But, on the presumption that it was an act of war, troops were massed along the border, Indian and Pakistani soldiers glowered at each other for nearly a year, enormous resources were sunk into aggressive posturing, soldiers lost their lives, over a hundred children reportedly fell prey to land mines, and many farmers along this mined, potential battlefield were left without a livelihood.'[5]

Noting that Mohammad Afzal, the prime accused, was a surrendered militant in regular contact with the Special Task Force (STF) in Kashmir, Ramanathan observed, 'A surrendered militant is no longer a militant but one who has chosen to return. The surrendered militant is in the uneasy zone where he is suspect on both sides of the divide. The militants see in him a turncoat. The security forces and the STF hold him in their thrall, while viewing him constantly with suspicion.'[6] Specifically, she notes, 'If a person under the watchful eye of the STF could be part of a conspiracy to wage war against the state, how can anything less than a public inquiry do? For this is not about the guilt or innocence of one man, but about how a system works and what it means, to democracy, sovereignty and the security of the state.'[7]

Yet, the 'astonishing fact', Ramanathan suggested, was that 'there has never been a public inquiry into the attack on Parliament: not by a parliamentary committee, not by the media, not an expanded search by the police, nor even a commission of inquiry. When we picture the parliamentarians huddled inside Parliament as the sounds from the battleground outside told them of their narrow escape, it is difficult to understand why no one, not in the ruling coalition, not in the opposition, not in the secretariat of Parliament, thought there should be an immediate and deep-reaching inquiry.'[8]

Elsewhere (*The Book Review*), Ramanathan wrote, 'The only inquiry of which the public has knowledge has been translated into criminal proceedings in the court. The microscopic nature of a trial in court, however, means that it is only the accused whose conduct will be interrogated and judged.'[9]

About the failure of the media to initiate a far-reaching inquiry, Gouri Chatterjee wrote in the *Telegraph:* 'The media's unquestioning acceptance of whatever the police fed them, no, directed them to say, and their complicity in the government's scheme of things are downright embarrassing.'[10]

Rajat Roy (*Anandabazar Patrika*) illustrated the complicity of the media with the police by recounting in detail the event of Afzal's forced confession before the media.[11] Subhendu Dasgupta (*EPW*, 22 July 2006) summed up the complicity as follows: 'The truth that the media presented was incomplete, partial, truncated, engineered and designed, and the judgement was made on the basis of this truth. The media came to its judgement before the judicial process started. The administrative truth was passed on to the media; the media took the official truth and transformed it into "media truth".'[12] Notice that Dasgupta maintained this nearly one year after the judgement of the Supreme Court.

Commenting on the entire episode in her article in the *Telegraph*, Gouri Chatterjee observed that 'the greater tragedy is, we are condemned to repeat all this the next time round too'.[13] After the judgement, Sukumar Muralidharan expanded on these themes (*Biblio*). 'The December 13 event,' Muralidharan observed, 'proved the pivot from which momentous consequences followed. These involved issues of war and peace, the security and well-being of the peoples of India and Pakistan, and the posture that national governments in the two countries would adopt towards the global struggle being waged between what was "civilization" and its supposed antithesis.'[14]

Needless to say, none of these momentous issues can be addressed without ascertaining the facts surrounding the event. More specifically, as Muralidharan puts it, 'a well-informed citizenry obviously owes itself the duty of unravelling the facts behind the attack on a central institution of its democracy. And an indispensable part of the process of ascertaining [the] facts would be to establish the motivations that led the Delhi Police into its sordid saga of fabrication.'[15]

After describing Afzal's predicaments as a surrendered militant, Muralidharan writes, 'Any Indian citizen with a basic level of civic involvement would be assailed by a number of questions if she were to take the statements by Afzal in their entirety.'[16] He goes on to say, quoting from a recent book on the subject:

'Indeed, the conclusions that any observer who has not surrendered his critical faculties to the cult of the nation state would be impelled to [draw are] fraught with immensely disturbing consequences for the functioning of the Indian state and, hence, for the health of Indian democracy.'[17]

Appeal for Inquiry

Going beyond printed words in the margins of the media, a group of citizens consisting of writers, academicians, lawyers and journalists has publicly appealed for a parliamentary inquiry into the entire episode. A committee chaired by Nirmala Deshpande, and with Mahasweta Devi, Rajni Kothari, Prabhat Patnaik, Ashish Nandy, Prashant Bhushan, Sumanta Banerjee, Mihir Desai and others as members, held a press conference within a week of the Supreme Court judgement. In its press statement the committee noted:

> Afzal has been convicted of conspiracy primarily on the basis of statements of police witnesses and seizures of materials from him shown by the police, which went un-rebutted during trial, because Afzal was practically unrepresented in the trial. Be that as it may, the fact remains that the court has acquitted three of the four persons charged of conspiracy and has held that the manner and circumstances in which the confessions were obtained makes them unreliable. However, it is only on the basis of these unreliable confessions that the then government immediately committed the country to a full-scale war mobilization against Pakistan, with the possibility that it might have escalated to a nuclear war. The mobilization was used by the NDA government for political

purposes. POTA was immediately enacted, and anti-Pakistan as well as communal feelings were whipped up in the war hysteria which was drummed up taking advantage of the attack on Parliament.

Soon after, the committee appealed to the members of Parliament in the following words, with supporting documentation:

> Members of the Committee as well as reputed human rights organizations have been raising serious questions on the conduct of the previous NDA government, especially the functioning of the investigating agencies, in the Parliament attack case. In the light of the Supreme Court judgement of August 4, 2005, we wish to draw your attention to these apprehensions.

> (1) The NDA government initiated a full-scale mobilization for war against Pakistan, saying that the terrorists were Pakistanis sponsored by the Pakistan government. The war-effort, which was sustained for nearly a year, had very serious consequences. We have mentioned them in our public appeal . . . The only evidence of terrorist conspiracy originating from Pakistan is Mohammad Afzal's confessional statement. The Supreme Court has held that the confession is unreliable. With the confession set aside, we do not know who attacked Parliament and what was the conspiracy.

> (2) Mohammad Afzal, the only person found guilty of conspiracy by the Apex Court, is a surrendered militant, who was not only supposed to report regularly to the Special Task Force of J&K, but was also under their surveillance. How could such a person mastermind and execute such a

complex conspiracy? How could a terrorist organization rely upon such a person as the principal link for their operation? On whose behest was he acting? Is there some credibility to Afzal's statement . . . that both the leader of the attack, Mohammad, and that one of the masterminds in Kashmir, Tariq, actually belonged to the Special Task Force? What is the significance of the press report that 4 terrorists including one Hamza—the same name as one of the terrorists killed in the Parliament attack and supposedly identified by Afzal—had been arrested by the Thane police in November 2000 and handed over to the J&K police for further investigation? . . . It will be a travesty of justice to hang Mohammad Afzal without ascertaining answers to these questions.

(3) With the acquittal of three out of four persons from the charge of conspiracy, it is clear that the investigating agency tried to frame at least three innocent persons. The high court had found the agency guilty of producing false arrest memos, doctoring telephone conversations, and illegal confinement of people to force them to sign blank papers. It is also clear that false confessions were extracted by torture.

In the absence of alternative explanations, it seems that the NDA government was massively fooled by its own police. The country must learn the truth behind the attacks. Responsibility must be fixed for those guilty of negligence, concoction of evidence and propagation of deliberate falsehood. Above all, those who almost took the country to war in such a reckless manner must be made accountable. To that end, the committee has already issued an appeal for Parliamentary inquiry . . . There have been other recent appeals for a public inquiry on the case . . . We urge you to institute a Parliamentary inquiry at least on the following questions:

(1) Who attacked Parliament and what was the conspiracy?
(2) On what basis did the NDA government take the country close to a nuclear war?
(3) What was the role of the Special Task Force (J&K) on surrendered militants?
(4) What was the role of the Special Cell of Delhi Police in conducting the case?
(5) What institutional and legal changes are required to prevent a government from going to war unilaterally without the consent of Parliament as in this case?

The political system has failed to take any steps to answer such serious questions. And time is running out for initiating any fruitful inquiry on these questions. From what we can see through the restricted legal window of the Supreme Court, just six persons are in view, five attackers and Mohammad Afzal. Since the attackers died on the spot, Mohammad Afzal is the only living soul who, according to the Supreme Court itself, might know something of what really happened. And as Nandita Haksar has observed (*Indian Express*, 30 September 2006), 'We have not even had a chance to hear Afzal's story. Hanging Mohammad Afzal will only be a blot on our democracy.'[18]

This essay first appeared, in a slightly different form, in *The Economic and Political Weekly*, 7 October 2006.

[16]

MULAQAT AFZAL

Vinod K. Jose

A rusted table, and behind it stood a well-built man in uniform holding a spoon. Visitors, all of whom looked habituated to the routine, queued up with their plastic bags containing food open for inspection. The security man stirred the thick curries—Malai Kofta, Shahi Paneer, Alu-baingan—mechanically separating each piece of vegetable from the other. Sometimes he smelt and even tasted the food. A middle-aged woman, an early-teenage boy, and then it was my turn. It was around 4.30 in the afternoon.

The security man put his spoon on the table and frisked me thoroughly, thrice. When the metal detector beeped, I had to remove my belt, steel watch and keys till the man, bearing the badge of Tamilnadu Special Police (TSP), was satisfied. This was the fourth security drill I had had to go through to get into the High Risk Ward of Prison No 3 in Tihar Central Prison. I was on my way to meet Mohammad Afzal, one of the most talked about men in recent Indian history.

In a room with many tiny cubicles, visitor and inmate were separated by thick glass and iron grills. There was a mike and a speaker fixed on the wall, but the sound was poor and people in all the cubicles put their ears to the wall to hear. Mohammad Afzal was waiting for me on the other side, a short man in his mid-thirties, wearing a white kurta-paijama, a Reynolds pen in his pocket. He appeared calm, and gave an impression of great dignity. He spoke in a clear, polite voice: 'How are you, sir?'

'I'm fine,' I said. Should I ask the same question of a man on death row? I was apprehensive for a moment, but then I did.

'Very fine. Thank you, sir,' he answered warmly.

We spoke for close to an hour, and continued a fortnight later with a second mulaqat. It seemed to me that he wanted to tell the world a great many things and felt helpless that he could not. I scribbled almost without pause in my little pocket book.

Excerpts from the interview:

There are so many contradictory images of Afzal. Which Afzal am I meeting?

Is it? But as far as I'm concerned there is only one Afzal. That is me.

Who is that Afzal?

(A moments' silence.) Afzal is a young, enthusiastic, intelligent, idealistic young man. Afzal is a Kashmiri, influenced like many thousands in the Kashmir Valley in the political climate of the early 1990s . . . [He] was a JKLF member and crossed over to the other side of Kashmir, but in a matter of weeks got disillusioned and came back and tried to live a normal life but was never allowed to do so by the security agencies. [They] picked me up, tortured the pulp out of me, [I was] electrocuted, frozen in cold water, dipped in petrol, smoked with chillies—you name it—falsely implicated in a case, with no lawyer, no fair trial, and finally condemned to death. The lies the police told were propagated by you [people] in the media. And that perhaps created what the Supreme Court referred to as the 'collective conscience of the nation'. To satisfy that 'collective conscience' I'm condemned to death. That is the Mohammad Afzal you are meeting.

(After a moments' silence, he continued.) But I wonder whether the outside world knows anything about this Afzal. I ask you, did I get a chance to tell my story? Do you think justice is done? Would you like to hang a person without giving him a lawyer? Without a fair trial? Without listening to what he had to go through in life? Democracy doesn't mean all this, does it?

Can we begin with your life? Your life before the case . . .

It was a turbulent political period in Kashmir when I was growing up. Maqbul Bhatt was hanged. The situation was volatile. The people of Kashmir decided to fight an electoral battle once again to resolve the Kashmir issue through peaceful means. Muslim United Front (MUF) was formed to represent the sentiments of Kashmiri Muslims for the final settlement of the Kashmir

issue. The administration at Delhi was alarmed by the
kind of support that MUF was gaining and as a
consequence we saw rigging in the elections on an
unprecedented scale, and the leaders who took part in
the elections and won with a huge majority were
arrested, humiliated and put behind bars. It is only
after this that the same leaders gave a call for armed
resistance. In response thousands of youth took to
armed revolt. I dropped out from my MBBS studies in
Jhelum Valley Medical College, Srinagar. I was also
one of those who crossed to the other side of Kashmir
as a JKLF member, but was disillusioned after seeing
Pakistani Politicians acting the same as Indian politicians
in dealing with Kashmiris. I returned after few weeks.
I surrendered to the security forces—and you know, I
was even given a BSF certificate as a surrendered
militant. I began a new life. I could not become a
doctor but I became a dealer of medicines and surgical
instruments on a commission basis! (He laughs.)

With my meagre income I even bought a scooter
and also got married. But never a day passed by
without the scare of Rashtriya Rifles and STF men
harassing me. If there was a militant attack somewhere
in Kashmir they would round up civilians, torture them
to pulp, but the situation was worse for a surrendered
militant like me. They detained us for several weeks,
and threatened to implicate us in false cases. We were
let free only if we paid huge bribes. I had to go through
this kind of treatment many times. Major Ram Mohan
Roy of 22 Rashtriya Rifles gave me electric shocks in
my private parts. I was made to clean their toilets and
sweep their camps. Once I had to bribe the security
men with all that I had to escape from the Humhama

STF torture camp. DSP Vinay Gupta and DSP Davinder Singh supervised the torture there. One of their torture experts, Inspector Shanty Singh, gave me electric shocks for three hours until I agreed to pay one lakh rupees as bribe. My wife sold her jewellery and my scooter. I left the camp broken both financially and mentally. For six months I could not leave my house because my body was in such a bad shape. I could not even share the bed with my wife as I'd been given electric shocks on my penis. I had to take medical treatment to regain potency . . .

Afzal narrated the torture details with such calm that it was disturbing. Unable to hear about the horrors perpetrated by the security forces that operate with my tax money, I cut him short and asked:

If you could come to the case . . . what were the incidents that led to the Parliament attack case?

After the lesson I had learnt in STF camps, which is that either you or your family members get harassed constantly for refusing to cooperate with the STF blindly, I had hardly any options left when DSP Davinder Singh asked me to do a small job for him. That is what he said—'a small job'. He told me that I had to take one man to Delhi and find a rented house for him there. I was seeing the man for first time, but since he did not speak Kashmiri I suspected he was an outsider. He told me his name was Mohammad [Mohammad is identified by the police as the man who led the five gunmen who attacked the Parliament. All of them were killed in the attack]. When we were in Delhi Mohammad and I used to get phone calls from Davinder Singh. I had also noticed that Mohammad used to visit many people in Delhi. After he purchased a car he told me now I could go back and gave me 35,000 rupees, saying it was a gift. And I returned to Kashmir for Eid.

When I was about to leave for Sopore from Srinagar bus stand I was arrested and taken to Parimpora police station. They tortured me, then took me to the STF headquarters and from there brought me to Delhi. In the torture chamber of the Delhi Police Special Cell, I told them everything I knew about Mohammad. But they insisted that I should say that my cousin Shoukat, his wife Navjot, S.A.R. Geelani and I were the people behind the Parliament attack. They wanted me to say this convincingly in front of the media. I resisted. But I had no option other than to yield when they told me that my family was in their custody and threatened to kill them. I was made to sign many blank pages and was forced to talk to the media and claim responsibility for the attack by repeating what the police told me to say. When a journalist asked me about the role of S.A.R. Geelani, I told him Geelani was innocent. ACP Rajbeer Singh shouted at me in full media glare for talking beyond what they had tutored me to say. They were really upset when I deviated from their story and Rajbeer Singh requested the journalists not to broadcast the part where I spoke of Geelani's innocence.

Rajbeer Singh allowed me to talk to my wife the next day. After the call he told me if I wanted to see [my family] alive I had to cooperate. Accepting the charges was the only option if I wanted to see the family alive and the Special Cell officers promised they would make my case weak so that I would be released after some time. Then they took me to various places and showed me the markets where Mohammad had purchased different things. Thus they made the evidence for the case.

Police made me a scapegoat in order to mask their failure to find out the mastermind of the Parliament attack. They have fooled the people. People still don't know whose idea it was to attack the Parliament. I was entrapped into the case by the Special Task Force (STF) of Kashmir and implicated by the Delhi Police Special Cell.

The media constantly played the tape. The police officers received awards. And I was condemned to death.

Why didn't you find legal defence?

I had no one to turn to. I did not even see my family until six months into the trial. And when I saw them it was only for a short time in the Patiala House Court. There was no one to arrange a lawyer for me. As legal aid is a fundamental right in this country I named four lawyers whom I wished to have defending me. But the judge, S.N. Dhingra, said all four refused to do the case. The lawyer whom the court chose for me began by admitting some of the most crucial documents without even asking me what the truth of the matter was. She was not doing the job properly and finally she moved to defend another fellow accused. Then the court appointed an *amicus curiae*, not to defend me, but to assist the court in the matter. He never met me. And he was very hostile and communal. That is my case, completely unrepresented at the crucial trial stage. The fact of the matter is that I did not have a lawyer and in a case like this, everyone can understand what it means not having a lawyer. If you wanted to put me to death what was the need for such a long legal process which to me was totally meaningless?

Do you want to make any appeal to the world?

I have no specific appeals to make. I have said whatever I wanted to say in my petition to the President of India. My simple appeal is, do not allow blind nationalism and mistaken perceptions to lead you to deny even the most fundamental rights of your fellow citizens. Let me repeat what S.A.R. Geelani said after he was awarded the death sentence at the trial court, he said, peace comes with justice; if there is no justice, there is no peace. I think that is what I want to say now. If you want to hang me, go ahead with it, but remember that it would be a black spot on the judicial and political system of India.

What is the condition in jail?

I'm lodged in solitary confinement in the high risk cell. I'm taken out from my cell only for a short period during noon. No radio, no television. Even the newspaper I subscribe to reaches me torn. If there is a news item about me, they tear that portion out and give me the rest.

Apart from the uncertainty about your future, what else concerns you the most?

Yes, a lot of things concern me. There are hundreds of Kashmiris languishing in different jails, without lawyers, without trial, without any rights. The situation of civilians in the streets of Kashmir is not any different. The valley itself is an open prison. These days the news of fake encounters is coming out. But that is only the tip of the big iceberg. Kashmir has everything that you don't want to see in a civilized nation. They breathe torture. Inhale injustice. (He paused for a moment.) Also, there are so many thoughts that come to my mind—farmers who get displaced, merchants whose shops are sealed in Delhi, and so on. So many faces of injustice you can see and identify, can't you? Have you thought how many thousands of people are affected by all this—their livelihood, family . . .? All these things worry me, too. (Another, longer pause.) Also global developments. I heard the news of the execution of Saddham Hussain with utmost sadness. Injustice, so openly and shamelessly done. Iraq, the land of Mesopotamia, the world's richest civilization that taught us mathematics—about the 60-minute clock, 24-hour day, 360-degree circle—is razed to dust by the Americans. The Americans are destroying all other civilizations and value systems. The so called War against Terror is only spreading hatred and causing destruction . . . I could go on telling you what worries me.

Which books are you reading now?

I finished reading Arundhati Roy. Now I'm reading Sartre's work on existentialism. You see, it is a poor library in the jail. So I will have to request the visiting SPDPR [Society for the Protection of Detainees and Prisoners Rights] members for books.

There is a campaign in your defence . . .

I am obliged, and really moved by the thousands of people who came forward saying that injustice has been done to me. The lawyers, students, writers, intellectuals, and all the other people involved are doing something great by speaking against injustice. The situation was such in the beginning, in 2001 and the initial days of the case, it was impossible for justice-loving people to come forward. After the High Court acquitted S.A.R. Geelani, people started questioning the police theory. And when more and more people became aware of the case details and facts and started seeing things beyond the lies, they began speaking up. It is natural . . .

Members of your family have conflicting opinions on your case.

My wife has been consistently saying that I was wrongly framed. She has seen how the STF tortured me and did not allow me to live a normal life. She also knew how they implicated me in the case. She wants me to see our son Ghalib growing up. I also have an elder brother who apparently is speaking against me under duress from the STF. It is unfortunate, that's all I can say. See, it is a reality in Kashmir now—what you call counter insurgency operations take any dirty shape. They field brother against brother, neighbour against neighbour. [They] are breaking a society with [their] dirty tricks.

What comes to your mind when you think of your wife Tabassum and son Ghalib?

This year is the tenth anniversary of our wedding. Over half that period I have spent in jail. And prior to that, I was detained many a time and tortured by the Indian security forces in Kashmir. Tabassum witnessed both my physical and mental wounds. I would return from the torture camp unable to stand [after] all kinds of torture, including electric shocks . . . she gave me hope to live . . . We did not have a day of peace. It is the

story of many Kashmiri couples. Constant fear is the
dominant feeling in all Kashmiri households.

We were so happy when a child was born. We
named our son after the legendary poet Mirza Ghalib.
We had a dream to see our son Ghalib grow up. I could
spend very little time with him. After his second birthday
I was implicated in the case.

What do you want him to grow to be?

If you mean professionally, a doctor. Because that is my
incomplete dream. But most importantly, I want him to
grow up without fear. I want him to speak against
injustice. That I am sure he will. Who knows the story
of injustice better than my wife and son?

*While Afzal continued talking about his wife and son,
I could not stop recollecting what Tabassum told me
when I met her outside the Supreme Court in 2005
during the appeal stage of the case. While the rest of
Afzal's family remained in Kashmir, Tabassum dared to
come to Delhi with her son Ghalib to organize the
defence for Afzal. At a tiny roadside tea stall outside
the Supreme Court New Lawyers Chamber, she chatted
in detail about Afzal. She told me how much he
enjoyed cooking. One image has remained with me, a
precious private moment from their life together—he
asks her to sit on a chair near him in the kitchen, and
ladle in one hand and a book in the other, reads out
stories to her as he cooks.*

**If I may ask you about the Kashmir issue—how do you
think it can be solved?**

First let the government be sincere to the people of
Kashmir and initiate talks with the real representatives

of Kashmir. Trust me, the real representatives of Kashmir can solve the problem. But if the government considers the peace process as one of the tactics of counter insurgency, then the issue is not going to be solved. It is time some sincerity is shown.

Who are the real people?

Find out from the sentiments of the people of Kashmir. I am not going to name x, y or z.

And I have an appeal to make to the Indian media: stop acting as a propaganda tool. They should report the truth. With their smartly worded and politically loaded news, they distort facts, make incomplete reports, build hardliners, terrorists and others. They easily fall for the games of the intelligence agencies. By doing insincere journalism they are adding to the problem. Disinformation on Kashmir should stop first. Allow Indians to know the complete history of the conflict, let them know the ground realities. True democrats cannot deny facts. If the Indian government is not taking into account the wishes of the Kashmiri people, then it can't solve the problem. [Kashmir] will continue to be a conflict zone.

Also, tell me how are you going to develop real trust among the Kashmiris when you send out the message that India has a justice system that hangs people without giving them a lawyer, without a fair trial? When hundreds of Kashmiris are lodged in jails, most of them with no lawyer, no hope for justice, are you not further escalating distrust of the Indian government among Kashmiris? Do you think if you don't address the core issues and do a cosmetic job you can solve the Kashmir conflict? No, you can't. Let the democratic institutions of both India and Pakistan start showing some sincerity—their politicians, Parliament, justice system, media, intellectuals [all of them].

Nine security men were killed in the Parliament attack. What do you have to say to their relatives?

I share the pain of the family members who lost their dear ones in the attack. But I feel sad that they are misled into believing that hanging an innocent person will satisfy them. They are used as pawns in a completely distorted cause of nationalism. I appeal to them to see through things.

What do you see as your achievement in life?

My biggest achievement perhaps is that through my case and the campaign about the injustice done to me, the horror of the STF has been brought to light. I am happy that now people are discussing the security forces' atrocities on civilians, encounter killings, disappearances, torture camps, etc . . . These are the realities that a Kashmiri grows up with. People outside Kashmir have no clue what Indian security forces are up to in Kashmir.

Even if they kill me for no crime of mine, it would be because they cannot stand the truth. They cannot face the questions that arise out of hanging a Kashmiri without [a fair trial].

An ear-splitting electric bell rang. I could hear hurried last-minute conversations from the neighbouring cubicles. I put my last question to Afzal.

What do you want to be known as?

(He thinks for a minute.) As Afzal, as Mohmammad Afzal. I am Afzal for Kashmiris, and I am Afzal for Indians as well, but the two groups have entirely conflicting perceptions of my being. I would naturally trust the judgment of Kashmiri people not only because I am one of them but also because they are well aware of the reality that I have been through and they cannot be misled into believing any distorted version of either history or an incident.

I was confused with this last statement, but on further reflection I began to understand what Afzal meant. The true history of Kashmir and the facts behind any ugly incident involving a Kashmiri always shock an Indian whose sources of knowledge on Kashmir are confined only to text books and media reports. Afzal had just done that to me.

Two more bells. Time to end the mulaqat. But people were still busy conversing. The mikes were put off. People finally stopped speaking. But I could see his lips still moving, and strained to hear. The guards came up, roughly asking people to leave. They put the lights out. The mulaqat room turned dark.

In the long walk out from Jail No 3 of the Tihar compound to the main road, I found myself among clusters of twos and threes, moving out silently—a cluster of mother, wife and daughter; or brother, sister and wife; or friend and brother; or no relation at all. Every cluster had two things in common. They carried empty cotton bags and the bags had food stains on them, the result, most probably, of rough frisking by the special police. And they all wore inexpensive winter

*clothes, many had torn shoes, and outside Gate No 3
they waited for Bus No. 588, Tilak Nagar-Nehru
Stadium, or any other that would take them, perhaps,
to the Dhaulakuan main junction. They were the poor
of this country. My interviewee was also one. When I
asked him how many 'tokens' (the form of currency
allowed in the jail) he had, he said, 'Enough to survive. '*

February 2007

PART TWO

THE HANGING

[17]

AN EXECUTION MOST FOUL

T.R. Andhyarujina

The execution of Afzal Guru on 9 February 2013 was an inhumane act by the Government of India. Afzal Guru was hanged seven years after the Supreme Court's pronouncement of the death sentence on him on 4 August 2005 and over six years after his clemency petition to the President of India on 8 November 2006. During this period, he and his family remained in agonizing suspense over his fate every day—a situation that is condemned by all civilized countries and our Supreme Court. The rejection of his petition by the President after over six years, on 3 February 2013, was kept secret and deliberately not communicated to his family, lest it become the subject of judicial consideration as has been done in other cases of delayed execution. Within a few days of the rejection of his mercy petition, the execution was carried out in secrecy on 9 February 2013 without informing his family, and his body was buried in equal secrecy in a grave inside Tihar Jail, New Delhi.

Six Years

A petition made to the President for pardon, reprieve or remission of punishment under Article 72 of the Constitution is a right of a convict and until the petition is rejected the government cannot carry out the sentence. In disposing of the petition under Article 72, the President does not act at his discretion but on the aid and advice of the government. This was held by the Supreme Court in Kehar Singh's case in 1989. The crucial question was whether the execution could be carried out after a prolonged delay of over six years from the day Afzal Guru made his petition to the President.

The disposal of Afzal Guru's petition became a political matter, with the BJP's unseemly demand for his execution and its making it an issue in the ensuing elections. For its own political consideration, the government did not decide the petition made to the President. In fact, between 2006 and 2008, the then home minister deliberately instructed the Government of Delhi to delay responding to the Afzal Guru file sent to it. In 2008 Afzal Guru made a statement that revealed his mental distress. He said in an interview, 'I really wish L.K. Advani becomes India's next PM as he is the only one who can take a decision and hang me. At least my pain and daily suffering will ease then.'

When the terrorist Ajmal Kasab was executed on 21 November 2012, immediately following the Supreme Court's verdict on him, the Opposition again renewed its demand for Afzal Guru's execution. Steps were then taken by the government to prevent the Opposition from exploiting the situation. Kasab's execution carried out in secrecy became the model for the execution of

Afzal Guru. On 15 November 2012 President Pranab Mukherjee sent Afzal Guru's file back to the home ministry for a fresh consideration of the mercy petition. On 23 January 2013 the home ministry recommended its rejection and on 3 February 2013 the President formally rejected the petition. The President's rejection was then implemented by the home minister on 4 February 2013 and five days later, in the early morning of 9 February 2013, Afzal Guru was hanged.

In executing Afzal Guru after a prolonged period in which he and his family suffered the agony of suspense, the government flouted a well-settled law laid down by the Supreme Court in several cases. In Edigma Anama vs. State of A.P. in 1974, Justice Krishna Iyer spoke of the 'brooding horror of haunting the prisoner in the condemned cell for years'. Justice Chinnappa Reddy in T.V. Vatheeswaran vs. State of Tamil Nadu in 1983 said that a prolonged delay in the execution of a sentence of death had a dehumanizing effect and this had the constitutional implication of depriving a person of his life in an unjust, unfair and unreasonable way so as to offend the Fundamental Right under Article 21 of the Constitution. He quoted the Privy Council's observation in a case of inordinate delay in execution: 'The anguish of alternating hope and despair, the agony of uncertainty and the consequences of such suffering on the mental, emotional and physical integrity and health of the individual has to be seen.'

Trauma of Convict and Family

In 1983, in Sher Singh vs. State of Punjab, the Supreme Court repeated the same observations, and in the larger

Constitutional Bench in Triveniben vs. State of Gujarat in 1989 to settle the law the Supreme Court again reiterated that a prolonged delay in execution would be unjust, unfair and unreasonable. The Supreme Court held that in the disposal of mercy petitions it has been universally recognized that the condemned person suffers a degree of mental torture even though there is no physical mistreatment. It held that if there was an inordinate delay in execution, the condemned prisoner would be entitled to move the court to examine whether it was just and fair to allow the sentence of death to be executed. The disclosure of the rejection of the mercy petition was, therefore, mandatory. In the case of Jagdish vs. State of Madhya Pradesh in 2012, the Supreme Court highlighted not only the agony of the convict by inordinate delay of execution but also the agony and trauma of his close relatives.

In 1994 the Privy Council adopted the observations of the Indian Supreme Court and stated in a moving part of the judgement that 'there is an instinctive revulsion against the prospect of hanging a man after he has been held under sentence of death for many years. What gives rise to this instinctive revulsion? The answer can only be our humanity; we regard it as an inhuman act to keep a man facing the agony of execution over a long extended period of time . . . To execute these men now after holding them in custody for so many years would be inhuman punishment.' The European Court on Human Rights in 1989 and the Canadian Supreme Court have also taken a similar view. In executing Afzal Guru, the government deliberately ignored the views of our Supreme Court and other courts in other jurisdictions.

Apart from the torment and agony suffered by the death row convict, it has been universally recognized that the agony is suffered also by his near and dear ones in the same manner by the delay. A leading textbook on death penalty states that 'the trauma for families is specially evident when the date of the execution draws near. In recognition of this, it appears to be the common practice in most retentionist countries to allow relatives to visit the condemned person prior to execution, to inform them of the date of the execution, and to deliver them the body for burial.'

In Afzal Guru's case, his family members were not informed of his imminent execution and were unable to meet him one last time before his execution. The government's claim that it informed them by a speed post letter dispatched on 8 February 2013 is meaningless. The letter was delivered to the family in Kashmir two days after his execution!

In March–April 2012, the Supreme Court heard petitions by two death convicts—Devender Pal Singh Bhullar and Narender Nath Das—on the validity of carrying out executions after mercy petitions were delayed for eight to eleven years. The court considered the cases of other death row convicts whose executions were prolonged and directed the Government of India to give details and files relating to the convicts. The government then gave the details of the death row convicts whose mercy petitions were pending with the President of India.

Legality of Prolonged Delay

One of the pending cases was that of Afzal Guru. The Supreme Court appointed me as amicus curiae to consider the larger question of the execution of convicts after inordinate delay. In the course of my submissions, I referred in particular to the facts of the Afzal Guru case. The hearing concluded on 19 April 2012, and judgement was reserved in the case. The government was fully aware that the legality of prolonged delay in the execution of convicts was pending consideration by the Supreme Court. It was incumbent upon the government to await the authoritative pronouncement of the Supreme Court on the pending petitions but the government carried out the execution of Afzal Guru on 9 February 2013.

Overall, Afzal Guru's execution will remain the most callous death sentence carried out by the Government of India.

This essay was first published in *The Hindu*, 19 February 2013.

DOES YOUR BOMBPROOF BASEMENT HAVE AN ATTACHED TOILET?

Arundhati Roy

What are the political consequences of the secret and sudden hanging of Mohammad Afzal Guru, prime accused in the 2001 Parliament attack, going to be? Does anybody know? The memo, in callous bureaucratese, with every name insultingly misspelt, sent by the Superintendent of Central Jail No. 3, Tihar, New Delhi, to 'Mrs Tabassum w/o Sh Afjal Guru' reads:

> *The mercy petition of Sh Mohd Afjal Guru s/o Habibillah has been rejected by Hon'ble President of India. Hence the execution of Mohd Afjal Guru s/o Habibillah has been fixed for 09/02/2013 at 8 am in Central Jail No-3.*
> *This is for your information and for further necessary action.*

The mailing of the memo was deliberately timed to get to Tabassum only after the execution, denying her one last legal chance—the right to challenge the rejection of the mercy petition. Both Afzal and his family, separately, had that right. Both were thwarted. Even though it is mandatory in law, the memo to Tabassum ascribed no reason for the President's rejection of the mercy petition. If no reason is given, on what basis do you appeal? All the other prisoners on death row in India have been given that last chance.

Since Tabassum was not allowed to meet her husband before he was hanged, since her son was not allowed to get a few last words of advice from his father, since she was not given his body to bury, and since there can be no funeral, what 'further necessary action' does the jail manual prescribe? Anger? Wild, irreparable grief? Unquestioning acceptance? Complete integration?

After the hanging, there have been unseemly celebrations. The bereaved wives of the people who were killed in the attack on Parliament were displayed on TV, with M.S. Bitta, chairman of the All-India Anti-Terrorist Front, and his ferocious moustaches playing the CEO of their sad little company. Will anybody tell them that the men who shot their husbands were killed at the same time, in the same place? And that those who planned the attack will never be brought to justice because we still don't know who they are.

Meanwhile, Kashmir is under curfew, once again. Its people have been locked down like cattle in a pen, once again. They have defied curfew, once again. Three people have already been killed in three days and fifteen more grievously injured. Newspapers have been shut down, but anybody who trawls the internet will see that this time the rage of young Kashmiris is not defiant and exuberant like it was during the mass uprisings in the summers of 2008, 2009 and 2010—even though 180 people lost their lives on those occasions. This time the anger is cold and corrosive. Unforgiving. Is there any reason why it shouldn't be?

For more than twenty years, Kashmiris have endured a military occupation. The tens of thousands who lost their lives were killed in prisons, in torture centres, and in 'encounters', genuine as well as fake. What sets the execution of Afzal Guru apart is that it has given the young, who have never had any first-hand experience of democracy, a ringside seat to watch the full majesty of Indian democracy at work. They have watched the wheels turning, they have seen all its hoary institutions, the government, police, courts, political parties and, yes, the media, collude to hang a man, a Kashmiri, who they do not believe received a fair trial. With good reason.

He went virtually unrepresented in the lower court during the most crucial part of the trial. The court-appointed lawyer never visited him in prison, and actually admitted incriminating evidence against his own client. (The Supreme Court deliberated on that matter and decided it was okay.) In short, his guilt was by no means established beyond reasonable doubt.

They have watched the government pull him out of the death row queue and execute him out of turn. What direction, what form will their new anger take? Will it lead them to the blessed liberation they so yearn for and have sacrificed a whole generation for, or will it lead to yet another cycle of cataclysmic violence, of being beaten down, and then having 'normalcy' imposed on them under soldiers' boots?

All of us who live in the region know that 2014 is

going to be a watershed year. There will be elections in Pakistan, in India and in the state of Jammu and Kashmir. We know that when the US withdraws its troops from Afghanistan, the chaos from an already seriously destabilized Pakistan will spill into Kashmir, as it has done before. By executing Afzal Guru in the way that it did, the government of India has taken a decision to fuel that process of destabilization, to actually invite it in. (As it did before, by rigging the 1987 elections in Kashmir.) After three consecutive years of mass protests in the Valley ended in 2010, the government invested a great deal in restoring its version of 'normalcy⁵ (happy tourists, voting Kashmiris). The question is, why was it willing to reverse all its own efforts? Leaving aside issues of the legality, the morality and the venality of executing Afzal Guru in the way that it did, and looking at it just politically, tactically, it is a dangerous and irresponsible thing to have done. But it was done. Clearly, and knowingly. *Why?*

I use the word 'irresponsible' advisedly. Look what happened the last time around.

In 2001, within a week of the Parliament attack (and a few days after Afzal Guru's arrest), the government recalled its ambassador from Pakistan and dispatched half a million troops to the border. On what basis was that done? The only thing the public was told is that while Afzal Guru was in the custody of the Delhi Police Special Cell, he had admitted to being a member of the Pakistan-based militant group Jaish-e-Mohammed (JeM). The Supreme Court set aside that confession extracted in police custody as inadmissible in law. Does what is inadmissible in law become admissible in war?

In its final judgement on the case, apart from the

now famous statements about satisfying 'the collective conscience of the society' and having no direct evidence, the Supreme Court also said there was no evidence that Mohammad Afzal belonged to any terrorist group or organization. So what justified that military aggression, that loss of soldiers' lives, that massive haemorrhaging of public money and the real risk of nuclear war? (Remember foreign embassies issued travel advisories and evacuated their staff?) Was there some intelligence that preceded the Parliament attack and the arrest of Afzal Guru that we had not been told about? If so, how could the attack be allowed to happen? And if the intelligence was accurate, and infallible enough to justify such dangerous military posturing, don't people in India, Pakistan and Kashmir have the right to know what it was? Why was that evidence not produced in court to establish Afzal Guru's guilt?

In the endless debates around the Parliament attack case, on this, perhaps the most crucial issue of all, there has been dead silence from all quarters—leftists, rightists, Hindutva-ists, secularists, nationalists, seditionists, cynics, critics. Why?

Maybe the JeM did mastermind the attack. Praveen Swami, perhaps the Indian media's best-known expert on 'terrorism', who seems to have enviable sources in the Indian police and intelligence agencies, has recently cited the 2003 testimony of former ISI chief Lt. Gen. Javed Ashraf Qazi, and the 2004 book by Muhammad Amir Rana, a Pakistani scholar, holding the JeM responsible for the Parliament attack. (It's touching, this belief in the veracity of the testimony of the chief of an organization whose mandate it is to destabilize India.) It still doesn't explain what evidence there was in 2001, when the army mobilization took place.

For the sake of argument, let's accept that the JeM carried out the attack. Maybe the ISI was involved too. We needn't pretend that the government of Pakistan is innocent of carrying out covert activity over Kashmir. Just as the government of India does in Balochistan and parts of Pakistan. (Remember the Indian army trained the Mukti Bahini in East Pakistan in the 1970s, and six different Sri Lankan Tamil militant groups, including the Liberation Tigers of Tamil Eelam, in the 1980s.)

It's a filthy scenario all around. What would a war with Pakistan have achieved then, and what will it achieve now? (Apart from a massive loss of life. And fattening the bank accounts of some arms dealers.) Indian hawks routinely suggest the only way to 'root out the problem' is 'hot pursuit' and the 'taking out' of 'terrorist camps' in Pakistan. Really? It would be interesting to research how many of the aggressive strategic experts and defence analysts on our TV screens have an interest in the defence and weapons industry. They don't even need war. They just need a warlike climate in which military spending remains on an upward graph. This idea of hot pursuit is even stupider and more pathetic than it sounds. What would they bomb? A few individuals? Their barracks and food supplies? Or their ideology? Look how the US government's 'hot pursuit' has ended in Afghanistan. And look how a 'security grid' of half a million soldiers has not been able to subdue the unarmed, civilian population of Kashmir. And India is going to cross international borders to bomb a country—with nuclear arms—that is rapidly devolving into chaos? India's professional warmongers derive a great deal of satisfaction by sneering at what they see as the disintegration of Pakistan.

Anyone with a rudimentary, working knowledge of history and geography would know that the breakdown of Pakistan (into a gangland of crazed, nihilistic, religious zealots) is absolutely no reason for anyone to rejoice.

The US presence in Afghanistan and Iraq, and Pakistan's official role as America's junior partner in the war on terror, makes that region a much-reported place. The rest of the world is at least aware of the dangers unfolding there. Less understood, and harder to read, is the perilous wind that's picking up speed in the world's favourite new superpower. The Indian economy is in considerable trouble. The aggressive, acquisitive ambition that economic liberalization unleashed in the newly created middle class is quickly turning into an equally aggressive frustration. The aircraft they were sitting in has begun to stall just after takeoff. Exhilaration is turning to panic.

The general election is due in 2014. Even without an exit poll I can tell you what the results will be. Though it may not be obvious to the naked eye, once again we will have a Congress–BJP coalition. (Two parties, each with a mass murder of thousands of people belonging to minority communities under their belts.) The CPI(M) will give support from outside, even though it hasn't been asked to. Oh, and it will be a strong state. On the hanging front, the gloves are already off. Could the next in line be Balwant Singh Rajoana, on death row for the assassination of Punjab's chief minister Beant Singh? His execution could revive Khalistani sentiment in Punjab and put the Akali Dal on the mat. Perfect old-style Congress politics.

But that old-style politics is in some difficulty. In the last few turbulent months, it is not just the image of major political parties, but politics itself, the idea of politics as we know it, that has taken a battering. Again and again, whether it's corruption, rising prices, or rape and the rising violence against women, the new middle class is at the barricades. They can be water-cannoned or lathi-charged, but can't be shot or imprisoned in their thousands, in the way the poor can, the way Dalits, Adivasis, Muslims, Kashmiris, Nagas and Manipuris can—and have been. The old political parties know that if there is not to be a complete meltdown, this aggression has to be headed off, redirected. They know that they must work together to bring politics back to what it *used* to be. What better way than a communal conflagration? (How else can the secular play at being secular and the communal be communal?) Maybe even a little war, so that we can play Hawks & Doves all over again.

What better solution than to aim a kick at that tried and trusted old political football—Kashmir? The hanging of Afzal Guru, its brazenness and its timing, is deliberate. It has brought politics and anger back onto Kashmir's streets.

India hopes to manage it with the usual combination of brute force and poisonous, Machiavellian manipulation, designed to pit people against one another. The war in Kashmir is presented to the world as a battle between an inclusive, secular democracy and radical Islamists. What then should we make of the fact that Mufti Bashiruddin, the so-called Grand Mufti of Kashmir (a completely phantom post)—who has made the most abominable hate speeches and issued fatwa after fatwa, intended to present Kashmir as a demonic, monolithic, Wahabi society—is actually a government-anointed cleric? Kids on Facebook will be arrested, never him. What should we make of the fact that the Indian government looks away while money from Saudi Arabia (that most steadfast partner of the US) is pouring into Kashmir's madrassas? How different is this from what the CIA did in Afghanistan all those years ago? That whole, sorry business is what created Osama bin Laden, Al Qaeda and the Taliban. It has decimated Afghanistan and Pakistan. What sort of incubus will this unleash?

The trouble is that the old political football may not be all that easy to control any more. And it's radioactive. Maybe it is not a coincidence that a few days ago Pakistan tested a short-range battlefield nuclear missile to protect itself against threats from 'evolving scenarios'. Two weeks ago, the Kashmir police published 'survival tips' for nuclear war. Apart from advising people to build toilet-equipped bombproof basements large enough to house their entire families for two weeks, it said: 'During a nuclear attack, motorists should dive out of their cars toward the blast to save themselves from being crushed by their soon-to-be tumbling vehicles.' And to 'expect some initial disorientation as the blast wave may blow down and carry away many prominent and familiar features'.

Prominent and familiar features may already have been blown down. Perhaps we should all jump out of our soon-to-be-tumbling vehicles.

This essay was first published in *Outlook*, 25 February 2013.

[19]

INDIA'S MESSAGE TO KASHMIR: THE NOOSE CAN EXTEND BEYOND THE GALLOWS

Mirza Waheed

A curfew is like a collective strangulation. You proscribe movement, talk, communication and assembly. You cut off the very sustenance of life: food, milk, medicine. You choke a people, because you fear, no, dread, what the curfewed other might say to the world. Indian-controlled Kashmir has been under curfew for the last five days; everything is shut down, locked up, besieged. Newspapers have been seized, editors verbally instructed by police officials not to print, TV channels, except of course the government-run ones, have been blocked. People are not allowed to travel except if you have a bullet in your body and are still breathing inside an ambulance. This latest imposition—Kashmir's modern history is bookmarked by chapter after chapter of sieges and martial-law-like curfews—came soon after Mohammad Afzal Guru was hanged by India for his involvement in the attack on India's Parliament in 2001 in which nine people were killed.

In a case widely criticized for its dodgy investigation, the absence of a fair trial and, most crucially, the lack of evidence beyond reasonable doubt, the Supreme Court of India, upholding sentences of lower courts, sentenced Afzal Guru to a double death sentence in 2005. There was only circumstantial evidence against him, the court admitted, but the 'collective conscience of society' could only be soothed with this execution. As soon as what many call a miscarriage of justice was performed in Delhi's Tihar Jail, the Indian government effectively shut off the Valley from the world. It was almost automatic, a reflex, and why wouldn't it be, for the powerful and increasingly militaristic Indian state is well rehearsed in dealing with the oppressed and weak of Kashmir.

So the run of play in this heartless display of retributive justice was this: you hang a Kashmiri in Delhi and then, to complete the picture, to make the performance full, immediately put Kashmir under a military siege. A country that needs to impose a curfew every time it fears what it calls 'unrest' in a region that it claims as an integral part should by now have learned that it is not an integral part. It never was.

It was not just the hanging but also the manner of it—executed while the world slept, in secret and in great haste, as thieves do when they embark on their dark deeds—that makes this execution a symbol of the deep moral rot at the heart of the Indian state. Indian authorities chose not to inform Afzal Guru's family prior to the hanging and quietly buried him in prison. His brother has said they learned of his execution on TV. A letter sent by the Government of India to Afzal Guru's wife reached her two days after the execution.

Even the public prosecutor responsible for Afzal Guru's trial has admitted that it was a violation of his rights as well as of India's prison manuals that state a person on death row must be allowed family visits.

What kind of state makes sure that the wife and young son of a man it is about to execute do not see him, touch him or hear him talk, one last time? Kashmiris, in mourning and in fury, erected a tombstone over an empty grave in the main martyrs' graveyard in the Kashmiri capital, Srinagar. The text of the epitaph was the same as that of another epitaph, erected in memory of Maqbool Bhat, the founder of Kashmir's main pro-independence militant group turned political formation, the Jammu and Kashmir Liberation Front, who was hanged in the same jail twenty-nine years ago. The epitaph reads, 'The martyr of the nation, Mohammad Afzal Guru, Date of Martyrdom: 9th February 2013 Saturday, whose mortal remains are lying in the custody of the Government of India. The nation is awaiting its return.'

On the morning of 13 February, Kashmiri news websites reported that the police had removed and destroyed the tombstone and then, after the news spread via Twitter and Facebook, a replacement tombstone mysteriously reappeared. The Kashmiri phrases Qabr Chhoor and Kafan Chhoor, titles for those who rob graves or shrouds, are deployed to describe the basest of thieves. The swiftness of the execution, and the macabre theatre that followed, which included an offer by the Indian government that Afzal's family will be allowed to pray once by his grave in prison, which the family promptly turned down, is disturbingly reminiscent of Franco's Spain.

I learned of the execution in London and struggled to make sense of it. I still do. It was, for reasons moral and legal—judicial review is available to even people denied a presidential pardon—somehow unbelievable, although by no means unexpected. Does the world's so-called largest democracy really want to be seen as a nation revelling in a retrograde, made-for-TV bloodlust?

I began to think of Ghalib, Afzal Guru's fourteen-year-old son, who, accompanied by his mother a few years ago, went to the head of the Indian state with a mercy petition, begging the President to pardon his father's life. Clearly, the President wasn't listening. He had to, as the judge had decreed in the Supreme Court of India's verdict, satisfy the 'collective conscience of the society', which will 'only be satisfied if capital punishment is awarded to the offender'.

It is of course impossible to understand the complex moral arithmetic necessary to arrive at the perfect potion needed to assuage the collective conscience of a billion people. I began to think of writing about it, answering an urge to say what I, and many others, felt. I struggled, despairing about the powerlessness, and perhaps pointlessness, of an op-ed or essay. I also began to feel lonely, for in spite of the proliferation of conversations on social media, a solidarity of the oppressed and the besieged is hard to find amid the buzz of the internet or a postmodern metropolis.

What was the Indian state trying to say, one must ask. Surely, it can't simply be explained, as some analysts have done, as merely a hideous expression of the compulsions of electoral realpolitik in which political parties in India become eager to sink to new moral lows to outdo their rivals. It's a message to the Kashmiri people, an occupying power yelling at the powerless natives that you must bow and genuflect, that the hangman's noose can extend beyond the gallows, casting its dark shadow over children's milk and medicines for old couples.

Two moments seem to have entered history. Kashmiris creating a hollow grave as a mausoleum to memory and resistance and India making a craven declaration: that a Kashmiri corpse can be seditious. It must remain in prison.

This essay was first published in the *Guardian*, 15 February 2013.

[20]

THE HANGING AS A MESSAGE TO KASHMIR

Mohamad Junaid

Several Indian commentators appear to have been shocked by the supposed 'secrecy' with which the Indian government executed Mohammad Afzal Guru. Some lament now that Afzal did not receive a fair trial, while others argue the execution could have been carried out in a more civilized manner, or at a different time. Either way, many of them agree that this incident is a blot on Indian democracy. Just a blot though—as if the rest of the record has been clean. Many tried to wash away the ghastly nature of this entire episode by blaming it all on 'politics'—petty party politics—exonerating the high politics of the state. India's prime minister, Manmohan Singh, unable to savour the moment completely, perhaps concerned about the reaction of offended liberal sensibilities around death sentences, chastised his Home Minister Shinde for not knowing how to conduct 'statecraft'. The state, he seemed to suggest, is subtle when executing people.

In my view, however, this execution is one of the most public events in recent memory.

Afzal's case was a high-profile one, constantly under media glare, and throughout considerable discussions took place around it. Several books were written about the flaws of the prosecution's case. For the previous twelve years, while Afzal awaited his fate in a tiny prison cell in Tihar, his name circulated regularly in the media or in speeches by Indian politicians. Prominent TV anchors frequently speculated about when Afzal was going to be hanged (and while breaking the news on the morning of 9 February they could hardly hide their glee). That the system was rigged against Afzal from the beginning was well known, if never acknowledged.

The execution itself took place in a very 'open' manner—each detail of the act of execution was made public, including Afzal Guru's final words and emotions at the moment of his execution. Most importantly, India announced the execution to Kashmiris in the most dramatic manner possible—by putting an entire nation under a clampdown, uniting Kashmiris simultaneously in grief, mourning and misery. Late letters, the indecency of not returning the body, the fact of not allowing his family members to meet him one last time, the February 9th of the execution (almost coinciding with Maqbool Bhat's death anniversary on 11 February, another Kashmiri hanged in the same prison twenty-nine years ago), all of it was made very public. Afzal's execution was meant to be a public event in India. Only in this public and brazen manner of execution, and not in any other way, could the 'national conscience' have been satisfied.

It was never a matter of justice but about the display of what Indian state officials call 'national will'—which is often what the state projects as the collective decision of the nation. The Indian nation can't be tough if the execution followed a procedure. National will is not displayed in following documents like the Constitution or international human rights norms; it is, rather, displayed in the ability to transcend such obstacles to sovereign action. TADA, POTA, AFSPA, etc. are all displays of such national will. Mohammad Afzal Guru's execution in this public and dramatic way is how sovereignty exercises itself—through an absolute, and extralegal, control over how, why, what, where and when of dispensing death. Sovereignty is above law and civility.

Many pro-India Kashmiri politicians, including a few unaffiliated commentators, are upset about the manner of hanging. They complain that Kashmiri sensitivities were not taken into account. It is surprising that at a time which could very well mark the most unapologetic and barefaced policy shift in India's efforts in Kashmir—forcing a resolution through demographic change (settlements and a possible annihilation)—these commentators expect the Indian state to worry about Kashmiri 'sensitivities'. Invoking sensitivities in the face of the state's open disregard for Kashmiri lives de-radicalizes the political understanding of the event in Kashmir. It softens the image of the state, even though the state has clearly declared that it will not be soft on Kashmiris. It is possible that by 'sensitivity' Kashmir's pro-India politicians just mean their own electoral calculations.

Instead of being a question of sentiments or conscience, the execution was a deeply political event. Political events bring to the fore fundamental contradictions that underlie political conflicts. Such events remove everyday obfuscations that blur the nature of the relationship between the contestants in a political struggle—here Kashmiri subjects and the Indian state. This execution clearly establishes the fact of Otherness of Kashmiris in the Indian political imagination, and towards whom the Indian state would act under no legality or norm of human rights, far less concern itself with questions of citizenship rights. Toward Kashmiris the Indian state can only exercise its sovereignty—every act of the state in Kashmir is such an exercise, and therefore each act a display of India's 'national will'. For instance, the arbitrary imposition of curfews is not done to maintain any law or order, but is an unambiguous threat to Kashmiris that the Indian state has the power to choke life in Kashmir any time it wants.

The event of Afzal's execution has effectively foreclosed any politics via elections. It has emptied more than anything else the rickety discourse of those who had suggested a move to 'governance'. I think at this stage the actual helplessness in Kashmir should be felt by those individuals or groups who had put at stake their social lives and political interests to argue that a hyphenated 'India-Kashmir' was a possibility. They had remained obdurate in their defence of the oppressive Indian state even in the face of terrible atrocities visited on their fellow Kashmiris. For them it is over in the political sense. If they still nurse illusions of any possibility of India agreeing to free Kashmir from its military stranglehold and allow decent life conditions in Kashmir, it would happen only at the cost of losing the last shreds of integrity from their politics, if there was any in the first place. Kashmir's pro-India politicians have been pretending, or perhaps sincerely lamenting, that they have no power over major affairs of the state, including the removal of AFSPA. But they have been unable, or lack the courage, to draw the necessary conclusions about the vacuousness of elections and democracy in Kashmir.

This event has reaffirmed resoundingly the thinking of those Kashmiris who have for long set themselves upon a course to create an independent destiny for Kashmir. Tehreek—the Movement—has always been based on the fundamental principle of the irreconcilability of Kashmir's future within India, and India has proved yet again how right Kashmiri pro-freedom leaders have been.

Since the ideological obfuscation should be over now, the only thing that keeps Kashmir territorially tied to India is brute force and arrogance. Shaheed Afzal's body in Tihar is an apt metaphor for Kashmir's territorial connection with India. It is a body that doesn't belong in that land.

This understanding must become the bedrock of Kashmiri resistance and politics.

This essay was first published on Kashmir Solidarity Network, an online community of Kashmir-related activism, 16 February 2013.

APPENDIX I

DETAILS OF CROSS EXAMINATION
SUBMITTED BY AFZAL WITH HIS PETITION TO THE PRESIDENT

Prosecution witness	Designation	Cross examination by Neeraj Bansal	Cross examination by Afzal	Remarks
PW 1 G.L. Mehta	SHO, Parliament Street PS	Nil	Nil	
PW 2 Sanjiv Kumar	SI, Parliament Street PS	Nil	Nil	Alleges that Afzal identified bodies of terrorists
PW 3 Rajinder Singh	SI, President's House security	Nil	Nil	Alleges Afzal identified Haider
PW 4 Yog Raj Dogra	SI, IGI Airport	Nil	Nil	Recovered slips with phone numbers; mobile
PW 5 ASI Jeet Ram	Security, Delhi Police	Nil	Nil	
PW 6 Constable Rajesh Kumar	Photographer	Nil	Nil	Alleges to have taken 184 photos
PW 7 Jasveer	HC, Parliament Street PS	Nil	Nil	
PW 8 H.S. Ashwani Kumar	HC, Parliament Street PS	Nil	Nil	

Prosecution witness	Designation	Cross examination by Neeraj Bansal	Cross examination by Afzal	Remarks
PW 9 Sukhbir Singh	HC, Parliament Street PS	Nil	Nil	
PW 10 Jagvir Singh	HC, Parliament Street PS	Nil	Nil	
PW 11 G.L. Meena	Deputy Secretary, Home	Nil	Nil	Court disallowed several questions; grant of prosecution sanction
PW 12 T.N. Mohan	DCP, Headquarters	Nil	Nil	Sanction for prosecution
PW 13 Dushyant Singh	Deputy Chief Security Officer, Ministry of Home Affairs	Nil	Nil	Issuance of sticker
PW 14 H.C. Malkit Singh	Parliament Street PS	Nil	Nil	
PW 15 Mathew George	Executive, Infrastructure Leasing and Financial Services Ltd.	Nil	Nil	Original owner of white Ambassador
PW 16 Dheeraj Singh	Peon, Infrastructure Leasing and Financial Services Ltd.	Nil	Nil	Buyer of the white Ambassador
PW 17 Satbir Singh	Shopkeeper	Yes	Nil	Bought the white Ambassador from PW 16
PW 18 Raghbir Singh	Motor mechanic	Yes	Nil	Buyer of the white Ambassador

Prosecution witness	Designation	Cross examination by Neeraj Bansal	Cross examination by Afzal	Remarks
PW 19 Harish Chander Jaggi	Proprietor, Jaggi motors	Yes	Nil	Bought the white Ambassador from PW 18
PW 20 Harpal Singh	Proprietor, Lucky motors		Afzal admits going to the shop of witness	Afzal truthfully owns up his role
PW 21 Constable Mahipal Singh	CRPF	Nil	Nil	Injured in firing
PW 22 R.S. Verma	Director, SFSL, Chandigarh	Nil	Nil	
PW 23 P.R. Nehra	Principle Scientific Officer, CFSL, CBI	Nil	Nil	Handwriting expert
PW 24 A. Dey	Senior Scietific Officer, Asst Chemical Examiner, CFSL, CBI	Nil	Nil	
PW 25 Jasvinder Singh	Computer Centre (Xansa Webcity)	Nil	Nil	
PW 26 Jibharam	Mechanic	Yes	Nil	Buyer of Yamaha motorcycle
PW 27 Salim	Junk Dealer	Nil	Nil	Purchased motorcycle from PW 26
PW 28 Babu Khan	Barber	Nil	Nil	Purchased motorcycle from PW 27
PW 29 Sushil Kumar	Gupta Auto Deals	Nil	Yes (Only one suggestion given)	Important witness on purchase of motorcycle

Prosecution witness	Designation	Cross examination by Neeraj Bansal	Cross examination by Afzal	Remarks
PW 30 SI Mahesh Kumar	Draftsman, Crime Branch, PHQ	Nil	Nil	
PW 31 Bal Raj	Property Dealer	Yes (Inadequate)	Nil	Court allows leading question; property dealer in regard to Indira Vihar
PW 32 Jagdish Lai	Owner of Indira Vihar house	Yes	Yes	Photos of five terrorists
PW 33 Davinder Pal Kapoor	Property Dealer	Yes	Nil	Not even a suggestion was put to the witness that he did not get the set premises on rent for Afzal or that he was deposing falsely
PW 34 Subhash Chand Malhotra	Owner of A-97 Gandhi Vihar	Yes (Inadequate)	Nil	Testimony regarding identification of Mohd. went unchallenged
PW 35 Capt. P.K. Guharay	Security Manager, Airtel	Nil	Nil	
PW 36 Maj. A.R. Satish	Sterling Cellular Ltd.	Nil	Nil	
PW 37 Prem Chand	Hostel owner, Christian Colony	Yes [one suggestion only)	Nil	Important witness
PW 38 Rajneesh Kumar	Runs STD booth, Christian Colony	Nil	Nil	

Prosecution witness	Designation	Cross examination by Neeraj Bansal	Cross examination by Afzal	Remarks
PW 39 Naresh Gulati	Landlord of S.A.R. Geelani	Nil	Nil	Landlord was on bail at the time
PW 40 Anil Kumar	Chemical business	Yes (Inadequate)	Nil	
PW 41 Ajay Kumar	Salesman, Dry fruits shop	Yes	Nil	
PW 42 Ramesh Adwani	Shopkeeper, Dyes and colours	Yes (Inadequate)	Nil	
PW 43 Sunil Kumar Gupta	Shopkeeper, Electrical gadgets	Yes	Nil	
PW 44 Sandeep Chaudhary	Shopkeeper, Mobile phones	Yes	Nil	
PW 45 Tejpal Kharbanda	Landlord, Shaukat (co-accused)	Nil	Nil	
PW 46 Usha Kharbanda	Wife of PW 45	Nil	Nil	Her testimony is not recorded
PW 47 Dr Upender Kishore	Senior Resident Lady Hardinge Medical College	Nil	Nil	Conducted postmortem on deceased terrorists; important witness,
PW 48 Dr Rajinder Singh	Expert, CFSL, CBI	Nil	Nil	
PW 49 Kamal Kishore Behal	Shopkeeper, Mobile phones	Yes	Nil	
PW 50 Sanjay Mani	Manager, Admin, Xansa India Ltd.	Nil	Nil	

Prosecution witness	Designation	Cross examination by Neeraj Bansal	Cross examination by Afzal	Remarks
PW 51 Dharampal	Clerk, District Transport Office, Faridabad	Nil	Nil	
PW 52 Charan Singh	Clerk, Registering Authority, Motor Vehicle, Faridabad	Nil	Nil	
PW 53 Mahesh Chand	LDC, MLO, HQ	Nil	Nil	
PW 54 Anil Ahuja	UDC, Transport Authority	Nil	Nil	
PW 55 Sham Singh	Sub-Inspector, Security, Vice-President	Nil	Nil	
PW 56 Constable Ranjit Kumar	Special Branch, Lodhi Road	Nil	Nil	
PW 57 SI Pawan Kumar	Special Cell, Lodhi Road	Nil	Nil	Laptop was in custody of this witness
PW 58 SI Neeraj Paliwal	CRPF, SDG, VVIP Security	Nil	Nil	
PW 59 N.K. Aggarwal	Senior Scientific Officer, CFSL, CBI	Nil	Nil	
PW 60 Ashok Chand	DCP, Special Cell	Yes	Yes	Witness states: 'I am not aware if on 20/12/01, accused Afzal was produced before

Prosecution witness	Designation	Cross examination by Neeraj Bansal	Cross examination by Afzal	Remarks
				the media or on any other date he was produced before media to tell media about his role in attack on Parliament.'
PW 61 Abdul Haq Butt	Deputy SP, SDPO, M.R. Ganj, Srinagar	Yes (Inadequate)	Nil	
PW 62 HC Mohammad Akbar	Parampura PS, Srinagar	Yes (one suggestion only)	Nil	Most important witness on Afzal's arrest
PW 63 V.K. Maheshwari	Addl. Chief Metropolitan Magistrate, Patiala House	Yes (Inadequate)	Nil	
PW 64 SI Hardaya Bhushan	Special Cell, Lodhi Road	Yes	Nil	Contradicts PW 61 and PW 62 on time, place of arrest
PW 65 SI Sharad Kohli	Special Cell, Lodhi Road	Nil	Nil	Important witness in regard to Afzal's arrest
PW 66 Mohan Chand Sharma	Special Cell, Lodhi Road	Nil	Nil	Crucial witness not cross-examined
PW 61 SI Bidrish Dutt	Special Cell, Lodhi Road	Nil	Nil	The witness stated that Afzal identified photograph of one Mohd@Bargar who was deceased

Prosecution witness	Designation	Cross examination by Neeraj Bansal	Cross examination by Afzal	Remarks
				terrorist and told he was hijacking of IC 814; someone objected but no cross examination
PW 68 Dr S.K. Jain	Asst Director, CFSL, Chandigarh	Nil	Nil	
PW 69 Inspector Santhosh Singh	CRPF	Nil	Nil	
PW 70 SI Harinder Singh	Special Cell, Lodhi Road	Nil	Nil	
PW 71 Rashid	Transporter	Nil	Nil	
PW 72 Vimal Kant	Computer engineer	Nil	Nil	On the laptop
PW 73 Krishnan A. Sastri	Bureau of Police Research and Development, Ministry of Home Affairs, Hyderabad	Nil	Nil	On the laptop
PW 74 Constable Shambir Singh	CRPF	Nil	Nil	
PW 75 K. Satyamurthy	Officer Commanding, BDU, NSG	Nil	Nil	
PW 76 Inspector H.S. Gill	Special Cell, Lodhi Road	Yes but inadequate	Nil	Crucial witness on whose testimony Afzal given a death sentence

Prosecution witness	Designation	Cross examination by Neeraj Bansal	Cross examination by Afzal	Remarks
PW 77 SI Lalit Mohan	Special Cell, Lodhi Road	Yes	Nil	
PW 78 Manjual Kapur	Manager, Siemen, Gurgaon	Nil	Nil	
PW 79 M. Krishna	Ministry of Home Affairs, Hyderabad	Nil	Nil	On laptop
PW 80 ACP Rajbir Singh	Investigating Officer, Special Cell, Lodhi Road	Yes but very inadequate	Nil	It is this officer whose investigation was found to be riddled with illegalities

APPENDIX II

CERTIFICATE OF INDIRA JAISING, SENIOR ADVOCATE, SUPREME COURT OF INDIA, CERTIFYING MOHAMMAD AFZAL's CASE MERITS CURATION BY THE SUPREME COURT

IN THE SUPREME COURT OF INDIA
IN ITS CRIMINAL ORIGINAL JURISDICTION
AND
IN ITS JURISDICTION UNDER ARTICLE 32 OF THE
CONSTITUTION OF INDIA
CURATIVE PETITION NO.——— OF 2006

In the matter of:

M. Afzal Guru

..................Petitioner

Versus

State NCT of Delhi & Anr

..................Respondent

CERTIFICATE OF MS. INDIRA JAISING,
SNR. ADVOCATE

1. This Hon'ble Court vide judgment dated 4.8.2005 in Criminal Appeal No. 381/2004 has found the Petitioner guilty, convicted and sentenced him to life sentence on three counts under Section 121–A, Section 3 (3) POTA and Section 4 (a) r/w Section 4 (i) of the Explosive Substances Act 1908, this life

sentence was merged with the death sentence on two counts under Section121 IPC r/w section 120-B IPC read with section 302 IPC. The appeal of the Petitioner was dismissed subject to setting aside convictions under Section 3 (2) of POTA and Section 3 of the Explosive Substances Act.

2. I have perused in detail the judgment dated 4.8.2002 of the Hon'ble Supreme Court as also order dated 29.10.2003 of the Hon'ble High Court in Cr. Reference No. 1/2-003 and Criminal Appeals No 59 & 80/2003 and judgment of the Ld. Sessions Court order dated 18.12.2002 in Sessions Case No. 53/2002 to the extent that they concern the right to legal representation through State legal aid.

3. A review petition was filed against the said order dated 4.8.2005 and rejected. The Petitioner has raised the ground of denial of effective legal representation in all his appeals including at para 1(vi) of the review petition.

4. I am of the opinion that the Petitioner's fundamental right to a fair trial and constitutional guarantee of effective legal representation, through State legal aid, as an accused in criminal trial, guaranteed under Article 21 read with Article 22 (1) and 39-A of the Constitution of India, has been violated in the present case, vitiating the trial and the consequent conviction and resulting in gross miscarriage of justice.

5. The procedure established by law under Article 21 and 22 requires that no person be convicted and condemned to death without adequate and effective legal representation through State legal aid. The Delhi High Court has framed rules, hereinafter 'High Court Rules', under Section 304 of the CrPC, which provide that if an accused is unrepresented and cannot afford a counsel, the sessions Judge shall make arrangements to employ counsel at Government expense. A list of 10-15 counsels willing to appear for the undefended (at State expense) is to be maintained and constantly revised in each district. The advocates placed on this list should be competent criminal lawyers not merely charity seekers (see rule 4 of Vol. III, High Court Rules and Orders, Chapter 24 relating to sessions cases, Part C). Strict compliance of the said procedure established by law is mandatory to fulfil the requirement of due process. However, the record bears proof of the fact that in the present case, the session's court failed to follow this

procedure. The detailed instances are raised vide the curative petition.

6. Having regard to the fact that the legal representation must be effective and adequate, especially in offences punishable by death, the state must take care to ensure that lawyers on the panel are sufficiently competent and that the scale of fee is such as is commensurate with the standing and experience of counsel. In my opinion an important question that has emerged from the present case and has serious ramification for the rule of law in India is with reference to the scale of fees fixed by the LASA for sessions court trials. The legal aid fee schedule, under the Legal Aid Services Authorities Act, provides for a paltry fee for Rupees 600 per effective hearing to the maximum of Rs 3000 for sessions cases (involving life imprisonment or death sentence) for the advocates. The 'High Court rules' referred to above, after amendment in 2003, for trials under Section 302 IPC, provide a fee of Rs 500 for preparation and first hearing in the murder trial and Rs 300 per subsequent effective to a maximum of Rs 5000. This fee schedule makes the right to fair representation illusory and a mockery of the right to effective legal aid and is therefore not in consonance with the right guaranteed under Article 21 of the Constitution of India. Anything short of appropriate and adequate fees for counsel for indigent and unrepresented accused results in two sets of standards of access to justice, one for the rich and the other for the poor.

7. Mr S. Murlidhar, (who is now an Hon'ble Judge of the Delhi High Court) in chapter 3 of his book *Law, Poverty and Legal Aid (Access to Criminal Justice)* has observed that it could be persuasively argued that the denial of these elements—(i) right to counsel immediately upon arrest, (ii) extension of the right to counsel to all subsequent stages where the arrested person will have to resist the consequences of his arraignment, trial, revision and appeal, (iii) the right of choice of counsel—of the right to a person who is unable to engage his own counsel, only on account of his being economically or socially disadvantaged, would violate the right to equality. Therefore the right to legal assistance at state expense if reconciled with the right under Article 22 (1) cannot partake of a different character in terms of scope and content. By pleading the inability of the state to

afford this right on equal terms, it is sought to be treated as a directive principle which, it is submitted, is inconsistent with its recognition as a non-derogable fundamental right.

8. In my opinion, the failure to provide effective and adequate legal aid has resulted in 'constitutional error' because it affects the framework within which a trial proceeds and requires no proof of prejudice.

9. The law laid down by the Hon'ble Supreme Court provides that denial of a fair trial simplicitor vitiates the trial and the question of prejudice does not arise when a citizen is deprived of his life without complying with the procedure prescribed by law. (*Bashira v. State of U.P.*, (1969) 1 SCR 32 and *Hussainara Khatoon v. State* 1980 (1) SCC 98.)

10. It is an established position at law that international conventions form part of domestic law which are enforceable in the absence of contrary statue (See *Visakha*) and can be used to interpret the width and breadth of fundamental rights in the Indian Constitution. Article 14 (3) (b) of the ICCPR provides that a person accused of a criminal offence has a right to be defended by an effective counsel during detention, trial and appeal.

11. In my opinion the judgement of this Hon'ble Court dated 4.8.2005 warrants curation since the appointment of amicus by the court of sessions in violation of the procedure prescribed by the Delhi High Court Rules has manifestly prejudiced the case of the accused. The Court erroneously concluded that the Petitioner was adequately represented based on a chart presented by the prosecution showing the number of questions asked in cross examination when a perusal of the questions itself reveals the manifest prejudice as is detailed vide the chart annexed to the curative petition. Moreover, at several places the accused Petitioner has himself been compelled to cross examine witnesses as he obviously perceived himself to be inadequately represented. Cross examination by the accused in a trial which could lead to a death sentence is no substitute for cross examination by a legally trained mind.

New Delhi   Indira Jaising
Dated   Snr. Advocate

APPENDIX III

TEXT OF A RECORDED INTERVIEW WITH DAVINDER SINGH, DEPUTY SUPERINTENDENT OF POLICE, SPECIAL TASK FORCE (STF) BY PARVAIZ BUKHARI

Parvaiz Bukhari: How do you know Mohammad Afzal Guru?

Davinder Singh: A source came to me and informed that one Afzal Guru is the top courier for Gazi Baba. I looked for him but could not capture him. When I got to know that Afzal works in Pattan area [Baramulla District], I contacted DSP in-charge of Pattan SOG camp, Vinay Gupta, and he captured him [Afzal]. After interrogating Afzal, Vinay called me and said that he could not get anything out from him. But I requested Vinay not to release him and send him to my camp at Humhama [Budgam District]. That is how I know Afzal.

PB: Once in your custody, what did he reveal?

DS: I did interrogate and torture him at my camp for several days. And we never recorded his arrest in the books anywhere. His [Afzal's] description of torture at my camp is true. That was the procedure those days and we did pour petrol in his arse and gave him electric shocks. But I could not break him. He did not reveal anything to me despite our hardest possible interrogation. We tortured him enough for Gazi Baba but he did not break. He looked like a 'bhondu' those days, what you call a 'chootya' type. And I had a reputation for torture, interrogation and breaking suspects. If anybody came out of my interrogation clean, nobody would ever touch him again. He would be considered clean for good by the whole department.

PB: So Afzal was freed?

DS: My SP, Mr Ashiq Hussain Bukhari, sent his own brother-in-law, Altaf and Afzal's brother Aijaz Guru, to the camp after calling me to meet Afzal. My SP said, 'If you have not found him involved in any way why don't you release him?' I told him let his [Afzal's] torture wounds heal so that he could be released. But since he was captured by the Pattan SOG camp, I sent him back there after he recovered. Afzal was released from there later.

PB: Have you had any contact with Afzal or any of his family members after that, as he has alleged?

DS: I have had no contact whatsoever with Afzal after I sent him back to Pattan camp. Not on phone, no meeting, nothing at all. I have seen his brother Aijaz only once when he was sent to my camp by my SP. And I have never had any contact with any of his family members either.

PB: Afzal in his letter has alleged that you asked him in presence of one Tariq to take one man to Delhi and help him?

DS: That is a lie. I don't know Tariq or Mohammad, but I know of them. Since I was working in counter-militancy, I know Tariq and Mohammad were 'A' category wanted militants with five lakh rupees reward on their head. If I knew them or had captured them do you think I would have released them? This is a concocted story. They come here from Pakistan for terrorism. Had I met them, do you think I would have spared them? Afzal wants clemency and he wants to gain sympathy of Kashmiri public and government of India by giving this story.

PB: Afzal alleges in his letter that you stayed in touch with him and that other man and Mohammad when they were in Delhi?

DS: It is not true. I never had his number and never called him. Why am I being suspected, it could be anybody else if at all calls were made to Afzal or any other person. Afzal was sent to Pattan from my camp in September 2000 and I was transferred out from Humhama SOG camp to CIK [Counter Intelligence Kashmir] Hari Niwas in February 2001. When I was in Humhama SOG camp, there was no STD dialling facility there. I have not even visited that camp after my transfer. If I called Afzal from there who will authenticate it?

PB: Did anybody pay you money for Afzal's release as he has alleged?

DS: No. Even if I wanted to take money, I could not have as my SP's brother-in-law was seeking his [Afzal's] release. At the same time I cannot guarantee that nobody else took money from his family.

PB: In the light of allegations by Afzal, do you think that you may have been used?

DS: It is a difficult time for me. I would expect my superiors to clear my name. But it is sad that nobody from my department has come forward so far. Even if I had an iota of suspicion that I had been used by anybody, I am not the type to keep silent. And I want to reiterate that I have not talked to, seen or met Afzal or any of his family members after handing him back to Pattan SOG camp.

PB: Then why is your name figuring in Afzal's letter and his wife's accounts?

DS: I am being victimized for having worked in SOG, for being very nationalistic. What am I getting in return? Bad name and a conspirator . . . It's really unfortunate . . . Also, to be candid with you, nobody would ever forget having been interrogated by me.

PB: You must also have seen Afzal's letter. Do you think the handwriting and the signature is his?

DS: The signature is but not the handwriting . . . Signature I haven't seen but the handwriting is not that of Afzal's. Signature could be his but handwriting I know is not his. I know because he was teaching somebody's children where I had seen his handwriting. That is all fabricated.

PB: Have you seen that carefully?

DS: Yes of course.

PB: You have handled Afzal. Do you think he is the kind of man who could be involved in the Parliament attack?

DS: He is doing this exercise saying that he took the man there and helped them. And helped them buy a car, etc. Why he did this he knows it better. If all this would have been established when he was captured by us . . . he would not have been knowing it. It ended for us when he could not be broken [by interrogation].

APPENDIX IV

MOHAMMAD AFZAL GURU'S LAST LETTER WRITTEN AN HOUR BEFORE HE WAS HANGED

9-2-2013

Bi-ismi-illahi Rahman-i-rahim (In the name of Allah,
the most gracious, most merciful)

6:25 in the morning

Respected members of my family and the Believers, Assalamu-alaikum (peace be upon you): My gratitude to Allah the pure, because He chose me for this destiny. And, I also congratulate you, the Believers, because we all stayed with truth and righteousness. May truth and righteousness be our destiny in the afterlife as well. My request to the members of my family is that instead of harbouring regret, be respectful of the destiny I met.

Allah is the protector and witness of you all.

Allah Hafiz (God be your protector)

Translated by Parvaiz Bukhari

NOTES

INTRODUCTION: BREAKING THE NEWS

1. Mohammad Afzal's statement under Section 313 of the Criminal Procedure Code in the Court of S.N. Dhingra, September 2002. Full text on www.outlookindia.com/fullprint.asp?choice=1&fodname=20061019&fname=nirmalangshu&sid=2

2. Full coverage of the press conference where Afzal was made to incriminate himself available online at http://timesofindia.indiatimes.com/articleshow/1600576183.cms and http//timesofindia.indiatimes.com/articleshow/1295243790.cms

3. Judgement of the Supreme Court of India on Mohammad Afzal vs. the State (NCT of Delhi): http://judis.nic.in/supremecourt/qrydisp.asp?tfnm=27092

4. Online petitions asking for clemency and retrial as well as an inquiry into the case: www.petitiononline.com/ekta1/petition.html and www.petitiononline.com/CMAG/petition.html

5. Speech made by Prime Minister Manmohan Singh (then the leader of the Opposition) on 18 December 2001 in the Rajya Sabha. For the full text, see *Rajya Sabha Official Day's Proceedings, December 18, 2001*' p. 430.

6. Davinder Kumar, 'The Ham Burger: Did Delhi Police Sleuths Jump the Gun with the Wrong One?' *Outlook*, 21 January 2002.

7. For the full text of the Parliament Attack chargesheet, see Nirmalangshu Mukherji's *December 13: Terror Over Democracy*, Promilla & Co. Publishers, New Delhi, 2005, 'Annexure 1'.

8. Indian Express News Service, 'Show No Mercy, Hang Afzal: BJP', *Indian Express*, 23 November 2006.

9. Chandan Mitra, 'Celebrating Treason', *Pioneer*, 7 October 2006.

10. Swapan Dasgupta, 'You Can't Be Good to Evil', *Pioneer*, 1 October 2006.

11. Available online at www.ibnlive.com/videos/27157/the-other-side-of-afzals-surrender.html and www.ibnlive.com/videos/27182/afzal-gets-mixed-bag-from-politcos.html

12. Siddhartha Gautam, 'Tortured, but Kept Alive for a Deal', CNN-IBN: www.ibnlive.com/videos/27164/tortured-but-kept-alive-for-a-deal.html

13. Siddartha Gautam, 'The Other Side of Afzal's Surrender': www.ibnlive.com/news/the-other-side-of-afzals-surrender/27157-3-l.html

14. 'Advani Criticizes Delay in Afzal Execution', *The Hindu*, 13 November 2006.

15 See judgement of the Supreme Court of India on Mohammad Afzal vs. the State (NCT of Delhi): http://judis.nic.in/supremecourt/qrydisp.asp?tfnm=27092

16. See the letter of N.D. Pancholi to NDTV, 26 December 2006. Full text of the letter available online at www.sacw.net/free/pancholitoNDTV.html

17. Despite the court judgements, the media continues to publish custodial confessions. See Mihir Srivastava, 'Inside the Mind of the Bombers', *India Today*, 2 October 2008.

18. Barkha Dutt, 'Death of the Middle Ground', *Hindustan Times*, 16 December 2006.

19. In November 2002, undercover Delhi police 'encounter specialists' killed two alleged Lashkar-e-Toiba terrorists. A doctor who witnessed the attack said the victims were unarmed and a number of holes quickly emerged in the official account of the incident.

20. Arundhati Roy, *Listening to Grasshoppers*, New Delhi: Penguin Books India, 2013. See pp. 56 and 57 ('And His Life Should Become Extinct') for details on the Iftikhar Gilani case and how it was reported in the media.

21. Maloy Krishna Dhar, *Open Secrets: India's Intelligence Unveiled*, New Delhi: Manas Publications, 2005, p. 20.

THE MANY FACES OF NATIONALISM

1. Coverage of the press conference where Afzal was made to incriminate himself completely in front of TV cameras and where he denied S.A.R. Geelani's involvement, from the *Times of India*: http://timesofindia.indiatimes.com/articleshow/ 1600576183.cms and http://timesofindia.indiatimes.com/ articleshow/1295243790.cms

2. The Prevention of Terrorism Ordinance/Act: www.satp.org/ satporgtp/countries/india/document/actandordinances/POTA.htm
   The act was repealed by the UPA government in 2004: www.hindu.com/2004/09/22/stories/2004092207420100.htm

3. Even the usually fair newspaper *The Hindu* carried sensationalist headlines. For example: Devesh Pandey, 'Varsity Don Guided "Fidayeen"', *The Hindu*, 17 December 2001: www.hin duo nnet.com/the hindu/2 001/12/1 7/stories/ 2001121700511100.htm

4. Anjali Mody, 'Three Sentenced to Death in Parliament Attack Case', *The Hindu*, 19 December 2002: www.hinduonnet.com/ 2002/12/19/stories/2002121905170100.htm

5. For more information on the support received from the student and academic community of West Bengal, see: www.thesouthasian.org/archives/2005/revisiting geelanis comments.html

6. Noam Chomsky wrote the foreword for Nirmalangshu Mukherji's book *December 13: Terror Over Democracy* (Promilla and Co. Publishers, New Delhi, 2005). He has also supported the petitions that have been taken out in Afzal's case.

7. For Geelani's statement after his acquittal by the High Court, see: Mukhtar Ahmed, 'Geelani Says He Will Work for Undertrials', *Rediff News*, 6 November 2003: www.rediff.com/ news/2003/nov/06parl1.htm
   For Geelani's statement after the High Court verdict was upheld by the Supreme Court, see: www.thesouthasian.org/ archives/2005/revisiting geelanis comments.html

8. Kuldip Nayar, 'Spoilers in the Peace Process', *Indian Express*, 4 November 2003: www.indianexpress.com/res/web/pie/archive full story.php?content id=34616

9. Ibid.

10. Once the Afzal hanging verdict was upheld by the Supreme

Court, the news media were replete with stories of the minutiae of the Afzal hanging, including who would be the hangman and who would supply the rope. See:

- PTI, 'Meet the Man Who Will Hang Afzal', *Rediff News*, 1 October 2006: www.rediff.com/news/2006/oct/0lafzal.htm
- Siddharth Kalhans/M.V.R. Rao, 'Meerut Hangman Mamu Gets the Call for Afzal', *Indian Express*, 12 October 2006: www.indianexpress.com/story/14509.html
- Indo Asian News Service, 'Bihar Jail Ready to Provide Rope to Hang Afzal', *Hindustan Times*, 2 October 2006: www.hindustantimes.com/news/1 8 1 1 8 10984, 000600030006.htm

11. Joint Statement/Resolution passed by Syed Ali Geelani, Shabir Shah, Mohammad Yaseen Malik, Mian Abdul Qayyoom and Nisar Ali: www.revolutionarydemocracy.org

12. Judgement of the Supreme Court of India on Mohammad Afzal vs. the State (NCT of Delhi): http://judis.nic.in/supremecourt/qrydisp.asp?tfnm=27092

MEDIA TRIALS AND COURTROOM TRIBULATIONS

1. I have relied extensively on the information (court records, deposition, etc.) and analysis undertaken, collected and collated in Nirmalangshu Mukherji's *December 13: Terror Over Democracy*, published by Promilla & Co. Publishers in association with Bibliophile South Asia, New Delhi and Chicago, in 2005. I have also relied on the report of the meeting to discuss the media trial of S.A.R. Geelani held at Sarai, CSDS, and on conversations I have had with Nandita Haksar and Vrinda Grover.

For more information on the 13 December case, see the website of the All India Defence Committee for S.A.R. Geelani. Also see Nandita Haksar's article in *Sarai Reader 04*, Tripta Wahi's article in *Sarai Reader 05* and an earlier posting by me on the Reader List: 'The Worst Is Always Precise': http://mail.sarai.net/pipermail/reader-list/2002-December/002080.html, which has links to several newspaper reports relevant to the 13 December case.

2. Readers interested in the murky history of the involvement of European State intelligence agencies under the ambit of 'Operation Gladio' to 'create' incidents of terrorism and sustain a 'strategy of tension' particularly in Italy are advised to refer to 'Fascism and the Establishment: Italy and the Strategy of Tension': http://struggle.ws/freeearth/fe3 italy.html. Google searches incorporating the words 'Gladio, P2, Italy, Belgium' are also likely to yield interesting results.

An equally interesting though less candid account of the work of intelligence agencies in India, particularly the IB, by a former intelligence operative, can be found in Maloy Krishna Dhar's *Open Secrets: India's Intelligence Unveiled*, Manas Publication, Delhi, 2005.

3. The films I watched while thinking about this text were *Dil Se* (Director: Mani Ratnam, 1998), *Mission Kashmir* (Director: Vidhu Vinod Chopra, 2002), *16 December* (Director: Mani Shankar, 2002), *Khakee* (Director: Raj Kumar Santoshi, 2003) and the Zee News Telefilm on 13 December, as well as the Zee News 'Inside Story' on the Al-Qaeda Terror Manual, broadcast on 24 July 2005, and the News at 9 and Special Programme at 9:30: *13 December Ek Saazish*, also broadcast on Zee News on the evening of 4 July 2005.

I also watched several news broadcasts on Aaj Tak, NDTV, Rashtriya Sahara and Zee News through the course of the successive trials in the special POTA court, the Delhi High Court and the Supreme Court.

MEDIA CONSTRUCTS A KASHMIRI TERRORIST

1. Arun Joshi and Neeta Sharma, 'Case Cracked: Jaish Behind Attack', *Hindustan Times*, 16 December 2001.
2. 'Past 24 Hours', *Hindustan Times*, 16 December 2001.
3. Ibid.
4. 'DU Lecturer Was Terror Plan Hub', *Times of India*, 17 December 2001.
5. 'The People', *Times of India*, 17 December 2007.
6. Devesh Pandey, 'Varsity Don Guided "Fidayeen"', *The Hindu*, 17 December 2001: www.hinduonnet.com/thehindu/2001/12/17/stories/2001121700511100.htm

7. 'Rajdhani Mein Ek Nahin Kai Thikane The Geelani Ke', *Rashtriya Sahara* (Hindi Edition), 18 December 2001.

8. Sutirtho Patranobis, 'Don Lectured on Terror in His Free Time', *Hindustan Times*, 17 December 2001.

9. Ibid.

10. Ibid.

11. Rajnish Sharma, 'Hunt for Teacher's Pet in Jubilee Hall', *Hindustan Times*, 17 December 2001.

12. 'Professor's Proceeds', *Hindustan Times*, 17 December 2001.

13. Sujit Thakur, 'Aligarh Se England Tak Chhaattron Mein Aatankwad Ke Beej Bo Raha Tha Geelani' (From Aligarh to England, Geelani Was Sowing the Seeds of Terrorism), *Rashtriya Sahara*, 18 December 2001.

14. 'Geelani Was in Bhuj with SIMI group', *Times of India*, 20 December 2001.

15. Neeta Sharma, 'Pak Uses Fanatics to Spread Terror in India', *Hindustan Times*, 21 December 2001.

16. Ibid.

17. Ibid.

18. Swati Chaturvedi, 'Terror Suspect Frequent Visitor to Pakistan Mission', *Hindustan Times*, 21 December 2001.

19. 'Person of the Week', *Sunday Times of India*, 23 December 2001.

20. 'Logic of an Anti-Terrorist Court', Lies of Our Times Exhibition, 2004.

THE STRANGE CASE OF QAYS AL KAREEM

1. S.A.R. Geelani, a lecturer in Arabic at Delhi University, was an accused in the '13 December 2001—Attack on Parliament Case'. Geelani, along with two others of his co-accused, was sentenced to death by a special anti-terrorism court under the Prevention of Terrorism Act (POTA; repealed in 2004). Geelani was arrested shortly after 13 December 2001 by the Special Cell of the Delhi Police and detained without trial under POTA (then an ordinance). The evidence produced by the Special Cell on the basis of which he was convicted by the POTA court consisted of a mistranslation of the transcript of a mobile phone conversation between Geelani and his stepbrother in

Kashmir that was recorded through an unauthorized act of telephone surveillance.

The verdict was challenged in the Delhi High Court. A protracted campaign by Geelani's friends, colleagues and human rights activists, together with his legal defence by a team of advocates, was able to reverse the POTA court's verdict. The 'evidence' was found inadmissible, and Geelani was acquitted on 29 October 2003, after spending nearly two years on death row in Delhi's Tihar jail.

Subsequently, the Delhi Police appealed against the acquittal in the Supreme Court. On 8 February 2005, Geelani was shot by unidentified assailants outside the house of Nandita Haksar, one of his lawyers. Haksar and her husband rushed Geelani to the All India Institute of Medical Sciences, where he was operated upon for three bullet injuries. Geelani survived this attack and is currently recovering. On 14 February 2005, Geelani issued a statement saying that he suspected the involvement of the Special Cell in this attack on his life.

The Supreme Court subsequently upheld the High Court's verdict and declared that Geelani was acquitted of all charges.

For a comprehensive timeline of the 'Parliament Attack' see: http://in.rediff.com/news/pat2001.htm

2. For more on the 'Media Trial' of S.A.R. Geelani, see:
   - Nandita Haksar, 'Tried by the Media: The S.A.R. Geelani Trial' in *Sarai Reader 04: Crisis/Media* (Center for the Study of Developing Societies, 2004, Delhi), pp. 158–164; also at www.sarai.net/publications/readers/04-crisis-media
   - Nirmalangshu Mukherji, 'The Media and December 13: Who Attacked the Indian Parliament and Why Don't Indians Have the Full Story', *Zmag*, 30 September 2005: www.zmag.org/content/showarticle.cfm?SectionID =32&ItemID=6332)

3. 'Hunt for Teachers' Pet in Jubilee Hall', *Hindustan Times*, 17 December 2001.

4. 'Produce Jordanian on Monday, HC Tells Police', *Indian Express*, 9 November 2002.

'AND HIS LIFE SHOULD BECOME EXTINCT'

1. 'Advani Criticizes Delay in Afzal Execution', *The Hindu*, 13 November 2006.
2. Details about Maqbool Butt available at www.maqboolbutt.com and www.geocities.com/jklf-kashmir/maqboolstory.html
3. Neeta Sharma and Arun Joshi, 'Case Cracked: Jaish Behind Attack', *Hindustan Times*, 16 December 2001.
4. 'DU Lecturer Was Terror Plan Hub', *Times of India*, 17 December 2001.
5. Devesh Pandey, 'Varsity Don Guided "Fidayeen"', *The Hindu*, 17 December 2001: www.hinduonnet.com/thehindu/2001/12/17/stories/2001121700511100. htm
6. Sutirtho Patranobis, 'Don Lectured on Terror in Free Time', *Hindustan Times*, 17 December 2001.
7. 'Professor's Proceeds', *Hindustan Times*, 17 December 2001.
8. Sujit Thakur, 'Aligarh Se England Tak Chhaattron Mein Aatankwad Ke Beej Bo Raha Tha Geelani' (From Aligarh to England, Geelani Was Sowing the Seeds of Terrorism), *Rashtriya Sahara*, 18 December 2001.
9. Swati Chaturvedi, 'Terror Suspect Frequent Visitor to Pakistan Mission', *Hindustan Times*, 21 December 2001.
10. 'Person of the Week', *Sunday Times of India*, 23 December 2001.
11. Neeta Sharma, *Hindustan Times*, 11 June 2002.
12. Pramod Kumar Singh, *Pioneer*, June 2002.
13. 'Gilani Ke Daamaad Ke Ghar Aaykar Chaapon Mein Behisaab Sampati wa Samwaidanshil Dastaweiz Baraamad' (Enormous Wealth and Sensitive Documents Recovered from the House of Gilani's Son-in-Law During Income Tax Raids), *Hindustan*, 10 June 2002.
14. Gilani, Iftikhar, *My Days in Prison*, Penguin Books India, New Delhi, 2005.
15. Full coverage of the press conference where Afzal was made to incriminate himself available online at http://timesofindia.indiatimes.com/articleshow/1600576183.cms and http://timesofindia.indiatimes.com/articleshow/1295243790.cms
16. Mohammad Afzal's statement under Section 313 of Criminal Procedure Code in the Court of S.N. Dhingra, September 2002.

Full   text   on   www.outlookindia.com/fullprint.asp?choice=
1&;fodname=20061019&fname=nirmalangshu&sid=2
17. Nirmalangshu Mukherji, *December 13: Terror Over Democracy*,
Promilla & Co. Publishers, New Delhi, 2005.

SHOULD MOHAMMAD AFZAL DIE?

1. Judgement of the Supreme Court of India on Mohammad Afzal
vs. the State (NCT of Delhi): http://judis.nic.in/supremecourt/
qrydisp.asp?tfnm=27092
2. Edit Page, *The Hindu*, 5 August 2005.
3. For more details, see my book, *December 13: Terror Over
Democracy*, Promilla & Co. Publishers, New Delhi, 2005, pp.
38–41.
4. Judgement of the High Court of Delhi on Mohammad Afzal vs.
the State (NCT of Delhi), Murder Reference 1 of 2003, 29
October 2003, para 448.
5. Judgement of the Supreme Court of India on Mohammad Afzal
vs. the State (NCT of Delhi): http://judis.nic.in/supremecourt/
qrydisp.asp?tfnm=27092 (pp. 158–159).
6. Ibid. p. 149.
7. Ibid.
8. Judgement of the High Court of Delhi on Mohammad Afzal vs.
the State (NCT of Delhi): The High Court had observed earlier
that Afzal's arrest memo was in fact signed by Geelani's
brother, Bismillah, while Bismillah was himself in 'illegal
confinement' and he was forced to 'sign papers' (judgement of
the High Court, para 251).
9. Judgement of the Supreme Court of India on Mohammad Afzal
vs. the State (NCT of Delhi): http://judis.nic.in/supremecourt/
qrydisp.asp?tfnm=27092 (p. 158).
10. Ibid. pp. 148 and 59.
11. *Tehelka: The People's Paper*, 16 October 2004, p. 21.
12. Basharat Peer, 'Victims of December 13', *Guardian Weekly*, 3
July 2005: www.guardian.co.uk/kashmir/Story/0,2763,
990901,00.html
13. Ibid.
14. Nandita Haksar and K. Sanjay Singh, 'December 13', *Seminar*
521, January 2003.

15. Judgement of the Supreme Court of India on Mohammad Afzal vs. the State (NCT of Delhi): http://judis.nic.in/supremecourt/qrydisp.asp?tfnm=27092 (p. 139).

16. Ibid. p. 140.

17. Ibid.

18. Ibid. pp. 141–142.

19. Written submissions on behalf of S.A.R. Geelani, Murder Reference 1 of 2003, presented by Ram Jethmalani, senior advocate.

20. Tabassum Afzal Guru, 'A Wife's Appeal for Justice', *Kashmir Times*, 21 October 2004: www.merinews.com/catFull.jsp?articleID=123536&category=India&catID=2&rtFlg=rtFlg

21. Judgement of the Supreme Court of India on Mohammad Afzal vs. the State (NCT of Delhi): http://judis.nic.in/supremecourt/qrydisp.asp?tfnm=27092 (p. 139).

22. Ibid. p. 161.

23. Afzal's Statement 313 of the Criminal Procedure Code from the magazine *Outlook:* www.outlookindia.com/fullprint.asp?choice=1&fodname=20061019&fname=nirmalangshu&sid=2

24. Judgement of the Supreme Court of India on Mohammad Afzal vs. the State (NCT of Delhi): http://judis.nic.in/supremecourt/qrydisp.asp?tfnm=27092 (p. 30).

25. Judgement of the Special Prevention of Terrorism Act Court—Judge S.N. Dhingra in the case Mohammad Afzal vs. the State (NCT of Delhi), para 222.

26. Onkar Singh, 'The J&K Police Reject Thane Police's Claim on Hamza', *Rediff News*, 20 December 2001: www.rediff.com/news/2001/dec/20parl3.htm

AFZAL MUST NOT HANG

1. Judgement of the Supreme Court of India on the Macchi Singh Case, 1983—Macchi Singh and Others vs. the State of Punjab: http://judis.nic.in/supremecourt/qrydisp.asp?tfnm=9766

2. Judgement of the Supreme Court of India on the Kehar Singh Case, 1989—Kehar Singh and Others vs. the State (Delhi Administration): http://judis.nic.in/supremecourt/qrydisp.asp?tfnm=8264

3. Black Warrant for Afzal: Judgement of the Supreme Court of India on Mohammad Afzal vs. the State (NCT of Delhi): http://judis.nic.in/supremecourt/qrydisp. asp?tfnm=27092

A DEATH SENTENCE AND A TEA PARTY

1. Tabassum Afzal Guru, 'A Wife's Appeal for Justice', *Kashmir Times*, 21 October 2004: www.merinews.com/catFull.jsp?articleID=123536&category=India&catID=2&rtFlg=rtFlg

2. UNI & PTI, 'Naxals Besiege Usur Village—KPS Gill Takes Over as Security Adviser', *The Hindu*, 19 April 2006: www.hinduonnet.com/thehindu/thscrip/print.pl?file=2006041917200300.htm&date=2006/04/l 9/&prd=th&

3.. Coverage of the press conference where Afzal was made to incriminate himself and where he denied S.A.R. Geelani's involvement, from the *Times of India* http://timesofindia.indiatimes.com/articleshow/1600576183.cms and http://timesofindia.indiatimes.com/articleshow/1295243790.cms

4. Tabassum Afzal Guru, 'A Wife's Appeal for Justice', *Kashmir Times*, 21 October 2004: www.merinews.com/catFull.jsp?articleID=123536&category=India&catID=2&rtFlg=rtFlg

HOUR OF THE HANGMAN

1. Judgement of the Supreme Court of India on Epuru Sudhakar vs. Government of Andhra Pradesh and Others: http://judis.nic.in/supremecourt/qrydisp.asp?tfnm=28103

2. The chief minister of Jammu and Kashmir, Ghulam Nabi Azad, is reported to have sought clemency for Afzal and spoken to the Prime Minister of India on the subject in view of the unrest in the Valley: www.ibnlive.com/news/jk-cm-seeks-clemency-for-afzal-speaks-to-pm/22767-3.html

3. The chief minister of Jammu and Kashmir then denied that he never asked the PM for clemency and that it was merely the media coming to its own conclusions: www.ibnlive.com/news/azad-takes-a-uturn-on-afzal-hanging/25119-4.html

HANG THE TRUTH

1. Judgement of the Supreme Court of India on Mohammad Afzal vs. the State (NCT of Delhi): http://judis.nic.in/supremecourt/qrydisp.asp?tfnm=27092
2. Ibid.
3. Onkar Singh, 'J&K Police Reject Thane Police's Claim on Hamza', *Rediff News*, 20 December 2001: www.rediff.com/news/2001/dec/20parl3.htm
4. Judgement of the Supreme Court of India on Mohammad Afzal vs. the State (NCT of Delhi): http://judis.nic.in/supremecourt/qrydisp.asp?tfnm=27092

GUILTY OF AN UNSOLVED CRIME?

1. Judgement of the Supreme Court of India on Mohammad Afzal vs. the State (NCT of Delhi): http://judis.nic.in/supremecourt/qrydisp.asp?tfnm=27092
2. Ibid.
3. Ibid.
4. Afzal's letter to his lawyer Sushil Kumar: www.revolutionarydemocracy.org
5. Afzal's Statement 313 of the Criminal Procedure Code from *Outlook*: www.outlookindia.com/fullprint.asp?choice=1&fodname=20061019&fname=nirmalangshu&:sid=2
6. Judgement of the Supreme Court of India on Mohammad Afzal vs. the State (NCT of Delhi): http://judis.nic.in/supremecourt/qrydisp.asp?tfnm=27092
7. Jake Khan, 'Thane Police Claim to Have Arrested Hamza Earlier', *Rediff News*, 20 December 2001: www.rediff.com/news/2001/dec/19parl19.htm
8. Onkar Singh, 'J&K Police Reject Thane Police's Claim on Hamza', *Rediff News*, 20 December 2001: www.rediff.com/news/2001/dec/20parl3.htm
9. Tabassum Afzal Guru, 'A Wife's Appeal for Justice', *Kashmir Times*, 21 October 2004: www.merinews.com/catFull.jsp?articleID=123536&category=India&catID=2&rtFlg=rtFlg
10. Judgement of the Supreme Court of India on Mohammad Afzal

vs. the State (NCT of Delhi): http://judis.nic.in/supremecourt/
qrydisp.asp?tfnm=27092

POPULAR FEELING IN KASHMIR IS
VALID GROUND TO GRANT AFZAL PARDON

1. President Ford's Statement granting pardon to President Nixon:
   www.ford.utexas.edu/library/speeches/740061.htm
2. Jaworski, Leon, 1976, *The Right and the Power,* Reader's
   Digest Press, New York.
3. Edmund Burke's speech on conciliation with America in Britain's
   House of Commons, 22 March 1775: www.britannia.com/
   history/docs/eburke.html
4. Judgement of the Supreme Court of India on Mohammad Afzal
   vs. the State (NCT of Delhi): http://judis.nic.in/supremecourt/
   qrydisp.asp?tfnm=27092
5. UNI, 'No Need for It: Venkaiah Naidu', *Tribune,* 2 June 2003:
   www.tribuneindia.com/2003/20030602/nation.htm#6
6. Judgement of the Supreme Court of India on Epuru Sudhakar
   vs. Government of Andhra Pradesh and Others: http://
   judis.nic.in/supremecourt/qrydisp.asp?tfnm=28103
7. Biographical Information on Baron Samuel Silkin, the Attorney
   General of England and Wales as well as a link to where his
   political writings can be found: http://janus.lib.cam.ac.uk/db/
   node.xsp?id=EAD%2FGBR%2F0014%2FSILK
8. Hamilton is credited with authoring many of the Federalist
   Papers. For further information on the Federalist Papers, please
   refer to: www.foundingfathers.info/federalistpapers/

   For the complete text from which the author has quoted,
   refer to Federalist paper no. 74: www.foundingfathers.info/
   federalistpapers/fed74.htm

SATYAMEVA JAYATE?

1. Barkha Dutt, 'A Battle for Life', *NDTV Columns*, 20 September
   2006: www.ndtv.com/columns/showcolumns.asp?id= 1061
2. Vir Sanghvi, 'The Complexity of Execution', *Hindustan Times*,

15 October 2006: www.hindustantimes.com/news/181 1820675,00300001.htm

3. Karan Thapar, 'Should Mohammad Afzal Be Hanged', *Hindustan Times*, 15 October 2006: www.hindustantimes.com/ news/181 1820688,00300002.htm

4. Nirmalangshu Mukherji, *December 13: Terror Over Democracy*, Promilla & Co. Publishers, New Delhi, 2005.

MEETING AFZAL

1. Coverage of the press conference where Afzal was made to incriminate himself completely in front of TV cameras and where he denied S.A.R. Geelani's involvement, from the *Times of India:* http://timesofindia.indiatimes.com/articleshow/ 1600576183.cms and http://timesofindia.indiatimes.com/ articleshow/1295243790.cms

2. Afzal's older brother Aijaz on CNN-IBN where he propounded his view of the whole case and of Afzal's behaviour: http:// www.ibnlive.com/videos/27157/the-other-side-of-afzals-surrender.html and www.ibnlive.com/videos/27182/afzal-gets-mixed-bag-from-politcos.html

LAST CHANCE TO KNOW

1. See 'Annexure 16', Nirmalangshu Mukherji, *December 13: Terror Over Democracy*, Promilla & Co. Publishers, New Delhi, 2005.

2. Nirmalangshu Mukherji, *December 13: Terror Over Democracy*, Promilla & Co. Publishers, New Delhi, 2005.

3. Reports of the People's Union for Democratic Rights: www.pudr.org/

4. Usha Ramanathan, 'A Case for Public Enquiry', *Frontline*, 6 May 2005: www.flonnet.com/fl2209/stories/ 20050506000307600.htm

5. Ibid.

6. Ibid.

7. Ibid.

8. Ibid.

9. Usha Ramanathan, *The Book Review*, 5 May 2005: www.thebookreviewindia.org/

10. Gouri Chatterjee, *Telegraph*, 30 June 2005.

11. Rajat Roy, *Ananda Bazaar Patrika*, 16 July 2005.

12. Subhendu Dasgupta, *Economic and Political Weekly*, 22 July 2006.

13. Gouri Chatterjee, *Telegraph*, 30 June 2005.

14. Sukumar Muralidharan, *Biblio*, September–October 2005.

15. Ibid.

16. Ibid.

17. Ibid.

18. Nandita Haksar, *Indian Express*, 30 September 2006: www.indianexpress.com/story/13656.html

NOTES ON CONTRIBUTORS

T.R. Andhyarujina is a Senior Advocate of the Supreme Court of India. He was formerly Solicitor-General of India and Advocate General of Maharashtra. He is a leading authority on constitutional law and public law. He is the author of two books on constitutional law, *The Kesavananda Bharati Case* and *Judicial Activism and Constitutional Democracy in India*.

Praful Bidwai, former senior editor of the *Times of India*, is a freelance journalist and regular columnist for several leading newspapers and magazines in India. He is also Visiting Professor at the Nelson Mandela Centre for Peace and Conflict Resolution, Jamia Millia Ismalia, New Delhi.

Syed Bismillah Geelani is a writer and columnist whose stories and features have appeared in the Urdu- and English-language press in Srinagar and Delhi. He also wrote a column on events in Kashmir for the Malayalam weekly *Free Press*.

Nandita Haksar was on the defence team of S.A.R. Geelani and represented Mohammad Afzal Guru at the time of filing of the mercy petition by Tabassum, Afzal Guru's wife, and later by Afzal. She is the author of *Framing Geelani, Hanging Afzal: Patriotism in the Time of Terror* (2007).

Sonia Jabbar is an independent journalist who has been writing on Kashmir since 1995. She is a receipent of the WISCOMP Scholar of Peace Award.

Indira Jaising is a well-known civil rights activist and a Supreme Court lawyer. She was awarded a Padma Shri in 2005 for public affairs.

Vinod K. Jose is the Executive Editor of *The Caravan* and an award-winning journalist. He has previously worked as a producer from South Asia for public radio stations in the US and Europe.

Mohamad Junaid is a doctoral student in Anthropology at The Graduate Center, City University of New York. He grew up in Kashmir.

Ashok Mitra is a former Rajya Sabha member and has been finance and planning minister of West Bengal. He has been a columnist for many years with the *Economic and Political Weekly* and the *Telegraph*. He is also a recipient of the Sahitya Akademi Award for his contribution to Bengali literature.

Nirmalangshu Mukherji teaches philosophy at Delhi University. He is the author of, among other books, *December 13: Terror Over Democracy.*

Jawed Naqvi is a veteran journalist who has worked with Reuters, *Gulf News* and *Khaleej Times*. He writes as a freelance journalist for *Dawn*, *New Age* and *Tehelka*.

A.G. Noorani is a Supreme Court lawyer and a leading constitutional expert. His columns appear in the *Hindustan Times, Frontline, Economic and Political Weekly* and *Dainik Bhaskar*. His published books include *Citizens' Rights, Judges and State Accountability and Indian Political Trials, 1775-1947.*

Arundhati Roy is the author of *The God of Small Things* (1997) and four volumes of non-fiction writing: *The Algebra of Infinite Justice* (2001), *An Ordinary Person's Guide to Empire* (2005), *Listening to Grasshoppers* (2009) and *Broken Republic* (2011). *The Shape of the Beast*, a collection of her interviews, was published in 2008.

Shuddhabrata Sengupta is a media practitioner, artist and writer with the Raqs Media Collective and one of the co-initators of the Sarai Programme at the Centre for the Study of Developing Societies (CSDS), Delhi.

Mihir Srivastava is the Assistant Editor at *Open*, and was formerly the principal correspondent at *Tehelka*.

Mirza Waheed is a novelist and journalist born and raised in Kashmir. His debut novel, *The Collaborator*, was shortlisted for the *Guardian* First Book Award and the Shakti Bhat Prize, and longlisted for the Desmond Elliott Prize. It was also book of the year for *The Telegraph* (UK), *New Statesman*, *Financial Times*, *Business Standard* and *Telegraph* (India), among others. Waheed has written for *Granta*, the *Guardian*, the BBC, Al Jazeera English and the *New York Times*. He lives in London.

Tripta Wahi teaches history at Delhi University. She is a convener of the Forum for Democratic Struggle (FDS).